THESE ARE AFRI
A Memoir

THESE ARE AFRICAN HANDS:
A Memoir

By Kevin Brewerton

PAIGE PUBLISHERS

For Kaivalya and Kolby.

I began writing this book out of the sheer frustration of not being able to find my father and losing my grandmother. If I could put it all on paper, then maybe it might make sense, I told myself. And if nothing else, maybe even more importantly, my children, or anyone else, could one day read my book. It would be a story that I could pass on to them; a way of seeing the family lineage through their father's journey, and perhaps somehow in the telling of the story something deeper might be mended. I'd once heard that writing is alchemical. So, I started to write, thinking that it couldn't be harder than fighting. Oh, how wrong I was about that. But what I learned is that if you write from your heart, then you can't go wrong. In that same token I could approach it through the logic of fighting: the technical stuff is secondary. If you have the heart for it, then nothing can stop you. A lot of hours and a number of years later, I've found out that writing is alchemical.

The peninsula curves like the palm of a cupped hand, as I drive north toward Point Dume. I feel the gap between my car seat for the house keys I'd been searching for all morning. It's the second time in the last week that I've lost them. The sky is cloudless, and I wonder why I'm being asked to secretly meet at this place in Malibu.

"We'll get him back on his feet, Kevin!" Alex, an old friend in Los Angeles and co-founder of the rehabilitation center, squeezed his hand on my shoulder. His electric blue eyes beckoned me. "Come to Higher Ground. It's not like any other rehab. You'll train him hard, help him get his life back. You're the man!"

I laugh as I turn my car onto Cavalleri Road. The man, huh? I'd planned to relax this morning with a cup of tea and write, but instead I'm driving to an entirely new destination. I wind through the acres of land towards the cobbled courtyard of a Tudor house. An oak door swings open and Alex steps out.

"He's inside. He's relaxed. It's just gonna be you and him. This is your time with him, and it's very important. The doc said you're the key!"

"I'm the key?"

Alex pushes open the door. I follow him, mentally tracing this morning's steps to determine if I'd left my house keys in the kitchen, or if my friend's three-year-old daughter, Pearl, hid them in the pocket of her stroller again. I remember her wispy blonde locks and her small feet tapping against the wooden floor as she ran away, clutching my keys as if they were a treasure.

"There he is," Alex whispers, pointing across the enormous living room to the back of an armchair that cradles a large figure of a man. "This is Kevin Brewerton!" he says.

The armchair rocks and a head turns slowly to reveal one of the greatest boxing heavyweight champions of all time. He looks up at me. "Nice to meet you, M" I say.

"Nice to meet you, too." His voice is almost a whisper. I feel the weight of his calloused palm as we shake hands.

"Kevin's the five-time kickboxing champ —"

"Please." I wave my hand at Alex, trying to stop him before he can say the word champion. "That's not important."

"Okay. Well, I think I'll just leave you guys alone."

Alex walks away and I sit down, facing him, in an identical swiveling armchair. He looks at ease, but his eyes are cautious. The strong ocean breeze wafts through the open patio doors, bathing us both as we sit in an awkward silence. Nothing is said. It's as if we are waiting for the first punch to be thrown to begin the conversation. My instincts tell me something quite unordinary is happening, and yet, there's a familiarity in the stillness between us. It's an outer calm, while an inner rage ripples deep within, patiently awaiting the opening bell to ring, where everything will be revealed. The silence around us is unnerving. He looks majestic. We continue to sit in stillness. And then he asks, "So, what made you a fighter, Kevin?"

I walked through the gates of Heaton High School with my chin up and my shoulders back, proudly blending into the collective mass of navy blazers. I was twelve years old; it was my first week of school, and I was thrilled to be wearing my new uniform. The button-down collar and blue striped tie meant I was part of something real and established. I felt a sense of security and that somehow, I was worthy of wearing the school's coat of arms on my breast pocket.

"You look handsome," my mother had said, as she brushed off the lint from my shoulder. She straightened my tie before sending me off with a packed lunch into the fresh morning air.

I was excited to be rushing to get to class on time as the bell shrieked. I imagined myself in a race, fighting my way to the winning post, immersed in the bustling flow of blue ~ the anticipation of my first day. I felt a push from behind, and I stumbled.

"Blacky!" I heard. At least that's what it sounded like amidst the laughter that rang through the hall.

I felt the hard floor against my lip and the bitter taste of varnish. I remembered sitting with my best friend, Sean Fineran, in primary school. We would eat cupcakes and sing "Morning Has Broken" on our way to assembly. The thought of cupcakes was now fleeting, as I watched my books being trampled and kicked along the polished wood floor. I wiped my mouth with the sleeve of my jacket and ran after the scattered pages.

Blacky. The word echoed within me, as I stood in the hallway that was now suddenly empty. I tried to reason with myself. Dad's voice flooded my memory, pointing out the fact, as he very often did, that he "looked like an I-tie"; and therefore, I did too.

"What's an I-tie, Dad?" I asked the first time he'd said it. We were sitting at a table in the King Arms, a crowded pub, while Mam was engrossed in a game of bingo.

"It means Italian," he replied. Dad rolled up his shirtsleeves, pushed the empty beer glasses out of the way, and stuck his hairy, sun-tanned forearm onto the table next to mine.

"You look just like me, Son. I've got the olive skin of an Italian. When I was in the army, they used to think I was Italian! In fact, when I was a prisoner of war, me and a bunch of men escaped. We had to get across the Alps to get to

Switzerland, but every time we walked through a little village, they'd send me out first, to make sure the coast was clear...because I looked Italian."

"Did they, Dad?"

"Aye, lad, they did."

In the corridor at school, I picked up the last of my books, but the word permeated my mind. The feeling inside me grew heavier. *Blacky.* It wasn't just the thought of cupcakes that had left the bitter taste. In primary school, I'd wrestled with a boy who had called me Mowgli and laughed in my face. This time was different. The wound reached deeper. Despite how much I reasoned or reminded myself of Dad's words, something just didn't feel right. I wondered why he always emphasized the fact that he had olive skin and was a darker shade of white. Although he was certainly white, as was my mother and their other children. Skin color had never been a question.

I pushed open the classroom door. "Brewerton, you are late!" Mr. Kirkpatrick shouted from across the room, and the class began to laugh.

"Sorry, sir, I dropped my books."

"Ya don't need books here, Lad. This is a woodworking class. Now hurry up and join the rest of 'em."

I rushed between the workbenches to join the group of boys. Mr. Kirkpatrick unbuttoned the jacket of his tight, brown suit and loosened his tie.

"Now, this is a dovetail joint, and you have to make sure it doesn't fall apart," he said, reaching for a pot of glue.

Someone nudged my arm, and I looked sideways. It was Jimmy Shelton. "Read it and pass it on," he whispered and handed me a crumpled piece of paper. Jimmy was the slickest kid in class with his cravat-like tie knot, trimmed spiky hair and a self-made, abstract tattoo on his knuckles. I unfolded the paper and read the tiny, scribbled letters:

Meet after school, football field.

I nodded my head in approval and passed the note to Paul Benedict, who was standing next to me.

"Now this is what it's supposed to look like," Mr. Kirkpatrick's handlebar moustache was perfectly framed in the wooden square he held up. "And if it doesn't, you do this with it." He laid the frame on the workbench and picked up a wooden mallet.

"Now you lot, watch carefully," he began tapping the frame. "Sometimes, if the joint isn't tight enough, it slips out."

I looked at Jimmy, who was looking across at Paul Benedict and making masturbation hand gestures.

"Now you have to be gentle with it. It's a delicate joint," Kirkpatrick said.

Benedict burst into laughter and the class followed. Kirkpatrick sprung up like a bolt, his eyes bulging like car headlamps.

"Benedict, come here at once!"

Benedict strolled with a smirk, emboldened by the class's brazen laughter. He threw his head back in a gesture that said, "You can't touch me," and Kirkpatrick lunged, grabbing his lapels with both hands.

The room shook and fell into silence as Benedict's body slammed into the wall, his eyes turning into blue marbles of shock. Kirkpatrick reached for the mallet and swung it like an axe, burying it into the wall, inches from Benedict's head.

Kirkpatrick's broad back stretched the seams of his suit jacket as he held Benedict by the throat. I watched the drops of sweat form on the end of Benedict's nose while he whimpered into the silence.

I was no stranger to this feeling. I wanted to run, but I was transfixed, a silent sideline observer. I had spent my childhood in dread of the clock reaching eleven o'clock on a Saturday night. That was the time my parents would return home from the pub. My mother called it "going to church," but it was a much more celebratory occasion than anything offered by the Catholic Church she knew as a child.

She didn't like institutional religion. She'd experienced enough of that being punished by nuns and filled with shame. She did believe in God, though, and spirits. Quite often she'd refer to a time when a framed picture of her mother that hung on the wall in the living room, fell to the ground, and jumped right back to its reserved spot.

"I saw it with my own eyes," she'd say and then laugh. It was that same God and those same spirits that I would pray to for peace in the home. In her prime, before she ever colored her gray hair or curled it into a perm, Mam resembled a movie star of the '40s. It was the sculpted brunette hair and long, elegant legs that Dad was too proud to point out. When she wore heels, she was taller than him. He was five foot eight at best, but he was boastful of his thick gray hair that covered his head like a lion's mane.

Together, they were renowned for dancing all night to the local band, on any given Saturday. They were almost a permanent fixture, if not the heart and soul of the pub. But it was always unknown whether their inebriated state would enhance their feeling of joy. The opposite was usually the case. I remember once waiting for them to return.

"They should be back any minute," said Sandra, my older sister. She was the youngest of four girls. The eldest was Joan, who we rarely ever saw, followed by Doreen and Sonia. Sandra was the only one who still lived at home. She was my first friend, my accomplice, and my big sister. She was a dozen years older than me, but age didn't matter. We'd play hide and seek around the house or walk together up through the wooded Dene to the corner shop in Jesmond, bringing back bags of coal or any other odds and ends that Mam would send us to get.

Sandra was a raven. Her long straight black hair, against her pale cheek bones was a striking contradiction. In the same way, her personality switched back and forth without a moment's notice. One day she would be filled with euphoria, and the next she'd shut down and isolate into her own world, talking out loud, only to herself.

It was three days before Christmas, and I'd been sitting on the floor in my faded, striped flannel pajamas. I was trying to guess where the presents were hidden while watching the hands of the clock turn, wondering what kind of mood my parents would be in when they arrived home.

"Watching the time makes it go slower, you know." Sandra grabbed a hairbrush from the top of the upright piano, threw her long black hair over her shoulder like a cape, and sat down on the brown tweed sofa.

Just then, the front door flung open and in they staggered, Mam and Dad, full of laughter. Dad pulled packets of crisps out of his pocket and threw them across the room at me: Cheese and Onion, Prawn Cocktail, Salt and Vinegar (my favorite) and Pickled Onion. I caught them with both hands.

"She's staying the night," Mam shouted as my older sister, Sonia, who we only sometimes saw, walked into the room, bobbed hair framing a bright, smiling face.

"Come here, Son!" Mam said, taking my head between her hands and planting a sloppy kiss, reeking of Brown Ale, on my cheek. I blushed with embarrassment but was overjoyed to see her so happy. When Mam stood up with a carefree smile, letting her coat fall from her shoulders and her red nylon scarf waft to the floor, I felt a stillness in the room and a sinking sensation in my stomach. I saw Dad's arm swing in a dark arc as the nylon scarf hit the ground. Mam cried out as his fist hit the side of her face.

"Stop it, Dad! Stop it!" Sandra screamed out. Sonia grabbed my arm and tried to turn me away, but it was too late. I'd seen it too many times before. Mam fell, her head hitting the side of the piano, causing a panel to fall open and the Christmas presents to come spilling out.

"Stop! Stop!" The words were stuck inside of me. I couldn't shout out loud. I was paralyzed.

"If you challenge me, lad, al put ya head in a vice and crack it like a nut! Do you understand me?" Kirkpatrick shouted into Benedict's face. He turned to the room as Benedict fell to the floor like a piece of rope.

"No one messes around in my classroom! I hope I've made that clear!" He paused and picked up the wooden frame. "Now, where were we? Ah yes, as you can see, gentlemen, the glue has set. And this is a perfect dovetail joint."

I slammed open the exit doors and leapt into the cold air. I was relieved to have survived the first day of high school. In front of me, a football field sprawled out like a bright green blanket, and three distant silhouettes stood by the goal posts. I reached into my pocket and pulled out the crumpled piece of paper that Jimmy had given me. I checked to be sure that the meeting place was on the football field, and then I ran towards the three figures.

"Excuse me!" I waved my hands. "Have ya seen Jimmy?"

"Jimmy who?" The tallest of the three boys squeezed his narrow lips together and shrugged off his blazer.

"Jimmy Shelton. Don't ya know Jimmy?"

"Na, never 'erd of him."

"Who are you?" A boy with short red hair asked me. He held a red striped ball in his hands. And behind him, a bald-headed kid peered at me.

"My name's Kevin. What's yours?"

"Malcolm Macdonald," the tall boy said. The other two boys laughed while they pulled off their shirts, exposing their stark, goose-bumped skin as they wrestled their arms into black and white football shirts.

"Malcolm Macdonald plays for Newcastle United," I said.

They kept laughing, and the tall boy replied, "Do ya wanna play? We're a man short."

"Really?" I smiled, feeling the waning sun against my face. "I don't have my kit."

"Ya don't need a kit! Just take off ya jacket, man."

"Okay!" I laughed with them and threw my blazer onto the grass. "Good," Malcolm prodded my chest with his finger. "You and me, two against two."

He dribbled the ball down the field and I followed, loosening my tie. We turned and faced the other two boys, who were crouched like sprinters in their blocks.

"We're on!" Malcolm kicked the ball toward me, and I felt a rush of heat sweep through my chest as the red-headed boy dashed at me like a bloodhound and lunged for the ball. I kicked it through his legs and ran around him, leaving his foot swinging into the air.

"Mop-headed bastard," he shouted as I took off toward the goal with my tie fluttering in the wind. I knew he couldn't catch me. I'd been running for as long as I could remember. Dad would line up the old oil barrels that the workmen had left behind in our back garden in the Dene. I would run and hurdle them, one after the other. He would sit watching with Mam, drinking tea and marveling my athleticism.

"Over 'ere!" Malcolm sprinted in a parallel line across the field.

I lobbed the ball high and he sprung off his feet. "Get in!" he grunted.

The ball ricocheted off his head toward the goal. The bald-headed boy dived, punching the spinning ball away, his body outstretched like a rod.

"I'll get it!" I lunged forward and kicked as hard as I could. The red- striped orb hurtled past the goalkeeper's fingers and crashed into the back of the net.

I raised my arms in the air. "Goal!"

"Fuck off, Darkie!" Someone pushed the back of my head.

"Fucking wog!" The red-haired boy snapped his jagged teeth. "You cheated!"

"No, I didn't!" I looked around for help and saw Malcolm running across the field, his eyes wild.

"Malcolm, tell him! Tell him I didn't cheat!"

"What's this?" Malcolm shouted as he punched me in the stomach. "That was my fucking ball, darkie."

The air gushed out of me and I fell. I lay curled on the grass, more ashamed and in shock than anything else. *Had I done something wrong? Was he mad at me for scoring the goal, or was it because my skin was darker?*

"Who wants to stick the boot in first?" Someone shouted. I closed my eyes waiting to be stomped into the muddy grass. Instead, I felt nothing but the cold wind sweep over me. When I opened my eyes again, I saw the three boys running away, scattering across the empty field. I wondered what had happened. *What would make them run?* I turned my head to see Jimmy and a mob of boys running across the field.

"Charge!" They shouted, bolting past me with their fists clenched and their heels tearing up the turf as they ran toward the three boys who had become specks in the distance.

"Why are you crying?" Jimmy had stopped and was standing over me with his hands on his hips.

"I'm not crying," I said, wishing I could explain the feeling of joy that made me burst into tears.

"Looks like it to me." Jimmy's ears jutted out beneath an egg-like dome, which sat on his head.

"What's that?" I said, pointing to the dome.

"To some, it's a football cut in half and turned inside out. But to others it's the Kojak!"

He reached into his back pocket and pulled out the other half of the yellow plastic dome that he was wearing. "Our lads are wearing them. Who loves ya baby? Catch!"

It spun like a pancake when he tossed it at me. I reached up and clutched it in my fist. I looked at Jimmy's egg-like head and then over to the cluster of boys who had run themselves into invisible shadows.

"Our lads," I whispered Jimmy's words, feeling a strange warmth envelop my body.

"Fucking hurry up and get it on ya." Jimmy shouted. I raised the plastic dome like a crown and placed it on my head, squeezing it over my recalcitrant locks of curly hair.

"Come on," Jimmy grabbed my hand and pulled me to my feet. "It's fucking freezing!"

He put his hands into his pockets, and we walked toward the school gates. I wondered if anyone could see how tall I felt. I kept walking, ignoring the pain in my stomach, and the question of why Malcolm had called me Darkie.

K evin!" Mam exclaimed as she opened the front door. The sun glistened on her forehead and her brown eyes reached out to me with great interest.

"How was school? And what the hell is that on your head?"

"It's nothing." I pulled off the sweaty dome that Jimmy had given me just as Dad walked in, his thick eyebrows raised into question marks. He rubbed his hands together, as if he were trying to warm himself up from sub- zero temperature.

"Well, how'd it go, Son?"

"It was..." I began but faltered. I had previously determined that when I got home, I would tell Dad about being called Blacky. I would tell him everything, but the words wouldn't come out. "It was just fine."

"Just fine? Is that all you have to say about your first day?" Dad said. Somehow, he seemed relieved.

"Yeah, just fine." I turned to escape up the stairs to my bedroom. Maybe it was the quiver in my voice or the shrug of my shoulder when I turned away that spurred Dad's heavy voice to catch me before I could get too far.

"Son, what do ya mean, 'just fine?'"

"It was fine. I was playing football."

"Playing football," Mam laughed. "He was playing football, George. He's just fine; he's as good as gold! Leave him alone. Let him get settled in."

"Yeah, I was playing football. Some boys called me names." Mam stopped laughing, and the hallway became a vacuum. "What kinda names, Son?" Dad said.

"Just names."

"I'll bloody kill them lads!" Mam shouted.

Dad put his hand on her shoulder. "He can take care of himself, Sally!"

"Yeah, I can take care of myself," I echoed. And in that moment, bolstered by Dad's words, the urge to say more melted away. "I'm okay. It was a good day at school."

I bounded up the staircase, leaving them staring after me. I ignored a strange feeling of curiosity as the floorboards creaked under my feet. *Why did they ask me so many questions?* It wasn't uncommon for them to inquire about my school experiences. They were protective parents. But this time their prodding seemed intentional and my responses, crucial.

I walked into my room, clutching the plastic half-football. I stared at the poster of Elvis Presley, hanging on my wall. His shiny black hair was greased back. I tried to envision myself as one of the lads. I am one of them. I needed to be sure of it. I threw off my jacket, turned to the mirror and examined my thick, unruly locks. There was nothing I could do to get my head to resemble Elvis's quaff or Dad's slicked back mane.

"Just something I'll have to live with. Not a big deal, not a big deal at all," I'd tell myself each time I slid out of the barber's chair, frustrated that no one ever seemed to know how to cut my hair.

"It's unmanageable, Kid," the barber would tell me. "I've never seen owt like it ..."

Of course, he hadn't seen the like before. After all, we were 300 miles northeast of London and 60 miles south of the Scottish border. Newcastle— a 2,000-year-old city, partly built by the Romans, and at various times was ruled by the Saxons and the Danes— sat on the bank of the River Tyne. The city played a major part in the Industrial Revolution. Its inhabitants, made up of coal miners, shipbuilders and various other types of working-class citizens, were known as Geordies. Why? No one exactly knew. However, it is said that people of Newcastle were so loyal to King George II, they were given the name in fortitude.

In the mid-seventies, bands like Queen and David Bowie ruled the airwaves. All I wanted to do was look like them or anyone else who sported a Bay City Rollers haircut, or another slicked back version of Shawaddy Waddy, or Elvis.

But now, I felt like I was part of something, and I had the football dome that Jimmy had given me to prove it. I placed it back onto my head, pressing down my hair. My goal was simply to cover my head as much as possible, so I squashed the cap and pulled it into place. I stuffed my curls into the sides of the dome. Perfect.

Sandra burst into the room. "Kevin! What do ya think ya doing?" She started to laugh, pointing at my head.

"Get out!" I yelled.

It felt good to be able to say that. It wasn't until we'd moved from the small house in Jesmond Dene to the three-bedroom flat on Barrack Road that my view of the world had changed. My twelfth birthday was coming up. The landscape outside my home abruptly transitioned from wildlife, trees and the river to the Black Bull pub, and the ubiquitous, smoke-billowing rooftops of the council house. And I had my own room.

We had lived in the wooded Victorian valley of the Dene where Dad was the park keeper. It was secluded, and nature was all around. Mam hated it because there were rats, and it was miles from her job, polishing floors and cleaning cars at the showroom on Elswick Road.

I loved the Dene, a canyon with its waterfalls and a million places to hide and play. It was more than a place to live. I could lose myself for hours: running with Jai, my Alsatian dog, climbing trees, following ancient paths by the Old Mill, discovering hidden caves and buried canyons, and scaling the banks of the waterfall. It nurtured me from the day I was born.

I remember Mam whispering lullabies, while the sound of the river flowed through my ears. The Dene was part of me. Then one day Dad came home and told us he was being promoted, and we were going to be leaving. "I'll still be cutting grass, but I'll get a raise and I'll get picked up in the mornings, if I want," he said. "We've done our time in the Dene."

I didn't want to leave; it was all happening at once. Within a few weeks I was living in a new home, in a different part of town, and walking through the halls of a new high school. I was discovering an entirely new world.

"Don't you know how to knock? Don't you have any manners?" I said to my older sister.

"Mam says your dinner's getting cold."

"Get out!" I pointed at the door.

"What's that on your head? You look like a madman. Did you steal Dad's oil, again? I'm telling him."

"No, I didn't steal Dad's oil! Now get out!"

The last time I'd reached into Dad's cabinet to grab his bottle of olive oil, it had ended with my hair sagging over my ears, oil dripping onto the flowery rug, and Mam's voice coming at me like a rocket, "What have ya done, Kevin!"

Sandra looked at me square in the eyes. "I'll tell you where Dad keeps his olive oil if you tell me where Mam keeps her cigarettes."

"I don't care where Dad keeps his olive oil," I said, wondering if I could believe her even if she did tell me. The problem with Sandra is what Mam had always said: "If she's not on the meds, Son, you just can't believe a word she says. It's a crying shame, a bloody crying shame. She's a twenty- something with the mind of a twelve-year-old."

It meant nothing to me as a young boy. Sandra was Sandra ~ full of stories and laughter and games and tears. But as a teenager, I questioned everything she said. Where we were once the closest of allies, seemed to have changed the moment we left the Dene. My big sister who watched over me, and who's mild, yet distinct mental disorder, which was once a comical normality, became a source of embarrassment.

"If I really wanted his olive oil, I could get it because I know where he keeps it," I told her.

"Well, you might know where he keeps it, our Kevin, but I know a secret about the family. Tell me where the tabs are, and I'll tell you."

"Is it about George? I already know," I said, remembering that Mam once told me that she had lost a baby soon after giving birth, and his name was George Jr. "I don't care about your secrets. Now get out! And I'm telling Mam you're stealing her tabs."

"You're mean, our Kevin," she shouted as she ran out of the room. I didn't care what she said, but when I pushed the door closed behind her, I couldn't help but wonder if there really was a secret.

Benedict stood by the old shed at the back of the school, waving his arm at me. "Quick, quick! The coast is clear!" he shouted, as I peered up into the canopy of a maple tree, where Jimmy was descending through the branches. In my pocket was the plastic dome that he gave me three days earlier. Although the novelty had mostly worn off, I'd been carrying my skullcap around wherever I went. I liked the idea of having it there, folded up in my breast pocket. The thought of being able to grab it as easily as reaching inside my blazer to snatch a pencil, or some other compulsory school supply, made me feel at ease.

Since the first day of school, I'd had a feeling that something was falling apart. I couldn't describe it. Fragments of space floated up inside me, like soft bubbles. Inside each one was the sound of the creaking staircase under my feet as I left Mam and Dad standing in the hallway, and then Sandra's voice whispering the word "secret."

"Come on! Quick! The coast is clear," I shouted up to Jimmy. Benedict ran over. "There's no one in sight for miles."

Jimmy jumped to the ground, landing in front of me, as he cupped his swollen mouth and spat into his hand. "That was fucking hard," he said, out of breath, opening his saliva-covered palm, where two brown speckled, pale blue eggs sat.

"They're beautiful," I said.

"Aye, blue tits!" Jimmy held them up with one hand and took a squashed packet of cigarettes from his breast pocket with the other. "Your turn to light up."

"I'll do it next time," I said, not sure if I wanted to smoke another cigarette. I'd only been smoking for two days, trying to fit into the group without anyone knowing that I wasn't really inhaling.

"Come on, Kev. Light up!" Jimmy shoved the pack into my hand.

"All right, all right," I pulled three cigarettes and wedged them between my lips. I'd seen Jimmy do it with five, lighting them up with ease and passing them out like a croupier dealing cards. How hard could it be?

"Give me a pin," Jimmy said to Benedict. I struck a match and lit the first cigarette.

"If I can get two more of these, I'll have ten of 'em," Jimmy said. He pierced a hole with the pin in one of the shells, pressed the egg to his lips and began blowing. A green liquid dribbled out.

"Eeehhh! It looks like snot," Benedict laughed, as I sucked hard on the tabs, sending smoke surging to the back of my eyeballs and through my nostrils. I yelped and spat the cigarettes out, spraying Jimmy and Benedict. Jimmy dropped the eggs. The blue shells splattered across the top of his black leather shoe.

"Fuck! Fuck!"

"Shhh, quiet!" Benedict tugged on Jimmy's arm. "I don't want to get caught by Kirkpatrick again."

"Me eggs, me fucking eggs." Jimmy shook his leg, trying to flick the shells off his shoe.

"Sorry, Jimmy," I wiped my eyes.

"Sorry! You're fucking sorry?"

"They're only eggs," Benedict reached to put his hand over Jimmy's mouth.

"Fair enough," Jimmy slapped Benedict's hand away and pointed at me, "But you've got to get me two more eggs."

"Me?" I looked into Jimmy's wild eyes.

"Yes, you."

"Have a look at that one," Benedict said, laughing and pointing into the sun. I squinted.

"What is it?" I asked, noticing a small round shadow at the top of the tree.

"That's another nest," he said. "But you'll need a helicopter to get to that one."

"Shit! I'm not going up there!" I said.

"Yes, you are!" Jimmy replied.

Benedict put his hand on my shoulder and whispered, "It's easy, Kevin."

"Well, if it's so easy, why don't you do it?"

"Because you made me drop the eggs." Jimmy spat on the ground. Benedict slapped my arm. "You can do it, Kev."

"No. I don't want to do it. I don't want to climb the tree for a bloody egg."

"What? Are ya a chicken?" Jimmy laughed.

"I'm not a chicken."

"He's a chicken." Benedict started flapping his arms.

I raised my hands in the air, "Okay, okay!"

I slipped off my blazer and threw it into Benedict's arms. In a second, my leg was wrapped around a branch and I was hoisting myself into the tree.

"Fuck me, he's quick," I heard Jimmy say.

My feet found every foothold, and my hands gripped each branch with certainty. I remembered the Dene—the smell of sap, the feel of bark in my hands, and how I'd climb to the top of every tree. I'll show them, I repeated to myself.

It wasn't fear that made my heart race as I climbed higher and higher, leaving Jimmy and Benedict flat-footed on the ground staring up at me in amazement. It was the feeling that I was showing them that I was good at something.

"Look at him go. He looks like a fucking monkey," I heard Jimmy shout.

I climbed with more vigor. *It's good to be a monkey*, I thought. But when I heard Benedict shout "jungle boy!" my foot slipped.

"Whoa!" Jimmy shouted. "He almost lost it! Are you okay up there?"

I held my breath, without answering, because I could feel those bubbles rising up inside of me. *Did Jimmy say I looked like a monkey because my skin was darker? Maybe he was impressed with my ability to climb.*

I felt weak as I hung with my arms wrapped around the trunk, while more strange bubbles rippled through my skin. *I could fall now*, I told myself. I decided to turn back down, but then Jimmy's voice called through the branches, "Are you okay, Kev? Are you okay?"

I felt the urge again, and I began my way back up the tree. I pulled myself upwards, until the woven loop of mud and twigs was above my head. I had to stop to catch my breath. When I looked down Jimmy and Benedict looked very small. I could see everything from up there: kids playing football in the school yard, clumps of people shuffling through the stone arch beneath the headmaster's office, the white shirts of the lunch workers walking out of the school gates, and the cathedral tower of the civic center reaching above the rooftops in the distance.

"Are there any eggs?" Jimmy shouted. I peered into the nest, wondering if I'd find anything. When I looked inside, I was taken by surprise: two sky-blue jewels lay in the brown nest.

"What's up there?" Jimmy shouted.

"Wow," I whispered. I stared at the eggs, wondering what to do as Jimmy kept hollering.

"What's up there?"

I reached inside and stroked the eggs. They were warm. I pulled my hand away, scanning the pale blue sky, looking for the mother. She must be close by. I could feel my body burning, and I could feel someone watching me.

"What the fuck is up there! How many eggs?"

"Hold on!" I searched the sky, the people below, and the cathedral tower in the distance. And then I reached into the nest.

"His cheeks look big," Benedict said, as I retraced my path through the branches.

"Aye, he must have a nice catch there," Jimmy clapped his hands. I jumped to the ground. The two boys huddled around me as I cupped my mouth and spat into my palm.

"One egg! Is that all there was? One poxy egg?" Jimmy shouted.

"Aye, there was only one egg. If you don't believe me, ya can go up and take a look for yourself."

"Fuck that!"

"Shhh! Someone's coming," Benedict squealed. We squeezed ourselves behind the tree as the footsteps became louder before coming to a halt right in front of us.

"Oh, shit. I bet it's Kirpatrick," Jimmy whispered.

My body tensed, and Benedict started sniffling as if he was trying to stop himself from crying. But when a velvet voice oozed, "What are you boys doing?" all three of us peered around the tree and laughed with relief.

"Well, look who it is, for fuck's sake!" Jimmy sniggered.

There before us, with his sculpted shiny black face and tentacle-like fingers clasping his school binder, stood Apea Corantin, the only African student in the whole school. "What ya looking at?" Jimmy pointed at him.

"Why is that boy crying?" Apea pointed.

"I'm not fucking crying!" Benedict said, wiping his nose with the sleeve of his blazer.

"But he looks..."

"He said he's not crying. Don't you get it? You people are all the same," Jimmy grunted. Then he spun around to me with his hazel eyes a squint, as if he had said something wrong. "Not you, Kev. I didn't mean you. You're not black. You're different. You're one of us."

"Aye, you're one of us," Benedict echoed as Jimmy spun back to face Apea, and a jolt of confusion swept through my body, sweeping my mind away in a torrent. *I have the skin of an I-Tie. I'm not black!*

I wanted to shout into Jimmy's face, "I've got Dad's olive skin. I'm not dark. I'm olive colored. Yes, I'm olive colored." The tears began to well up, and I wasn't sure why. As much as I wanted to scream at Jimmy, I wanted to hug him and express my gratitude. He said I was one of them, and Benedict had echoed it. It was all confusing.

"You looking for trouble?" Jimmy took a step forward, and Apea clutched his binder and took a step back. "I told you he's not crying, Blacky!"

"Yeah, I'm not fucking crying," Benedict sniffled. While we all stepped forward towards Apea, I could feel the surge of all those ripples reaching the top of me, like a wave roaring into my head, bulging my neck at the collar and emptying my lung.

I filled the air with a scream that made everyone freeze: "Blaaaaaacky!"

It was strange. I felt empty and filled as the word came out. I looked at Jimmy's stunned face and Benedict's surprised smile. And then Apea turned and tore down the cobbled path like a whippet, his binder falling to the ground.

"He's not crying, Blacky! He's not crying, Blacky!" I shouted, still holding the egg, feeling powerful as we ran after him. Our shoes echoed on the concrete, as the three of us galloped shoulder to shoulder like a six-legged monster.

"Go back to Africa!" Jimmy shouted.

"Yeah, go back to Africa!" We all wailed in fits of laughter as we saw Apea get further away from us.

"Let him go!" Jimmy flailed his arms, out of breath.

"We showed him," Benedict said.

"Did ya see his face, Kev, when you started shouting?" Jimmy patted my shoulder.

"Yeah, I did, Jimmy. It felt good," I said, even though I ignored the disjointed feeling in my gut. But what did it matter? What was done, was done, right? If it got me closer to my friends, it would indeed serve a greater purpose in exchange for a brief discomfort. I carefully placed the egg into his palm as we walked back toward the tree.

"Let's light up before the bell rings. I'd better do it this time, so we don't get egg on Jimmy's shoe," Benedict said, and we laughed, throwing our arms over each other's shoulders. When we turned the corner towards the tree the laughter stopped, seeing a familiar face.

"Well, well, lads, what have we here now?" Mr. Kirkpatrick was standing before us, holding up a cigarette butt.

I could still feel the sting of the headmaster's cane as I walked home from school at the end of the day.

"Six of the best for you, Brewerton." He had almost whispered it as he stood up and moved around his desk, a dignified silhouette against the bay window of his study. Anticipation proved worse than the beating as I bent over to receive the first lash of his cane. The act itself seemed to pass with ease. His regal voice tempered the lash of his whip, leaving me with a warm sting in my rear end.

I stood straight and said, "Thank you, sir," then left his office.

It was the same feeling that I had when Jimmy said, "You're one of us," ~ a comforting sting that I'd gratefully swallowed. That sting lingered, building inside of me as I reached my front door. I turned the key and walked inside looking for Dad, for some sort of answer.

"Our Kevin's home," Sandra shouted the moment I walked into the house. She breezed past me on her way to the kitchen.

"Where's Dad?" I asked.

"Don't I get a 'hello'?"

"Where's Dad?" I demanded.

"You're in a fine mood." She kept walking. "He's where he always is this time of day."

I had a picture in my mind of him leaning back with his stocking feet up on the glass coffee table and his shoulders sinking into the armchair. I made my way to the living room. *I'll just tell him straight out that I feel weird and something isn't right and that I can't tell what it is, because it's just a feeling I have that makes no sense. I don't even know if it's worth talking about, but if it is, I want to know what it is that's bothering me.*

When I pushed open the living room door, Mam was sitting in Dad's chair, and Dad was standing by the window.

"Hey, our Kevin. Look who the cat dragged in." Mam pointed across the room to Sonia. She looked different, but I couldn't tell why. Maybe it was the uncomfortable way she was sitting, upright, on the edge of Mam's reclining chair, with her palms resting on her knees and her short brown hair pinned behind her ears.

"Hello, our Kevin," Sonia said.

"Hello." I glanced at her, not wanting to lose momentum in my mission to talk to Dad. I wondered how I'd be able to talk to Dad, with Sonia sitting right there in Mam's chair. At least she didn't have her children with her— two girls and a boy: Shona, Zhora and Saif. Their father, Hanif, was from Pakistan. He'd moved to Scotland after they divorced. If they were here, it would be impossible to talk to Dad.

"Is that it?" Mam laughed. "You haven't seen Sonia in months. Is that all you have to say?"

"I just wanted to talk to–", I began, but Mam jumped right back in and my words were swept away in the conversation.

"Look at the size of him," she told Sonia. "You just can't take your eyes off him for a second. He doesn't stop growing."

"You are looking much taller, our Kevin." Sonia put her hand out to wave me over, but I turned back to Dad, who had neither moved nor spoken.

"Kevin!" Mam's voice cut through the room again. "You must be hungry, Son, are ya?"

"Yeah, but…"

"How's school treating ya?" Sonia leaned forward. Her eyes seemed wistful and vulnerable. "It must be treating you well because you look happy. Are you happy, our Kevin?"

"Happy?"

I was thrown by the question. I felt the urge to blurt out, "Yeah! I'm really happy. The headmaster just gave me six of the best!" But I couldn't. The fear of Dad finding out that I'd been smoking tabs and stealing eggs made me freeze. I abandoned the reason why I'd stormed into the living room as the fear of revealing my shortcomings crumpled my resolve like a piece of paper.

"He's a happy boy," Mam said.

Dad stood in an unusual stillness, before breaking his silence. "You look like you have something to say, Kevin."

"Yes, I do."

"Well, what is it then? Speak your mind, boy." Dad stepped forward, and the words in my head slowed to a crawl.

"Am I olive-skinned or colored?" No one spoke. Dad frowned.

"Why are you asking such a question?"

"Because Jimmy said I'm colored."

"Who's Jimmy?"

"Aye, who's Jimmy?" Mam repeated.

"Jimmy's me mate at school."

"It's his mate from school, George," Mam repeated, as she often did, as if to buffer the explanation. Dad took a deep breath. He was trying to fill his lungs to their limit, while Sonia sat in silence.

Then he stepped forward and exhaled. "Tell him Sally. Tell him now."

"Okay, then. I'll tell him, George." Mam stood up, her chin quivering. "Well, the truth of it is, our Kevin, I'm cooking a pie and pea supper, and it's probably getting burnt by now."

"I'll check on it." Sonia stood up, covered her mouth with her hand, as if she was trying to hold something in, and slipped out of the room.

"Now tell me about Jimmy. And what made him say you're colored?" Dad said.

"He was just saying..."

"Saying what?"

"It's all right, George," Mam said.

"He was just saying that I'm the same as him." I said, wondering what happened to Sonia, and if the way she was holding her mouth was to stop her from being sick.

"You're as good as anybody, Son. Don't you forget that." Mam stood up.

"I told him that I've got olive skin."

Dad started blinking. I wanted to keep talking, but I could feel the questions tumbling down on me with the memories of Kirpatrick and the headmaster's office. I found myself mirroring Dad and stepped backward.

"Now the trouble is," Mam said. "If the pie is overcooked it won't be worth eating. And the peas will be all black and shriveled up."

"I'm hungry." I looked at Dad. "I better go and eat."

I turned and walked out of the room, my brow furrowed, trying to fathom if somehow, I'd been denied something. And then it was gone, washed away in the relief that my secret had not been discovered.

Stealing takes skill, and skill comes with practice." Jimmy rubbed his hands together as we strolled through the Eldon Square shopping center. The burn of the cane had faded away in the past week, and he was looking for a chance to put his light fingers to work—an opportunity to prove that we were not restricted by the boundaries of the school gates.

It seemed to be the natural thing to do: defy the teachers, defy Kirkpatrick, defy the headmaster's cane, and defy those feelings trapped inside of me like effervescent reminders that something was out of control. Nothing could be better than to stride around with Jimmy and Benedict, not caring about anything else.

At home, the flushed faces and awkward silences had been replaced with a lingering thin line of tension, along with the occasional urge within me to find out what Dad would have said had I not turned away for the pie and pea supper. It's all in my head. Life was easing back into its usual ebb and flow.

"It's as simple as plucking apples from a tree," Jimmy said, putting his hand on my shoulder and waving Benedict closer until the three of us stood huddled together amid all the shoppers.

"So, what's the plan?" whispered Benedict.

Jimmy looked up and stared across the floor at the flashing lights on a giant Christmas tree. He laughed, then said, "Here's what we're gonna do. We'll all go into a shop and see how much we can nick."

"Is that a plan?" I said.

"Sounds like a plan to me," Benedict chimed.

"It's a plan all right," Jimmy said. "We'll go in one at a time, so they won't know we're together."

"That bit does sound like a plan, but I think I'd be better off waiting outside," I said.

"Waiting outside?" Jimmy looked at me. His hair sheened. "Are you scared?"

"No, I'm not scared."

Benedict slapped my shoulder. "We all get scared the first time."

"I told ya, I'm not scared. I just don't want to go in."

"You won't get caught. It's easy, Kev, it's easy. All ya have to do is stick something down your pants or up your jumper or in your pocket if it's small enough. And then you just walk out of the fucking shop. Bingo," Jimmy said.

"I'll think about it."

"What's there to think about? Look." Benedict pointed through the crowd. "And we can meet over there, at the Christmas tree."

"I don't know why there's a fucking Christmas tree. It's far too early for a Christmas tree," Jimmy snapped.

"I do like a Christmas tree. It adds a bit of festivity to the occasion," Benedict continued.

"I hate festivities," Jimmy pointed in the air. "And I hate this song. Ya hear that? They're playing 'Away in a Manger'."

"It's Christ-massy, man. It's a good Christmas carol," Benedict smiled.

"What's a stupid manger anyway?" Jimmy said.

"Baby Jesus. It's baby Jesus." Benedict started rocking his arms. "I love Christmas."

"Yeah, me too!" I said, looking over his shoulder at a mob of elves wearing red hats and yellow tights who were dancing around the tree.

"Do you really believe that crap? There's no fucking red-nosed reindeer," Jimmy shouted over the din of the shoppers.

Benedict looked at Jimmy. "Eh, watch ya fucking mouth. It's about the spirit of good will. Didn't ya mother teach ya anything?"

"Yeah, she did. She taught me that Christmas is a big fat lie."

"Shut up or I'll kick your fucking head in!" Benedict retaliated.

Jimmy slapped Benedict on the side of the head, knocking his woolly hat askew. I jumped between them. "He's kidding, Benedict! He's just kidding."

"I'm not kidding. I'm telling the truth. It's a fucking BIG FAT LIE!" Jimmy screamed. Benedict's face was red, and his eyes were bulging as he straightened his hat.

"But the plan. What about the plan?" I shouted.

"Fuck the plan!" Jimmy said.

I put my hand on Jimmy's shoulder. "It's only a Christmas tree. What's the big deal?"

"It's his old man," Benedict shouted. "It's because his old man fucked off on Christmas day!"

"He didn't fuck off on Christmas day. Get ya facts straight. It was Easter!" Jimmy shouted as he threw a punch that flew over my shoulder, missing Benedict by inches. Shoppers walked by, staring.

"Whoa, stop it! Stop it!" I pushed Benedict back and I stood between them. Benedict and Jimmy stood with their teeth and fists clenched. "What about the plan? I thought we had a plan." Nobody answered. I said it again, "What about the plan? I'll go in. I'm not scared to go in."

Finally, Jimmy said, "All right. I'll keep to the plan if he will, but I still don't believe in Christmas. And ya can't make me."

"Okay, I'll keep to the plan." Benedict pulled his hat over his ears, and I took a deep breath. Relief settled as we walked through the flow of shoppers.

"Look over there!" Jimmy pointed. "It's the Tyneside Clothing Co. I wonder what's in there?"

"Clothes—what ya think?" Benedict said.

"Very funny, Benedict." Jimmy patted him on the back and looked at me. "You go first, Kev."

"Me?"

"Yeah, you."

"Okay, I'll do it," I muttered. I strode a straight line toward the mannequin-filled window and the red banner that hung above the door: BIGGEST SALE EVER. I looked back to see if Jimmy and Benedict were watching, but they had already melted into the crowd. Clever. They must be hiding. As I walked into the shop, a tall man wearing a purple shirt and black leather pants headed toward me.

"Can I help you?"

"I'm just looking for now," I said, noticing the circles of sweat under his arms.

"Is it for yourself?"

"Yes, it is." I avoided his glaring eyes and focused on his name tag, which read, JASPER.

"Very good, but we might not have what you're looking for. It's quite expensive here." His voice dropped to a mumble, "At least for the likes of you."

"Likes of who?"

"All I'm really saying is that it's quite expensive."

"Well, that's fine by me," I said.

"Very good," he smiled. "You'll find young men's clothing to the left at the back of the shop. If you need assistance, just let me know."

"I definitely will," I said and walked determinedly towards the racks of clothing, passed the cashier with the pigtails and Ferris wheel hoops that hung from her ears.

The young men's section was well stocked: shirts, jackets, pants, shoes, woolly hats, boots, scarves, socks, ties, and underwear. I took a deep breath. Plenty to choose from, I wondered where Benedict and Jimmy were.

I reached up and pulled a jacket off the rack. I liked the way the rich suede felt in my hands. *Maybe I can nick this one?* I slipped off my coat, letting it fall to the floor. I plunged my arms into the sleeves and shrugged it over my shoulders. It engulfed me like a blanket, reminding me of my Dad's worn-out work jacket that always smelled of grass. He'd drape it over me when I was little, and I'd run around the house until I got tired.

Laughter swept across the shop floor. *Bet that's Jimmy.* I spun around to wave them over, but it was a young couple walking into the shop.

I hanged the suede up and headed toward a row of trousers. I wondered where my mates were as I flicked through the hangers and stopped at a pair of sky-blue corduroys. I held them up, admiring their gold-stitched seams and traced my fingers around the shiny silver belt buckle. It all moved so quickly, initiated by my speeding heart. I told myself that I didn't need to wait for Jimmy or Benedict. *I'll steal these without being noticed and surprise them both when I meet them at the Christmas tree.*

I glanced around the shop. The couple was talking to the cashier and Jasper was folding shirts. I turned the belt buckle over in my hand, ignoring the strange queasiness in my stomach that said, *Maybe don't do this. Not today. Maybe not ever.* Those thoughts flew passed me with little delay and I stormed into the dressing room with the corduroys under my arm. I kicked off my jeans, jumped into the sky-blue trousers, fastened the belt buckle, and pulled my jeans back over the top of them. I looked in the mirror. *Great! That was easy.* I stepped out onto the shop floor and headed toward the exit, my heart pounding within my chest.

The cashier was still counting money and the young couple was nowhere to be seen. "Did you find anything you like?" Jasper said as I cruised past him.

"No, not this time. Thank you very much."

Sweat dripped down my face, and my legs swelled. The ends of the corduroy trousers were stuffed into my socks and the pants twisted tight around my knees. The plan seemed to have come together. When I took the first step out through the open glass doors and saw the flashing lights across the way on the Christmas tree. I chuckled. *This is easy! The easiest thing in the world!*

But then an alarm sounded, and a hand grabbed my shoulder, yanking me back.

"You're under arrest, boy!"

The squad car came to a stop outside Percy Street Police Station. The two towering policemen opened the back door of the car. I slid myself off the hard seat, my head low. I followed them into the grey, stone building. "Empty your pockets, Son." The taller of the two towers tapped the desk with his pen, and I emptied my pockets: a glow-in-the-dark skeleton keychain, a penknife, bubblegum, some coins.

"What's your name, Lad?" he said, his voice smooth and caring. I didn't answer. I didn't want to say my name out loud. *If I don't tell him my name, how could he find me? How could he find my parents and tell them what I've done?* I wanted to hide, being nameless for as long as I could and fade into the stale smell of cigarettes that filled the room.

"Did you hear me? I said, 'What's your name, boy?'" He tapped harder on the desk, leaving an echo in the room and a hopeless feeling in my gut that forced the word out of my mouth.

"Kevin," I whispered.

Then it all collapsed, falling in on me. The "information", as he put it, flowed out of me like a confession: the phone number, the address, the description of my criminal act, and the names of my parents—yes, the names of my parents. The thought of my Dad hearing the news made me want to faint.

"Have a seat over there," he ordered, sliding a box of tissues across the desk and pointing to a wooden chair. Then he walked out of the room, leaving me to sit in silence and imagine my fate. Through a small window, I could see him in the next room. He was straight as a rod, a black uniformed exclamation mark in the surroundings of his grey office. He picked up a telephone and dialed a number. I knew the number he was calling. Every turn of the rotary dial cut me inside, and an unfamiliar paradox befell me. I wanted nothing more than my mam to come and get me out of the mess I was in, but at the same time, I didn't ever want to see her again.

I sat there for at least half an hour. Then the door swung open, and I bolted upright in my seat. My heart raced at the sight of Dad as he walked into the room, shoulders hunched like a bull and fists stuffed into the depths of his coat pockets. *He'll kill me. I've seen what he's done to Mam for nothing. He'll kill me as sure as anything!*

"That's not your lad, is it?" The policeman entered the room.

"That's him," Dad said.

"I see." The policeman's eyebrows clenched as if he were unraveling something in his mind. He turned and exited the room as Dad wedged his foot against the door and waved me towards him. I slid off the chair and ambled across the room, my head down and my eyes following the cracks in the concrete floor. I could hear him breathing through his nostrils, almost snorting, but his face remained still when I stepped in front of him.

"Let's go home," he said, finally.

"What, Dad?"

"Let's go." He turned and started to walk.

How can we be leaving? A wave of confusion and relief swept over me. He led the way out of the station and down the steps onto the dark, deserted street. I pictured Dad explaining to the policeman that his punishment would be far greater than any time spent in jail, and it all made sense.

"Right. Stop where you are!" Dad turned; his white face distorted by shadows from the light of the moon. "I'll make a deal with you."

"A deal, Dad? What kind of deal?"

"If you don't do this again, I won't tell your mother. If she finds out about this, it will kill her. Do you hear me?"

"Yeah, Dad. I hear ya." I felt his thick hands grab my neck as he pulled me into him and squeezed me. I heard his heart beating through his thick jacket. I smelled the grass.

Why'd you leave me?" I looked at Jimmy, as we stood on the street, an endless flow of cars whisking passed us.

"I didn't leave you." He retrieved a handkerchief from his back pocket, bent over and wiped the steel toecaps of his new Doc Martens.

"So, where were you then?"

"I told ya already. Benedict was getting on me nerves, so I went to the bog, and when I got back, there was no sign of him. And you were being dragged out of the shop by a big fucking copper with a stupid grin on his face. Now, what do you think of the boots? Do you like them, or don't you?"

"They look too big. Actually, in fact, they look enormous, Jimmy. They look like elephant boots."

"Does that mean you don't like them?"

"No. I don't mean that," I said, trying to figure out if the boots made Jimmy seem different or my rage for him not being around when I was arrested. "I mean, I do like them. I'm just not used to seeing bright red boots."

I didn't know if I liked them. In the same way, I didn't really know if Jimmy was lying to me. What he said made perfect sense; I wanted to believe him.

"Ha ha! That's the best thing about them. Ya can see me coming a mile off."

We broke into laughter, and Jimmy seemed like Jimmy again—all fun and games.

"Me mother bought me them, an early Christmas box." He rolled up his jeans, and I compared the gigantic toecaps of his boots to my flat, broken down plimsolls.

"Come on!" Jimmy winked at me. "Let's get going."

He bounded down the road, past a row of brick council houses towards a one-story community hall that stood at the end of the street. Jimmy's strides were passionate. His boots pounded the pavement, red juggernauts lighting up the grey concrete.

"Wait for me!" I shouted, inhaling the metallic fumes of a double-decker bus as it rumbled by. There I was, running off after Jimmy, trying hard to hold onto something that seemed to have slipped away.

Dad had said, "You're growing into a man now, Son," as we walked through the moonlit streets on our way home from the police station. I'd taken it to be the reason for everything over the past three months or so that I had been feeling—the things that I couldn't quite put my finger on. A bond replenished itself with Dad's willingness to keep my secret, but the bond with Jimmy was the one I felt the need to hold on to.

"It looks deserted!" I shouted, as we neared the windowless building.

"It better not be. I've been waiting all week for this," Jimmy ranted.

He pulled open the big double doors. Music and laughter washed over us and spilled out onto the street. "Bingo! There's nothing like a good teenage disco!" Jimmy started clapping to the rock 'n' roll music the moment we walked inside the darkened room. I stood behind him, tracing the muddled shapes that danced on the floor in a red hue.

"Jimmy Shelton!" A tall blonde boy emerged with a shout. "Jimmy, Jimmy, Jimmy. Where ya been?"

"I've been around!"

"Well, Jimmy, Jimmy. I'm glad you're here. The place is packed. There's at least a hundred kids here, and we're all having a laugh. Who's this?"

"This is Kev."

"Hello, Kev," the tall boy said. He pulled Jimmy into the room before I had a chance to respond. I was left standing against the wall, watching Jimmy's boots, which had become fluorescent, disappear into the crowd. Go after him. I set off as a burst of strobe lights flashed through the room, shattering us all into fragments.

"Jimmy, wait for me!" I squeezed and nudged my way through the huddle of bodies, getting closer to him. Each time I reached out to grab his shoulder he disappeared. Off to a different part of the dance floor, waving his arms and laughing at the way our faces looked in the flashing white light.

I followed in search of him until I heard, "Kev! Kev!" I turned around to see Jimmy, smiling at me, his face merging in and out of focus. "Fucking cool, isn't it?"

"Yeah, it is, Jimmy. It's great." I said, wondering where the blonde boy had gone as I swung my arm around Jimmy's shoulder.

"Ha way." Jimmy tugged me toward the snack bar as the strobe stopped flashing and the light returned to red. "Drinks?" he cheered, throwing the coins onto the table and grabbing two cans.

"I could go for a can of pop."

"Here, it's cherry flavored." He passed me the cold can.

I tipped my head back, the bubbles cutting into my throat, washing away the residual taste of the metallic bus fumes I'd swallowed. It tasted sweet. At last

Jimmy and I were standing side by side, and I felt fulfilled. It was just the two of us. I no longer needed to chase after his red boots. The fear of something slipping through my fingers was gone, washed away with the taste of cherry and flattened into the palm of my hand as I squeezed the can into a knot and threw it into the rubbish bin.

"That was great, Jimmy! The best cherry pop I've ever had."

"Way aye!" He let out a long, raspy burp.

"Pig," I exclaimed, chiming in with a belch of my own.

"Mmm. That smells good." Jimmy lifted his nose in the air as if to sample a fine aroma. "It smells like a cherry fart." We broke into fits of laughter as the house lights rose, revealing a room full of sagging wet hair and eyes squinting in the harsh incandescent light.

"Five minutes!" a voice spewed through the speaker, followed by a crowd of boos.

"Fucking hell, that was quick! We got here too late. We've only been here half an hour." Jimmy nudged me. "Come on. Let's get out of this shit hole."

My skin tightened when we stepped out into the cold air, but my spirit was still filled with festivity. A long row of lamp posts bathed us in an orange light as we shuffled down the street. Jimmy rubbed his hands together and blew into them like a trumpet.

"It sounds like a strangled duck," I laughed, clapping my hands and singing while Jimmy continued playing his hands, rocking his head from side to side. We marched through the orange light until we ran out of lamp posts. The road got darker and the laughter stopped when we turned into a back alley to take the shortcut towards home.

"That was good, Jimmy." I noticed my friend studying his boots as we walked side by side.

"You can still see them in the dark," I laughed.

"What's that supposed to mean?" he said, without looking up. "You trying to be funny?"

"Not in a bad way, Jimmy. Just saying what we said before. Just trying to be funny in a good way."

"Well, it's not fucking funny," Jimmy spun around, grabbed my wrists, and pushed me into the wall.

"What're you doing, Jimmy?"

"What do ya mean 'not in a bad way'?"

"Get off! Get off!" I tried to break loose, but his hands were strong and my wrists were bent.

"I'm not getting off." He squeezed harder. I'd never seen him like this. His eyes were blank and indifferent.

"Why you doing this Jimmy? Stop playing around now. It's not funny anymore. Get off me!"

"Shut up." He slapped my face. "Come on dark man. See if you can escape. If you can get out of this, I'll let you go home."

"What... What?"

"What are you crying for, dark man?"

"Why are you calling me 'dark man'?"

"Try to escape, dark man," he laughed.

"I don't want to escape, Jimmy."

"Fuck off—you're gonna try and escape." He twisted my wrist, and I dropped my head to hide my face. Tears fell onto his boots. He pulled my head up and looked at me.

"I'll let ya go if you try to escape."

And just as I thought there was no way out, I heard the clanking metal crash of a dustbin lid in the alley. Jimmy turned his head. His grip loosened and his attention drifted, so I pushed him away and sprinted as fast as I could without looking back.

I kept running. I could sense him chasing me, his air-cushioned boots springing him forward, with his hand reaching out to grab me. I kept going, with the sound of my plimsolls slapping against the pavement. I saw Queens Court and my bedroom window on the top floor. I ran up the stairs of the building and down the narrow corridor. As I charged through the front door, Sandra screamed, spilling her cup of tea all over the beige-colored carpet.

"What's all the noise?" Dad shouted from the living room as I ran up the stairs. I was too angry to wonder why Jimmy attacked me, or why he called me dark man. The rage I had in that alley, while he restricted my hands, left me helpless. I wanted to fight back, but I just couldn't do it. I ran into my room and slammed the door behind me.

"Our Kevin's crying!" Sandra shouted. "He's upset! I think he's crying!"

We had come to an abrupt stop. "End of the line. Everybody off!" the bus driver shouted.

"I'm not getting off!" groaned the old lady, shaking her head of pink and white rollers. Although we were the only two passengers, she was pressed up against me, as if the bus was crowded. I would have gotten up and moved away when she first sat down, trapping me in my window seat, but I didn't want to make her feel bad. So, for the past eight stops I had sat with my school bag on my lap and my face pressed against the glass, trying to memorize the number plates of the passing cars. She was comforting, in a strange way. It had been a long night of being locked in my room, not wanting to face my parents' questions. Then, after a day at school avoiding Jimmy and staying secluded, this woman made me feel less lonely.

"Sorry, Mrs." The driver threw his coat over his shoulder. His voice was a strained, high pitch of urgency. He held up his forearm and glanced at his watch. "You gonna have to change buses here!"

"Well, I am not changing!" Her sagging chin was resolute. She gripped her shopping bags. "Av been getting on this bus for fifteen years, and 'av never had to change before. Why should I have to bliddy change buses now?" The driver stood at the end of the aisle, unbuttoning his collar and loosening his tie.

"Excuse me." I raised up and scooched past the old lady.

"There'll be another bus along in five minutes," the driver explained.

"Five minutes! Five minutes!" She slid over into the seat I vacated and stacked her shopping bags next to her, piling them up like a wall. "I refuse to get off! I refuse to get off this bus!"

I dropped down onto the pavement and walked away, inhaling the fresh air as her voice faded behind me. I didn't mind getting off the bus; I'd had enough of the stale cigarette fumes I'd inhaled while my nose was pressed against the window. Only one stop away from home, I gladly took the short stroll.

It had stopped raining and thick shafts of light seared through the grey clouds, parting them like flimsy pieces of cotton and scattered them across the sky. I walked up Barrack Road, past the empty football grounds and past the fort-like walls of the brewery. I glanced back a final time to see the bus still hadn't moved. I turned the corner, feeling a tension in my stomach as I neared my house.

I knew there'd be questions about last night. Our family routine of carrying on the morning after a big fight between Mam and Dad had become a necessity. They would hide the evidence and act as if everything was normal. Broken furniture would be put back together, shattered glass swept up, stains, where plates of food had been hurled across the room, were wiped clean. Even Mam, cleverly concealed the bruises and cuts with makeup or skewed her head in a certain way to hide parts of her face and averted her eyes so I couldn't see her pain. However, in this case, there would be none of that.

I threw my school bag over my shoulder and continued the rest of the way home. I walked through the front door and looked at the carpet. There was no sign of the spilled tea from the night before. My mouth watered as the smell of chopped onions wafts from the kitchen. "What's for dinner?" I shouted.

The living room door opened and Mam stepped out to greet me in her faded rose-petal blouse. "Hello, Son."

"Hello."

"Can I come down now, Mother? Can I come down?" Sandra's voice pleaded from upstairs.

"No, stay in your room, Pet. I'll tell ya when ya can come down!"

"Why is Sandra in her room?" I asked.

"That's not important. Now, come on. We've been waiting for ya, Son."

"Waiting for me?"

"Aye Son, we've been waiting."

Dad sat in his armchair peeling a blood orange—his favorite. He didn't look up when we entered the living room.

"Am I in trouble, Dad?"

"You're not, Son," Mam whispered as she crossed the room and sat down. I watched the red juice drip through Dad's fingers and onto the carpet as he ripped open the orange. I knew he was going to ask me about the night before or worse yet, break his silence and tell Mam why we walked home in the moonlight. I looked out over the rooftops where more clouds had been thrown like torn rags across the sky.

"Am I in trouble for something?"

"No," Dad laughed, but his eyes watered. "You've done nothing wrong, Son."

"Aye. You've done nothing wrong, Son," Mam echoed. Her voice sounded different.

"All right then." I breathed a sigh of relief, eager to leave, but Mam started sobbing into the palm of her hand.

"What's the matter, Mam?"

"Tell him, George. Tell him now, for Christ's sake!" She wrung her hands together, as if to squeeze something out of them.

"Tell me what?" I turned to Dad.

"Me and your mother love you very much, Son."

"Just say it, George. Tell him the truth." Mam stood up, dropping her hands to the sides of her body, giving up on something.

"The truth? What do ya mean, the truth?" I asked.

"The truth is—" Dad paused.

"The truth is what?!"

"Say it, George!" Mam cried, but to no avail. She stepped forward. "The truth is, Kevin, we're not—"

"Wait!" Dad raised his hand in the air and cut her off with a firm voice. He looked around the room and then at me and said, "All right, I'll say it. Kevin, we're not your real parents."

"What?"

"Me and ya mother are not ya real parents," his voice softened to a whisper.

I could see the words slipping from his mouth, a stream of soft white letters floating toward me in slow motion. I froze in fascination. I bent over in humorous relief, "That's funny, Dad!" I didn't quite understand the joke, but I didn't care. It was hilarious! An unmistakable sign that I really wasn't in any trouble. "That's funny, Dad! That's funny!"

But as I straightened up, wiping the tears from my eyes, I realized Mam and Dad's stoic faces. Dad's eyes flickered for a moment, and in that flicker, a voice in my head recognizes: this is not a joke. Those innocuous, soft white letters that had floated towards me crash into me like a sledgehammer.

"Not my real parents?"

The words collapsed in on me as a trillion memories shot through my head like sheets of microfiche. "It's impossible!"

"We're your grandparents, Kevin. So, it's like being your real parents. It's the same thing really, in a way." Dad stumbled with the words, as he tried to explain. "Sonia's ya real mother,"

A wave of sobs came from Mam. "Who's Sonia?" I asked.

Dad's eyes darted back across the room to Mam. "It's all right, George," she said.

"Your sister, Sonia. She's really your Mam," he went on.

"Sister Sonia?" I asked, trying to fathom the story.

"Aye," Mam continued. "She was only fifteen when she had you. That's not far off the age you are now, Son. She was still a baby."

More microfiche flashed through me. Pictures of Sonia spun in my head. I used to see her when she'd visit us in the Dene.

"Can Sister Sonia sleep in my bed tonight?" I would shout. We'd sleep at opposite ends of the bed, and I would dig my toes into her armpit and fall asleep. Sometimes I would wake up and find my foot in her crotch or stuck under her chin. But she'd never say anything. She would just lie there, never caring where my restless feet ended up.

"Sorry to have told you like this, Son," Dad admitted.

"Does anyone else know?" I asked.

"Everyone knows."

"Everyone?"

"Yes, everyone." Dad turned away.

I had felt strangely calm up until then. The thought of everyone knowing except me filled me with anger, betrayal. I sensed something closing inside me as I stared out of the window. I turned over memories of Sonia. I thought of our last encounter, when she slipped out of Mam's chair, with her hand over her mouth to escape the room and check on my pie and pea supper. The questions surged forward and it all became clear.

"But what about her kids?" I said.

"What about them?" Dad looked at me.

"You're their brother," Mam said.

"I'm their brother?" I pictured Shona and Zhora, with their red ribbons and long black hair and Saif's boisterous smile. It all seemed unnatural. *Could I live with the idea of being their older brother?*

"Next time they come to visit, you can all get along," Mam said, hopeful.

"Get along?" I answered. "What about my father? Is it Sonia's husband, Hanif?"

Dad looked at me, his shoulders collapsing. "We don't know who your dad is. It's not Hanif."

I pictured Hanif, the white turban bound over his head, his pockmarked cheeks, and the brown, almost red, skin of a Pakistani. There was no connection or any tug of curiosity, only nothingness. I was relieved he wasn't my father. But a tension pulled. *Who is my father?*

I smiled, unsure of an alternative reaction. I nodded my head as if I had just been told that we were going to spend the day at the mouth of the Tyne or Whitley Bay, as we'd done many times over the years, hunting for crabs on the beach. I looked at my hands. For the first time I saw that they were brown, not white. "I have brown skin!"

"Are you alright, Kev?" Dad asked.

I felt stupid. *How could I have not noticed that I didn't have the skin of an I-Tie? How could I have not known that my skin was brown?* The look on the policeman's face when he handed me over to Dad, the words of Jimmy– "You're one of us"– and all of those feelings inside that I couldn't explain surfaced one after another. The sun beamed stronger than ever. It burst through the window, like a kaleidoscope of yellow light. It enveloped me and filled the room.

"Are you sure you're alright, Son?" Dad asked. "We just think it's the best thing for you to get to know your sister, I mean Sonia, your mother, a bit better."

Is that all I had to do, just get to know Sonia? The solution seemed so simple, so doable. *This will be easy. I'll smile more when I see her and be polite. If we're in the same room, maybe I'll stay a few minutes longer. I can do that.*

I stood there, managing all of the thoughts in my mind. It occurred to me that in order to forego a catastrophe I'd have to go and live with her, with Sonia. Every ounce of mounting security inside of me plummeted, and a wave of anxiety crashed over me. "Do I have to go and live with Sonia? I don't want to go, please don't make me go?"

"No, Son," Dad reached out and held my shoulders with both hands, as if to keep me from falling.

"Can everything stay the same?" I pleaded.

"Yes, Son." They said in unison, relief in their voices. For them, the worst was over.

"You don't have to live with her. This is your home," Mam assured, reinforcing the fact that nothing had to change.

"Okay, okay, Dad. I can do that," I smiled at the thought. My composure returned gradually, and I thought about the old woman on the bus, holding onto her seat with both hands. I sighed, feeling at ease, all of those strange feelings stuffed back down inside of me.

"Can I come out me room now? I want to come out now!" Sandra's voice drifted down from above.

The room remained silent.

"Give me a minute," Mam said and rushed out of the room, her slippers chafing the carpet as she went. Dad and I stared at each other. His eyes strained, and his lips pressed shut. He still looked like Dad.

Mam flew back into the room and slid the steaming plate onto the coffee table. "It's hot. Watch the plate. Your favorite, lamb chops and mashed potatoes. And ya can use your fingers." She sat me down in Dad's chair, as if nothing had happened. I picked up the giant shank with my hands and bit into the meat, while looking out through the window. Across the sky the torn clouds now resembled fibers of thread. I wondered what to do about my brown skin.

THE SPANIARD

The ball of his bare foot sunk into my navel and I thrust backward, blowing out into the static of the crowd. The 5,000-plus were in a frenzy, waving their flags, blowing their whistles, spurring on the stocky Spaniard. He barreled forward like a rabid dog. I grinned as I reeled backwards, sending a message: I've got it all under control, but I was angry with myself for letting him hit me so easily. This was not the time to be making mistakes. *This is for the world—don't blow it!*

It was my opening match of the World Championship. I had just turned twenty-three and I was fighting for my dream. Two days of opponents lined up, with two rounds against each one in the form of point fighting, also known as kickboxing or sport karate. It resembles fencing in the way one accumulates points for every punch or kick that effectively lands on your opponent.

Point fighting was born from traditional Japanese Kumite, which literally means 'grappling hands.' It later evolved into the more dynamic sport of Freestyle Kickboxing Karate. It's skillful, it's hard, it's fast, brutal, and it's honest. This sport holds to only one truth: win, move forward, win, until you're fighting for gold in the main stadium.

I was no stranger at working my way toward victory. I'd been ranked number one in the U.K. for the past two years. I revolutionized the sport throughout Europe by introducing a technique called the Blitz. Steve 'Nasty' Anderson, America's all-time, number one point fighter taught me the technique of pushing off the front foot to propel forward in attack. His six- foot-three frame resembled that of an N.F.L. running back. He taught me in the parking lot of Heathrow Airport when I'd been randomly asked to pick him up. I took it from him and re-invented it, making it my own while influencing a new generation of sport karate fighters. I traveled to and from the U.S., fighting independently. I led the way in shaping the very essence of the sport.

What makes Kevin Brewerton so special? Well, for start, he keeps on winning. Not only that, but he makes it look easy, which is something only the very best can do. Technically, he has brought freestyle karate fighting up to the level of fine art. He has the speed, the precision, the energy necessary to make him a champion, and in a sport forced into anonymity by the apathy of the press, he is a definite personality.
- Combat Magazine

I shook off the stiffness: the unfamiliarity of Budapest, the foreign crowd, the concrete room, the smell of disinfectant, the voices I couldn't understand, and the smooth wooden floor that made it difficult to gain my usual traction. These details didn't matter. It was now or never. I had to adjust or be sent home early with nothing. Nothing.

My opponent ran forward, cutting the ring off. He was trying to trap me in the ropeless corner and force me out of bounds, where points would be deducted. I moved around him, throwing out a long, left jab that glanced his glove. Arched eyebrows and wild eyes revealed his anxiety to win.

Another front kick powered toward me. I pushed it away with the palm of my glove, as I stepped to the side, looking for an opening to hit him with my right hand. He swung his arm into a wild careless hook, grazing my shoulder and forcing me to snap my head back. It sent the crowd into mania, making the Spaniard look impressive to the outside world. Inside, however, I knew that I'd eventually break him down, and make him pay the full price of losing. The referee threw his white-gloved hand into the air, punctuating the point. The Spaniard, who had become inspired, swung again, filling the air with a salty odor and the blurred red of his glove. He wasn't slowing down. Another punch launched at me. It brushed my cheek, sending me back on my heels, and back to Newcastle. A teenager, waking up in a boxing ring with the taste of leather in my mouth after being knocked out. *Never again*, I told myself on the way to school the following day. My front teeth were loose, but I convinced myself not to give up.

"Move," shouted Neville, my coach and teammate, from the sidelines. "Move, Move! Move!"

I danced around the Spaniard, throwing a cluster of punches, all three of them bouncing off his gloves. But then a fourth squeezed past his guard— a direct hit. His fleshy cheek absorbed my fist.

"Yes! Blitz him!" Neville's voice fueled me to go after my opponent with more vigor and punches that baffled his cumbersome body. Two more jabs snapped against the side of his head. The referee's hand flashed in the air, marking the points to get me closer to my dream.

"Watch him!" Neville shouted as the Spaniard thrust his stocky legs, propelling himself across the ring at me. I moved to the side, but my feet were losing grip. I couldn't counter punch without falling down, so I let him come and waited for him to stop. But he didn't. He was a spoiler, one of the worst kinds of fighters: spoiling everything with his mistimed, clumsiness of movement. I had to be careful not to get thrown off by it. Spoilers are notorious for ruining a fighter's poise. I threw a left hook. It landed on his shoulder. Then I threw a right which just kissed his shiny forehead. The crowd cheered, and his eyes lit up. He was determined. And I had yet to find my usual rhythm.

"Move!" Neville continued shouting. "Stay outside. He's a brawler!"

My left hand smashed into his face and then my right hand into his thick body. He grunted and swung, wrapping his arm around my neck. We were tangled in the middle of the ring. His short, spiked hair grated my face.

"Break! Break!" the referee shouted. His black bow tie twisted as he tried to pry us apart. The Spaniard refused to let go. His hot breath on my neck and his heart pounded against my body. He's punched himself out. *He's tired,* I told myself.

"Break!" The referee found the strength to push us apart. There wasn't much time left in the round—the only round. The Spaniard looked away, trying to hide his wearied eyes from me. But it was too late. I knew he was finished. I flicked out jab. It landed flush on his chin. The referee marked another point.

He grunted and came swinging back at me. The crowd cheered. He moved forward, as his corner men screamed into the ring. He swung a left hook, hauling all of his weight to gain momentum, but I leaned back, and it flew right past me. I smiled and shook my head at him, as I moved away, blocking all of his punches. He slowed with fatigue. I had found my usual flow.

The arena was on fire. There were two inches of snow outside, but inside it was an inferno. Nothing could be heard from Neville. The noise drowned him out.

I curved around the Spaniard in a big arc. *I want this. I want this. I have to win.* He bounced towards me. I threw a side kick into his body. He bent at the waist and dropped onto one knee, shaking his head at the floor. The crowd booed, the referee gave the point, and the Spaniard stood up, hunched, holding his rib cage like a lost boy. *I've got him. I've got him.*

"Fight!" The referee waved.

I ran at him. The Spaniard remained unmoved until my fist smashed into his jaw. He wobbled backward, his eyes staring at me, as if questioning "Why'd you do that?" The bell rang and the referee vaulted between us, preventing me from throwing another punch.

"Yes!" Neville ran across the ring raising his hands.

"Corners please!" the referee demanded.

"Just breathe, Kevin! Suck it in. Breathe." Neville walked me to my corner, spraying cold water into my mouth. "You took him apart."

Did I do enough? I asked myself, even though I knew I'd won. Neville faced me, the hot lights scorching down on us. It was a lot different than the time we first met, when I was 18 years old. I stood in the shadows of the old church car park, urinating against the wall, and Neville, the six-foot-two-inch Jamaican shouted, "Don't piss there, use the toilet!"

I'd come looking for a new martial arts teacher after moving to London. Neville, who was several years my senior, was once the teammate of Steve Babbs. He was also the British team coach, and a seasoned fighter. And there he was, framed in the church doorway, a black shadow of stone in the fading light of dusk.

"Gentlemen!" The referee waved me back to the middle of the ring for the obligatory announcement. The Spaniard was already there, bound in a red and yellow flag. The referee stood between us, holding our wrists, ready for the official announcement to lift the victor's arm. The crowd was silent, at last.

The speakers crackled and an eastern European woman's voice filled the room: "The winner is, Brewerton! Great Britain!" The Spaniard dropped to his knees as the referee lifted my arm.

I flew across Byker Bridge, the wind stinging my face as I pedaled my bike over the iron arch. "Newcastle's full of bridges," Dad would say when he used to take me to the Quayside on Sunday mornings to watch the tall ships sail past the Tyne Bridge. He had a love for ships and a dream to sail the seven seas. He'd told me many times that if he had his own way, he would have been a sailor, instead of an artilleryman. "The Germans blew up a lot of bridges in the war. Bastards. Bridges unite people, Son."

I pedaled as fast as I could, trying to catch up to the cars that blurred past me. I intended to ride to Sonia's house, except I crossed the bridge in the wrong direction. It had been almost a week since I learned Sonia wasn't my sister. "Ya can go see her anytime you want, Son. Whenever ya feel like it, and only if you want to," Dad said.

But each time I got on my bike to ride to her house, I'd found myself somewhere else. I would ride for miles, crossing all of the right bridges but always heading in the wrong direction. I gripped the handlebars, raised myself off the saddle, and churned the pedals harder. Even on a grey afternoon, the dim sunlight made the chrome on my handlebars glint like a freshly minted bar of silver. I panted hard and my legs burned as a wall of wind resisted me. Byker Bridge seemed longer than ever. I was like a leaf blowing over the side of the bridge into the ravine, a hundred feet below, where the atrophied arm of the River Tyne trickled its way through the dumping grounds of the council houses.

Cars zoomed past, leaving me to struggle against the added turbulence. I grew frustrated and felt stuck — on this bridge and in the questions swarming my mind for the last week. *Why had Sonia given me up? Who was my father?*

I rode harder through the cold wind, my hands chilling to the chrome handlebars, my face molding into a numb grimace. I hadn't felt anything about being Sonia's son. I didn't want to. The emotions of it all had frozen somewhere in the synapses of my brain when it tried to send the message to the rest of my body. It served me better to stay frozen and forgotten.

I shivered as I crossed the line where the bridge ends and Osborne Road began its endless incline. I didn't worry about having to weave my bike up the slope of penguin-like Saturday shoppers. My eyes were fixed on the marquee of a tall red-brick building: ODEON CINEMA PRESENTS BRUCE LEE IN ENTER THE DRAGON.

I turned down an alley and slumped back into the saddle. The scream of the wind was gone and replaced by the squeaking of my front wheel. I glided to the back of the cinema. Squeezing the brakes, I glanced over my shoulder and hopped onto the pavement. No one noticed me propping my bike against the wall and concealing it behind the rubbish bins. Nor did they see me climbing up the drainpipe toward the small toilet window of the men's lavatory.

A slight stench of sewage wafted up from the gutter as I twisted my feet around the pipe. Guilt was there, but like the smell from the gutter, it wasn't strong enough to stop me from continuing my ascent. I had already rationalized that it wasn't my fault the legal age to see Bruce Lee was eighteen. And since I had already snuck in to see the movie four times in the past five days, I assumed one more time shouldn't really matter.

I tugged at the window frame, but nothing happened. It was stuck. The trick was to close the window and leave it unlocked for future visits. *Had someone foiled my plan?* I pulled harder, and the window burst open. A rush of warm, urine-scented air hit my face, forcing me to turn my head. I took extra care not to fall into the urinal, as I had on my last visit.

I jumped to the floor and closed the window behind me. I peeked under the cubicles, looking for feet, and then I opened the door to see if the coast was clear. There was no sign of anyone, so I ran across the hallway and slipped through the doors into the dark cinema.

Bruce Lee's face filled the screen. Blood dripped from his cheek. It was the last fight scene of the movie. I scooched through a row of recalcitrant knees. "Hurry up, man! I can't fucking see! I'm missing the best bit," someone shouted from the darkness.

"Shhh! Fucking shut up!" yelled someone else.

I sat down in one of the few empty seats. The smell of sweat and popcorn filled the air. My arm brushed against the old man sitting to my left. He pushed his elbow further across my side of the armrest, marking his territory.

"You have offended my family, and you have offended the Shaolin Temple," Bruce Lee said. He clenched his fist. This was the best scene—he was about to fight Han, the drug lord who had murdered his sister.

A longhaired boy to my right chuckled as Han pulled off his prosthetic hand and replaced it with a four-bladed butcher's knife. I felt the old man's arm stiffen, and for a moment, there was not even a whisper in the cinema as the two men faced each other.

And then, Bruce exploded across the screen, unleashing a flurry of kicks. A volley of solidarity swept the aisles. "Chin him!"

"Stick one on him!"

"Watch that fucking hand!"

A roar rose up as Bruce smacked Han in the face with a kick, then another, and another. Every time Han received a blow, the person sitting in front of me twitched his head to the left and right.

Although I had missed most of the movie, this was worth climbing up the drainpipe. My body was hot and the back of my neck tingles. Bruce clenched his fists, so I clenched mine. He threw a kick at Han, and I kicked out under the seat in front of me. I rose from my chair as Han fell to the floor. Bruce gritted his teeth. A flood of anger poured out of his eyes. If Superman could burn through a wall with laser vision, then Bruce Lee could burn through a hundred walls, two hundred. I stared right into those eyes, the core of them, beyond the physical matter, further than the eye can see. A fire burned out of control, my fury and his meeting.

"The bastard! The bastard!" someone shouted from the back row. Han had picked up a spear and was charging. He missed and the spear lodged itself into the wall. Bruce danced around him and released his war cry – a high- pitched shrill that hoisted the hairs on my neck.

"Whoop, Whoop!" he cried.

Someone in the theatre whooped back, and a cacophony of the sound spread through the audience like a herd of ostriches.

"Whoop! Whoop! Whoop!" high and low pitches bounced back and forth.

In a panic, Han ran, disappearing through a concealed door. Bruce, with his chiseled torso, followed. A wave of silence fell across the cinema as Bruce found himself standing in a labyrinth of mirrors, puzzled. The sides of my neck were pounding. *Where is the enemy? Where is the target at which to unleash the rage? Where are the two hundred walls?* Everywhere Bruce turned, his own face stared back at him. All of that anger projected and returned by each mirrored wall.

Out of nowhere, Han attacked. Bruce threw a punch but missed, and Han was gone again. I was trapped in my seat. Bruce began to smash every mirror, destroying his reflection. Shards of glass scattered across the screen and cut into me. The cinema screen retracted into the size of a television, then a postage stamp. An entire world of pain was contained in that tiny shard of glass. I had this urge to push the old man's elbow away, stand on my seat and shout, "There's a whole world that you can't see, and it's trapped inside that tiny shard of glass!"

I jumped back as the screen abruptly expanded. Han attacked, but Bruce turned with hurricane force. Kicks and punches jolted Han as if he were being tattooed with a cattle prod. I jolted with him. "Yes, yes, yes," I shouted, cheering on Bruce to annihilate him.

The crowd roared, stomping our feet in unison. More hits bounced off Han, then the stomping ceased. My skin tightened. Bruce stood, watching Han stagger like a drunk. Time expanded as we watched each twitch of Han's body attempt to stay on its feet.

"Looks like he's had a pint of Brown Ale, and he can't handle it!" someone shouted. A roar of laughter broke out but was quickly silenced.

Bruce turned his body to the side and crouched like an animal ready to kill its prey. He lunged forward and kicked. Han's body flew backwards like an inanimate object traveling through space. He crashed into the wall and the spear that was lodged there skewered his chest, leaving him hanging like a torn doll.

The crowd gasped. A rush of heat swept down my arms and discharged into my fingertips. I was a prism of light reflected in the screen, into Bruce Lee's eyes. I was on fire; I felt everything he felt.

Applause erupted. Some spectators stood, others sat, motionless. I stared at the screen, filled up to the brim, intoxicated, yet simultaneously craving more, needing more, to quench the fire. No one left their seats until the final credits rolled and the lights went up.

"Everybody out. We've got to clean up!" shouted a red-pigtailed usher. I dodged through the foyer of people and burst onto the street, invincible. That was, until I ran down the alley to find someone had stolen my bike.

I jumped out of the empty lift and watched it continue up to the fourth floor, and then I ran to the stairway and raced it to the top. It was a game I used to measure my speed when we lived on Queens Court. There were eight flights of stairs and I was determined to see if I could reach the top faster than a cumbersome machine pulled by cables.

Though I knew the empty box was ascending effortlessly, at a steady pace, the lack of knowing exactly where the lift was at a given moment intrigued me. It proved more difficult as I scrambled up the stairwell, racing after, what seemed, a meteorite hurtling past me.

I reached the top, out of breath, and looked at my watch. *Nineteen seconds.* Slower than my usual time. Perhaps the incident with Jimmy or losing my bike the week prior had its effects. Since then, my feet had become my main mode of transportation, and I'd just run home after viewing Enter the Dragon for the ninth time.

I walked down the narrow corridor of council flats. The lift chimed behind me as it docked on the top floor. It was an invitation for me to race again, but I declined. I reached my front door—112 Queens Court—and knocked, expecting Sandra to answer. When the door opened, it was Sonia.

"Hello, Kevin."

We stood there, her hands holding each side of the doorframe and mine holding the sides of my trousers. I was stuck. *What do I do? What do I say?* I looked into her eyes to see that she was stuck, too. *Were we supposed to scream in anger or laugh hysterically? Do we run into each other's arms and cry with joy?*

"Hello," my voice measured, like a spurt of air escaping a balloon while the rest stayed sealed inside. She smiled, so I smiled back. It was an automatic response. I had already told myself that I would be polite.

"Well, are you coming in or not, our Kevin?" She sunk her hands into the pockets of her tweed overcoat. *She's wearing her coat, maybe she's leaving soon.* I didn't want to move, but I prayed for a short-lived encounter and stepped inside. Sonia closed the door behind me. The door of the living room opened, and Mam stepped out, trapping us all together in the small hallway.

"You want some tea, Son?" she prompted. "Have some tea and biscuits."

"Okay, Mam," I whispered, standing between two mothers. Calling my mam "Mam" in front of Sonia made me feel uneasy. I didn't want to hurt Sonia's feelings. She seemed unmoved, so I repeated myself.

"Okay, Mam," I said, biting down harder on the word, establishing my boundary. We walked into the living room.

"Hello, Kevin!" a trio of voices rang out. Saif was sitting on the sofa between his sisters—my sisters—all three with straight, shiny black hair and pearly white smiles.

"Howay, Kev, you're just in time," Dad reclined in his armchair in his usual manner, both feet resting on the glass coffee table. His green socks matched the teapot, and the table was cluttered with cups and saucers. Though the scene was familiar, something seemed artificial. Mam and Sonia appeared carefree, but I felt the inevitable torque of rope pulling me in either direction.

Sonia rested her hand on my shoulder. "We all wanted to come and say hello, our Kevin."

"Look at me hair!" Sandra shouted. She'd been sitting on the floor, crossed legged, flipping through the family photo album. "I don't remember me hair being that short!"

No one paid attention to her. It was as if she was sitting alone, going through her own personal memories, while the conversation continued around her.

"The girls are getting more and more beautiful every time I see them," Mam laughed, and they blushed. "Come over here and sit next to ya Nana. I haven't seen you in months." They sat perched on the armrests of the chair, framing Mam, like exotic birds in flowered dresses.

The room was full and cluttered. There wasn't a space for me to go, so I stood in the center of the room, watching Sonia spoon sugar into the teacups. Dad remained reclined, as if he were having the best day of his life. "Saif, get over there!" he suggested. "Stand next to our Kevin. He's getting taller, Kev. He's catching you up."

"He's only up to my shoulder," I responded, looking down at Saif. His scruffy face and big brown eyes looked back at me. He wanted to play, but I was focused on holding my tongue. *Why didn't you tell me that I wasn't really your uncle? When I taught you how to ride my bike, and when we played in the Dene, and I showed you my secret hiding places. Why didn't you tell me?*

"Saif! Saif!" Sonia held out a cup and saucer with two biscuits balancing on the side. "Give this to your Nana, and don't spill it."

"There's a picture here of you, Dad! It's when you were at war, away in the army!" Sandra held up a photograph. No one replied.

"Our Kevin, do you want some tea?" Sonia suggested.

"No thanks."

"Go on have some tea, Kev." Dad bit into a biscuit, the crumbs fell into the creases of his brown cardigan.

"I'm not thirsty," I answered.

"He's not thirsty, George. He's teetotal!" Mam burst into laughter and the girls chuckled with her. The rest of the room joined in joyously. Mam was an expert of making light of a serious situation and steering a conversation out of danger. Our home was celebratory, and I wondered if the family was gathered to mark that the secret was out.

"There's me and Sonia!" Sandra forced her voice through the laughter and hoisted a photograph. "School picture day. That was just before Sonia got pregnant with our Kevin."

I felt a jolt in the room that couldn't be ignored by anyone. We'd been turned upside down with Sandra's innocent ramblings of nostalgia and were now falling into a void – the black hole of a moment's silence stretched through the room. The force prompted everyone to drop their heads, stir their tea and fuss with their cups and saucers, pretending nothing had been said. Sandra went on merrily, flicking through the photo album, unaware of her power to derail the family gathering at any moment.

"Mmmm. I'm telling ya—they're much better soggy!" Mam held up a droopy biscuit, rerouting the conversation. Zhora and Shona giggled and Saif bent over laughing. They were ignorant of the silent war taking place.

"Bastard tea's hot!" Dad shouted.

"Watch your language, George," exclaimed Mam. "I burned me lips!"

"Serves you right, George!"

"Kev, go in the kitchen and brew a fresh pot, will ya?" Dad stood up.

"I'll go!" Sandra closed the photo album.

"No, you won't!" Dad corrected. "You'll stay where you are!"

I grabbed the teapot from him, eager to leave the room and grateful to Dad for recognizing my need to escape. When I walked into the kitchen, the door swung shut behind me. I looked out of the window as I emptied the teapot into the sink. Across the street, the floodlights from St. James Park, the football stadium, were lit, giving the grey sky a synthetic glow. The kitchen door creaked open. "Da?" I turned around.

"No, it's me." Sonia walked in, unbuttoning her coat. Her voice was soft and her eyes cautious. "Do you need any help?"

"No, thank you. I'm alright." I turned and grabbed the tea caddy.

"I just wondered if you wanted to talk about anything, Kevin?" She stood next to me, and I pulled the lid off the caddy, inhaling the fragrance as it escaped the tin. "Kevin, do you want to talk?"

I glanced at her eyes, then down to the yellow buttons on her coat. I wished to smile at her the way I did when she was my sister. I liked her better as my sister.

"I wanted to tell you," she confessed. "But now you know. The girls are excited, and Saif's been telling all his friends." Her voice lifted into a forced chuckle and then dropped back to its previous monitored tone. "I'm proud of you, our Kevin."

Why? I wondered. *Because I'm her son?* We had fewer memories to share than most in the way that a mother and son would recollect, except on one occasion. When I was younger and Sonia came to visit in the Dene, she taught me how to memorize the two times table. She sat with me until I knew it all. *I remember that.* Maybe she was proud of me for that.

She smiled at me. I smiled and turned back to the teapot. I didn't want her to get to the part where she might say that I can call her "Mam". I scooped the tea into the pot.

"That's a lot of tea," she laughed. "That'll put hairs on ya chest."

"My Mam likes her tea strong," I said.

"Mam!" Zohra shouted and ran into the kitchen. Her hands flailed and her eyes darted back and forth towards me, Sonia, and where she had just come from. "Saif knocked over Nana's tea! It's all over her dress!"

"I told him! I told him a hundred times," Sonia stepped forward, grabbing a dishcloth from the sink and ran into the living room. "Oh, no, no, no!"

The sound of her escalating protest, while she disappeared into the other room seemed unnatural. It was as if she was redirecting all that she wanted to say to me towards the spilt tea on Mam's dress. Her voice sounded powerless. Or perhaps that was just how I felt inside.

I turned and finished pouring the hot water into the teapot, leaving it on the side for Dad. Then I slipped out of the front door, as a distant applause rippled across from the stadium. I headed towards the lift.

The hallway at the Quaker meeting house was filled with people of all ages and sizes. On the wall hung a sign that read: The doctrine of the inner light is working through the soul. It was an unlikely venue to learn an ancient Chinese art of self-defense. However, since Enter the Dragon had made its debut, martial arts schools were popping up all over the country in the most religious of locations, such as church halls or meeting rooms, like the one I was fighting to get into.

Shouts came from the street: "Move up! It's starting to fucking rain!" Everyone tried to move inside the building, but it was too crowded. I hadn't seen people queue with this much enthusiasm since going to see the Bay City Rollers perform at the city hall. I dug my hands into my pockets and held onto the newspaper clipping Dad had given me. SELF-DEFENSE CLASS–FREE KUNG-FU SUIT. It was the reason I was there, to get a free kung-fu suit, so I could parade around like Bruce. I wasn't even sure I wanted to learn martial arts. I told myself that I would try it out, put my toe in the water. But it was the suit that attracted me.

"Here," Dad had said, tearing the ad from the newspaper. There was something in the tone of his voice that took me by surprise. "You wanna learn?" he said. I hesitated, assuming his gesture was sparked by guilt for not telling me about Sonia. Or maybe somehow, he knew I had climbed through a toilet window thirteen times to see Enter the Dragon.

"Yeah, Da. I wanna learn." I snatched the paper from his hand, and imagined myself, kicking in the air, like Bruce.

"Alreet! Get in here and line up!" A thick Geordie accent flew over our heads. Attached to the voice was a tall, blue-eyed man. He was lean and muscular with short-cropped hair. We moved into the room, hustling ourway in, not knowing what to expect. I thought I felt a nudge from behind. Darkie flashed through my mind and rapidly disappeared.

"Take your shoes off and line up! I want eight lines of people. As quick as you can!" I threw down my jacket and slipped off my shoes and socks. I stood at the back of the room, tall as I could, trying to blend in. The room was filled with all kinds of people, from school kids to grown men who look like they'd just come from laboring all day in a shipyard. A few women were scattered about. Most of us first-time participants wore regular clothes: T-shirts, shorts, rolled-up jeans. I stood in my turned-up school trousers, imagining where the kung-fu suits were being stored and if I would get mine by the end of the class. Two rows down, a man stood in white work overalls splattered with paint.

A voice cut through the noise, "Me name's Ian Walker, and I will be assisting the teacher. This is Lau-Gar Kung-Fu."

He couldn't have been doing this for much longer than anyone else that was there, but he had the presence of a foreman, assuming the position of authority while bridging the colloquial language to something seemingly foreign. He pointed to the side of the room, where a door opened. Out walked an Asian man with silky black hair that matched the sash around his waist. We watched in awe as he sprung onto the stage like a cat and turned to face the crowd, looking down at us through his square, wire-framed glasses.

"My name is Mr. Tin!"

Wow, I thought. *He looks just like Bruce!*

Tin pushed his glasses up the bridge of his nose, punctuating his monosyllabic sentence: "First-we-bow!" Mr. Tin raised his hands, making a fist with one and placing it into the palm of the other hand.

"Stand straight. We're gonna start!" Walker shouted from the side of the room and then joined the ranks as one of the students. The mob stirred with excitement, and the clapping sound of fists against palms echoed in the meeting house. We followed Mr. Tin and bowed before him.

"Now you run!" Mr. Tin instructed, as he straightened his black sash.

"It's time to get warmed up. Everybody run around the hall!" Walker echoed. We looked at each other for a moment, unsure what to do. Then, realizing that we had been given free reign, we stampeded. Fifty or more unruly Geordies ran bare-footed, pushing, and elbowing each other. Some fell over and clambered back on their feet, while others maintained a steady pace. We each marveled at Mr. Tin, who was stretching and throwing warm up kicks at the side of the room.

"Slow down! You're just supposed to be warming up!" Walker shouted. After waiting more than an hour in a queue, each member of this boisterous mob was determined to prove their worth in the presence of a kung-fu master.

"Out me way!" A thick body barreled past me. I was running in step with this rapid flow. A hand grabbed my collar from behind, trying to pull me back. Without looking, I swung my arm behind me, slapping someone in the face. I felt the fleshy cheek and saliva on the back of my hand. It was strangely satisfying.

Is this kung fu? It resembled more like Murder Ball, a game the P.E. teachers occasionally allowed us to play at school. We'd run around the gym floor in a free for all, trying to grab hold of a medicine ball. The object was to keep possession of it, while everyone randomly kicked and punched at each other. The teacher would stand to the side, entertained by the carnage. I continued my stride, glancing over at Mr. Tin, who was now standing like the general of an army, scanning the ranks. I ran harder. There was chaos all around, but I felt free.

"Everybody get back in your lines! Now!" Walker's voice echoed. "Hurry it up! Ya got ten seconds!"

We scrambled to get back in line. A strong hand grabbed my shoulder, guiding me in the right direction. There was power in this grip, and when I turned to look, it was a muscular man. Everything about him looked hard, except for the nurturing look in his eyes. I thought of Dad, his mercurial temperament, and how he could move from gentleness to all-outrage in the blink of an eye.

"Ya better hurry up!" I was nudged as another voice broke my thought. It was the man in the painted overalls, smiling as he walked past and pointed to an open space where the lines were forming. Mr. Tin clapped his hands three times and the room quieted to random sniffles and a throb of heavy breathing.

"First lesson. You must learn. Self-control!" Mr. Tin's voice cut through the air like a scalpel. I felt awkward. *Could I really learn? Could I really be like Bruce?* Out of the corner of my eye, the yellow sign of the exit door illuminated. I dismissed the urge to leave and kept my focus on Mr. Tin. This was a lot different than Murder Ball, where the chaos was without purpose. There was a method here, and a way of mystique.

"This is left fighting stance." Mr. Tin stepped forward and raised his clenched fists. Gasps spread around the room as we stepped forward, trying to copy Mr. Tin's move.

"No. No. No." He jumped down from the stage and started down the lines of people, twisting wrists, slapping and squeezing arms, like a farmer inspecting crops in a cornfield. No one was overlooked as he floated along the rows.

He stood in front of me. I didn't know what to do. I tightened my jaw as hard as my fists were clenched and stared at his protruding Adam's apple with intensity. He moved my fist an inch with his finger as if to peek through a curtain. Then he left, a scent of carbolic soap and garlic trailing behind him. "When I give order, you take one step, one punch." He jumped back onto the stage.

"Wait! Wait for my count," he urged. "It takes strength to use control!" But we were foaming at the mouth, and my heart was racing.

"Hup," Mr. Tin shouted, moving with the grace of a dancer as he punched into the air. His body was a whirling instrument of destruction. Ian signaled us to follow Mr. Tin's lead, but before he lifted his hand high enough to extend his finger, we had already moved like Frankenstein's monster taking its first step. I swung as hard as I could, trying to exhale in the same modulated way that Mr. Tin had. Instead, a wail came out of me that fused with the dissonant chorus and soared into the roof of the meeting room.

"Hup," Tin commanded. I stepped and punched, but I strained my neck and my elbow trying to coordinate my fists with my footsteps. It was not as easy as it looked on screen or watching Mr. Tin.

"Keep straight!" he ordered. Up and down the hall we moved, veering left and right as Mr. Tin led us in broken English, his body moving in swift smooth lines.

Then came the kicks. I saw the muscular man lunging down the side of the room, thrusting kicks into the air, knocking down a series of invisible doors. His thick thighs struck a greater force than air, signifying a power I'd not yet seen. I wanted it. I wanted to fly through the air like Bruce Lee, smashing all of those mirrors until they're gone, every last bit, destroyed and gone forever. I could barely move my heavy body, my head feeling light from the muggy room. The walls were damp and the smell of sweat hung in the air.

Mr. Tin sustained a relentless pace, intent on sifting out the weak. Several people stepped out of the room and picked up their shoes on the way to the exit door. I struggled against the urge to do the same, reminding myself of the prize, that free kung-fu suit.

Finally, after more than an hour, Mr. Tin shouted, "Finish." He clapped his hands three times. "Quiet!" He hushed the room from the stage. "Stand and breathe," he demanded.

The deep breathing, random coughing, and rain tapping at the windows was melodic. I took inventory of my aching body. I was a rag that has had all the sweat wrung out of it. And yet, as I stood there full, I felt something inside, an intuitive whisper, "I think you should come back and do this again." It's visit was short, overtaken by anger and a deeper sense of betrayal. My surroundings shifted and somehow, I was standing in front of Mam and Dad. *How could they all keep this secret from me for so long?*

I know where your real Dad's from," Cookie said. I looked back at him as we stood on the patch of grass outside Queens Court. Cookie was an old friend of the family. He was seventeen, tall and brimming with swagger. He had a full smile and big sparkling eyes that together formed a crafty expression. The son of Pakistani parents, who were friends of Hanif, Sonia's husband, Cookie showed up at our door a day earlier, looking for a place to stay. I'd never seen Cookie outside the context of his own family setting. But when he showed up at the front door in need of a place to stay, my parents didn't hesitate to let him in, and of course, I gladly shared my room.

"What? What are you talking about?" I said.

"I know," he smiled again, this time bigger and more telling.

"You know nothing. You're a liar."

"No, I'm not." He stood between a tree and a wall, which had served as our goal posts during a one-on-one game of football.

"How do you know?" I asked.

"Sonia told me a long time ago."

"I don't believe you."

"It's true."

"Who is he then, my father?"

"I don't know."

"You just told me you know who he is?"

"What I mean is, I know where he's from." Cookie clarified, in a care- free, matter of fact, way.

"What?"

"Haven't you ever wondered why you're darker than Saif, Shona and Zhora, and why their hair is straight and yours is curly?"

I reached up and grasped my hair. "So? What does that mean?"

I stood, looking at Cookie. My eyes descended the curve of his large bent nose and down his gawky frame, right down to the bottom of his flared trousers. I was in search of a lie, a flinch or a wink that might contradict his speech. But his body remained straight and upright and his eyes wide, staring right back at me. The fact that someone who wasn't a direct family member possessed more knowledge about my father than I did infuriated me. A warmth rolled upward from my stomach and into my chest. I stepped forward until I was nose to nose with him. A cool wind brushed against us.

"Ok," he relented, his warm breath on my face. "I'll tell you where he's from. He's from Africa."

"Africa?" I repeated. The shape of the word widened my mouth into the grimace of a silent cry, not produced by anger. This sigh was one of pure joy. A bell rang through every cell of my body, the convulsion of a slot machine spitting out a torrent of silver coins to an unsuspecting gambler. JACKPOT! The part of me that was frozen, the part of me that had said NO, now said YES to Africa. *Yes! Yes! Yes! Yes!* Somewhere in my DNA, a compass had been aligned.

"Get out, Kevin. I need to use the toilet," Sandra shouted through the bathroom door. "You've been in there for bloody ages!"

"I'm nearly finished." I rinsed my hands in the sink.

"Mam! Mam! He won't listen to me," her voice retreated down the stairs.

I dried my face and looked in the mirror, studying my skin and wondering if Cookie had really told me the truth. I wanted to ask him one last time, but when I woke the next morning, his blankets were neatly folded at the foot of my bed. I knew then that he wasn't coming back. Perhaps the purpose of his visit was purely to give me the news of my father.

I rinsed my hands again, scrubbing them like a surgeon and holding them up to the light. Mam noticed me staring at my palms while we sat at the breakfast table. "What's the first sign of madness?" she said to me.

"I dunno, Mam."

"Hairs on the palms of ya hands, and the second sign is looking for them," she burst into laughter. No one but me knew what I searched for. It had been two days since Cookie left, and I'd become obsessed with the thought of being African. It was like I'd discovered something magical. Finding out the truth made everything come into focus.

On the surface, I was relaxed and unchanged, but inside I erupted with imagination. I sat, pondering the thought of being part of Africa. I scoured our family tree foraging for someone I could trust to confirm Cookie's news. I was afraid to ask Dad, not because of his rage, but because he might tell me it wasn't true.

"You've been a bit quiet, Kev. Are you all right?" Dad picked up his cup of tea.

"Yeah, I'm fine."

"Leave him alone, George. He's having his breakfast." Mam walked over holding a frying pan and flipped a fried sausage onto my plate.

I gazed in the mirror, looking for a trace of Africa in my small straight nose. Or was it in the curve of my English lips that made me different? Or was it the thick, black curls of my hair that proved my bloodline? The back of my hand was where I'd seen the most hope. My eye traced its shape, like an astronomer lost in the lens of a telescope. The reddish tint and the way the skin formed over my knuckles into tiny creases of dark brown encouraged me to declare over and over.

"These are African hands. These are African hands..."

W hat are you writing?" he asks me.

"I'm writing a memoir."

"I was once offered ten million dollars to do a memoir," he says.

"Ten million? Did you do it?"

"No. They had a writer who came to meet me. We sat down. It was okay at first, and then he started asking me personal questions. I said, 'Fuck. No way.' That shit was too hard."

I can't help but notice how open he is with me. We seem to have gotten closer. I've been coming here every day for the past four months, with the intention of training, but we never quite get there. We usually just sit here spending hours talking about everything else.

"Wow," I say, envisioning what it would be like to be offered ten million dollars to write a book, while remembering that vulnerability is of no use to a fighter.

"This might sound strange to you, but believe it or not, in art, vulnerability is a strength."

"What?"

"Crazy, right? That's the first thing I learned when I started acting."

"Really?" he says, looking uncomfortable and uninterested in the subject. He shifts his weight around in his chair.

"People see themselves in the struggles. That's why we love the underdog,"

He looks right at me without blinking, and says, "I got into fighting because I wanted to be someone else. I was ashamed."

"So did I," I realize how easy it is to admit that to him. "Fighting gave me a new identity. I could be someone else, and yet completely be myself. The more victories I had, the more I could hide all of the things I didn't like about my past. Early in my career, once I'd moved to London, at the age of seventeen, I realized that I could start a new life. When I was in college, everyone was from somewhere else. Whether it was the West Indies, or Africa, or other places. It was exciting. No one knew me or had any idea where I was from. It was a new world. It occurred to me that I could be anyone I wanted to be.

"One day, I'd told someone that I was American. It seemed so natural to say that. It stuck, and I began building a new identity. I told people that I was from

Miami. I said that because Miami was the first American city I ever visited. At the time it all made perfect sense. It empowered me. And in my position as a champion no one ever questioned me. Even friends from Newcastle who knew me, seemed to accept a different reality. Perhaps it was out of love, or just simply not knowing my past. I wasn't saying that I never grew up in Newcastle, I was saying that I was born in America.

"I had created an enigma, and the newspapers, magazine, and interviews made it all real and substantial. It was a rebirth. A chance to wipe the slate clean and start anew. I felt like I had total command of my life. The more I think about it, I must have needed to take back control and be in possession of my own identity. I had the power. I was both the author and the protagonist, re-writing my own story."

I stop and pause for a moment, feeling slightly embarrassed. I swivel my chair a few degrees to look upon the horizon. There is a clean line that separates the ocean from the sky. My discomfort is growing, and yet, there is something very freeing about being able to speak openly. A part of me questions if I sound crazy, or if he understands. Then, I feel my chair turn. I look down and notice his leg extended and the tip of his bare toe rotating my chair back into direct alignment with his. There is a pause, and a recognition as we look at each other. I'm not sure what to say or feel. I just allow myself to be open.

"How did you get into art?" he asks, laying back and grounding himself into the chair. He's engaged by the conversation.

"I had an acting teacher who was also a director and painter. His name was Milton Katselas. He was from an era when American art was redefining itself in society and the artist was becoming a new archetype of change. He's the one who taught me about vulnerability. He was a guru, but not the obvious type in robes. He was a tough Greek guy from Pittsburgh. He seemed more like a fighting coach. He was rugged and straight to the point. He used to say, 'It doesn't hurt to leave a little blood on stage.' He meant that metaphorically, but you never knew with him. He called me The Warrior. He talked in a way that I could relate and helped me to understand what art really is. It's the same as fighting. It's all about having a purpose and being a pro and breaking through your own limitations."

"Sounds like Cus Damato. He was like that. Tough guy."

"Being vulnerable is being willing to let your guard down," I try to explain.

"Cus would shout at me every time I dropped my guard. 'Keep your god damned hands up.'" We sit back in our armchairs and look at each other without saying a word.

I stood outside 39 Haggerston Crescent. The three-story house reared up above me. It was the second to last house on a cul-de sac, opposite a busy road. Barking came from inside and the tip of a wet snout forced its way through the letterbox.

"There's nobody there! Stop ya barking!" A voice shouted from inside the house. It's Doreen's voice. The dog barks louder, and its nose attacks the letterbox again. I stepped back, hiding myself in the shape of the overgrown ivy that hung at the side of the door. Should I call her Auntie Doreen now that I know Sonia isn't my sister? Am I making the right choice to come and speak to her first? She'll understand, I determined.

She had been my big "sister" for so long, with the house full of pets and people and music and food from the West Indies, where her ex-husband, Rocky, came from. He was a limbo dancer with midnight skin and a mouthful of gold teeth. She had to understand.

My main reason for coming to her house was the fact that her children—my cousins, who I once thought were my nieces and nephew, Mark, Alison, Cheryl and Debbie—looked like me. Debbie, the eldest, was eight days younger than I. Eight days was all that stood between us. It was easy for me to conclude that Doreen knew who had made her sister pregnant. I stepped forward. The dog barked louder, and the door cracked open. The black head of a Labrador squeezed through the gap.

"Who's there?" The door swung wide open and the Labrador pounced at me, licking my face.

"Eee, our Kevin!" Doreen's eyes lit up, her long false eyelashes flickered as her full frame stumbled through the door in a lime green dress.

"Kingsley! Stop licking our Kevin's face!" She grabbed his collar and yanked him back into the house. "I'll just be a minute!" The door closed and opened again with just enough time for me to wipe my face with the back of my hand.

"There, I've put him away!" She stood in the doorway. "What a surprise, our Kevin. Come on, Son, quick. I've got the stew simmering." She walked into the house, and I followed along the narrow corridor of soft carpet and orange wallpaper. We passed the open door of the living room with its black leather sofa and red lava lamp. Hanging beads clanged as we enter the kitchen. A melody of sweet spices wafted in my face.

"Nobody's here. They're not back from school yet," Doreen said. I sat down at the kitchen table.

"The food's nearly ready." She walked over to me and placed a bowl of grapes on the table. "Help yourself. I'm so pleased to see you, Kevin."

I plucked a grape and tossed it into my mouth, feeling exhilarated by the moment.

"So, what brings you over, Kev? Haven't seen you in months." She picked up an onion and turned to face the counter.

"Oh, well, I just ... well, I just felt like popping in." I stared at the back of her head where a whirl of hair was rolled into a bun.

"I hate chopping these onions. They're making me cry. The trick is to chop them quick. Get it over with. Get it done." She chopped and sliced, her head rearing back from the fumes of the onion. My heart raced at the sound of the knife on the chopping board.

"Do you know who my dad is?" I said, involuntarily slapping my knee with the palm of my hand. The knife stopped and the room fell still. My heart beat stronger. I was terrified that everything I had been dreaming could be proven false.

She turned around, knife in hand and mascara streaking down her cheeks. She looked directly at me, paused for a moment, and then with reverence in her voice, as a deep reflection passed across her eyes, "I knew this day would come."

Warmth flooded my body, and a sense of relief, as I wondered what day it was that she knew would come?

"Do you know I'm not your sister?" she questioned cautiously.

"I know," my voice was strong and clearer than ever. Her eyelashes flickered as I continued, "And I don't care about that."

It was true. I didn't care. She was the same as she'd always been, as was everyone else. They were the same people, in the same positions, just with different labels. Nothing had changed in relation to them, and yet everything was changing within me and how I viewed myself. "I want to know who my Dad is. That's why I'm here."

"What made you come to me, our Kevin?"

"I thought you'd understand because your children are like me."

She hesitated. I noticed her gathering her thoughts, her mind reaching back all of those years, before I was born, before any of her children were born.

"Oh yes. Oh yes," she said passionately, clearing her conscience. "Sonia and me were hanging out with the same crowd; he was a friend of a friend. We were all spending time together, our Kevin. That's how it all began." Then she stopped and took a deep breath before continuing. "But I think the best thing for you to do is to go and talk to Sonia. She'll tell you everything that I can and more."

"Just tell me one thing, just one thing," I requested. "Was he from Africa?"

"Yes! He was from Africa; he was from Africa indeed, but you need to talk to Sonia. That'll be your best bet." She wiped the mascara from her cheek.

Relief settled, amidst the sweet-smelling spices of West Indian cuisine, as she confirmed my belief with such clarity. My father was from Africa. *This is as good as it gets,* I told myself, knowing that I could always come back. I could always rely on Doreen, my sister, my aunt. Her title didn't matter. I'd become closer to her in that moment than I'd ever been before.

"Thanks so much," I said, longing to wrap my arms around her. But a stronger urge pulled me along to the next stop in my journey, facing Sonia.

"I'm glad you came to me, Kevin. You can always come and ask me anything." Doreen's words reached out, but I was already out of the kitchen, almost running, the hanging beads swinging behind me.

The sky was a pale blue sheet, pressing down on the jagged rooftops of the council houses. I walked down the empty street; the concrete echoed the brisk pace of my footsteps. I could feel a momentum building within, and I was armed with a truth that even Sonia couldn't deny. As much as I wanted to believe that I could have gone to talk with her first, instead of going to Doreen, the fact of the matter was that I didn't think Sonia would tell me the truth.

Since learning that she had kept the secret from me, it had been hard to trust her. It was the smiles that bothered me the most, and her subtle ways of being elusive. In retrospect, I could see it all —how she had avoided me all of those years without once raising my suspicion that anything could have been different. It bothered me to my core.

The echoing sound beneath my feet grew louder. It was a persistent tapping of heel against stone, the rhythm of a drum preventing me from turning back. It felt good, effortless. It carried me down the empty street until I reached Sonia's front door. *There's no turning back now,* I told myself, although the melody beneath my feet had ceased. I rapped on the door before I could change my mind.

My shoulders were rigid, my palms were sweating, and tiny waves rippled through me like a tide creeping in. *Will she tell me the truth?* The door opened.

"Kevin?" Sonia stood with a pink feather duster in hand, her brown hair tousled. "I don't believe it!" Her smile widened. "Well, come on in, our Kevin." She stepped to the side and waved the duster, as I walked into the house. The perfumed smell of floral air freshener filled the passageway.

"I was just spring cleaning." She tucked the duster into her apron and brushed her hair to the side. "I wish I knew you were coming. I'm a mess. Go in and make yourself at home."

She laughed as I walked into the blue and grey living room and sat at the edge of the couch, where a small square coffee table held a bowl of red apples. I looked around. Not a stitch was out of place, from the wool fibers of the couch and two matching chairs at perfect right angles to the polished glass ashtray on the window ledge. The navy-blue curtains were trimmed and tucked to the side to reveal a small brick backyard.

"Can you smell cigarette smoke?" She wafted at the air with her duster and sat at the opposite end of the couch, turning to face me.

"No, I can't smell anything." I looked at the bowl of apples.

"Are you hungry, our Kevin?"

"No, not really."

"Good, 'cos I hope you realize them apples are plastic," she chuckled and reached over to dust the tops of the apples. "See?"

I smiled, "They look real."

"That's the point," she bellowed. "I'm tickled pink." Her laughter increased as if she'd heard the funniest joke in the world. It sounded as artificial as the apples.

Is she that happy to see me? I wondered, *or was she as nervous as I was?*

"Tickled pink, you get it?" She waved the duster. "I'm tickled pink. Now, what can I get you to eat, our Kevin?"

"Nothing. I just wanted to ask you a question."

Her eyes became still. "Oh, really? What did you want to ask?"

"Who's my real dad?" The words blurted out before I could stop them. Her gaze turned downward and her shoulders retracted into the couch. A calm and measured smile told me she was now focused and defensive.

"Your dad?" her voice reduced to a whisper.

"Yes, my dad." My voice swelled, as Doreen's words echoed in the back of my head, *I knew this day would come.*

"Is he from Africa?" I leaned forward.

Her hand clutched at the feather duster laying in her lap. She paused for a moment, then she said, "Yes. He's from Africa."

My heart exploded like a rocket crashing through my chest, tearing through the roof of the house and hurtling toward space. We sat in the neat, tidy, blue and grey living room. Her face was pale, but I couldn't stop the questions.

"Which part of Africa?"

Her shoulders retracted again, and her lips seemed to tighten. "Ghu...Gi," She stumbled with the words, forcing them out of her mouth. "Ga, Ga, Ghana... I think it was Ghana."

"Are you sure?"

"Yes, he told me Ghana. That's what he said. Ghana." There was a sweetness that entered my ear in the awkward way in which she pronounced, "Ghana." It was the foreign-ness of it, the incongruence of a word sounding like that in a place like Newcastle that reassured me. I belong somewhere else.

"Ghana." I repeated, sounding the word like a food taster, savoring the first bite. It was delicious. "Tell me about him."

"It was a long time ago, Kevin."

"What's his name?"

"His name is Addo. And he was going to the university."

"Addo! Is that his first name?"

"I don't know. I just knew him as Addo."

"Why was he at the university?"

"I think he was going to be a doctor."

"A doctor?"

"Yes."

"Do you know where he is?"

"No."

"What does he look like?"

She glanced down at the feather duster. I wondered if she was reconstructing his face or inventing a lie. "He looked good."

"Looked good?" *Had she forgotten what he looked like?* I wanted more than that. I wanted to see the shape of his jaw, his nose, his eyes. Anything.

"What do you mean?"

"Doreen introduced us. And when I got pregnant, I stopped seeing him."

"What do you mean, you stopped seeing him?"

"I just did."

"Why?"

"Listen, Kevin. It was a long time ago."

"But I need to know. I need to know. It's not fair!"

I was outraged that I had to reason with her to find out the most rudimentary aspects of my existence. *Shouldn't it have been given to me freely? Should it not be my birthright?* My mind whirled in all directions. I needed to know so many things. I wanted to ask why she hadn't spoken to Doreen in so long, but the impulse retreated as I looked down at the feather duster.

"Did he know that I was born?"

Sonia paused and her body seemed to tighten. Her eyes were opaque. "He didn't know that I was pregnant, Kevin. I didn't tell him."

"What?" I stood up. Anger rose in me and my body tensed. "Why didn't you tell him?"

"I just didn't. It was a long time ago, Kevin. I just don't remember. I wish I could tell you more."

"How come you don't remember?"

She was silent. I waited for an answer, while I tried to make sense of the conversation. *Could she have actually forgotten what my father looked like?* I recognize the tightness in my gut. It was the same feeling I'd get when I'd see Mam's face in the aftermath of violence. It was the knowledge of having to live with an unchangeable narrative I had no choice but to accept. *Should I just agree with Sonia? Should I just agree and carry on with the way things are?*

"No. No. I don't believe you!" I spat the words out. Tears welled up in my eyes.

"But Kevin. It's true."

"Why didn't you tell me? How come everyone knew but me? You didn't say anything. You never said a word!"

Sonia stood up. The feather duster pointed at me. "I wanted to tell you. I wanted to say something."

"Why didn't you?"

"I was scared! I wanted to call you my son, but me Mam wouldn't let me. She took over right from day one and she wouldn't give you back."

"What?"

"I was young, our Kevin. I was just a little girl."

"Why won't you tell me?"

"I've told you all I know, there's nothing else to say. That's it, Kevin." I looked straight at her. She forced a smile to cover an overwhelming frown. *Was she lying about wanting to call me her son, or was she just saying that to distract me from asking about my father?*

"Who else would know him?"

"Who?"

"My father! Who else would know where he is?"

"No one else. That's all I know."

"That's all you know? How can that be? How long were you together? Was it just once?"

She began to speak and then paused, as if she had changed her mind about something. Then the words spilled out, "He loved me."

"What?" I was bewildered. "Then why didn't you tell him?"

"I don't know, Kevin. It was a long time ago." I thought I could see a tear roll down her cheek. "That's all I know. That's it!" She punctuated the end of the sentence, closing a door.

I tried to stay calm, but inside my mind was wheeling and a surge of confusion escalated inside of me. Sonia was silent; she looked like she was stuck in time, trapped by my incessant need and a maternal debt she was trying to negotiate. In the same way Doreen had known that this day would come, I was certain that Sonia must have also known, but to a greater consequence. I could see it in how uncomfortable she was, the feather duster gently trembling in her hand.

"I wish I could tell you more, Kevin. That's all I can say."

I waited for a moment, deciding what to do next, and as the undulation of confusion reached its peak, I surrendered, "Okay."

I waved at her, as if I were wiping the air clean between us. It was clear to me that, for the moment, I didn't need anything else from her. Despite all the secrecy, she had confirmed the one thing that mattered the most: my father was African. I heard what I had come to hear, and that alone made me feel unstoppable.

"Thank you," I said. I turned and walked toward the front door, with only one thought in mind. *I have to find him.*

I stood at the back of the yellow double-decker. The bus was crammed, standing room only. It swerved onto Market Street. "For fuck's sake," someone shouted, as the bus tilted, throwing us to the side and forcing everyone to grab for the handrails in fear.

"Did ya see that? He just flew past the bus stop. He better not miss my stop," yelled a large, square-shaped man in front of me. His neck bulged out of his stained white collar as he wobbled back and forth.

Muttering voices and gasps spread through the lower deck of the bus as it rumbled down John Dobson Street. It bore Monday morning's fill of council workers, laborers, and school kids. The swaying heads, smell of smoke, and the driver flying past the previous bus stops didn't bother me. In fact, I didn't care if we flew past ten bus stops because, as we hurtled through Newcastle, I was too busy staring out of the window looking for black faces on the street. I had counted two in the last several miles. Though I couldn't be certain, because one of them looked Indian. In the past week, since finding out that my father was African, I had counted six men of color in random places.

The small amount of information that Sonia had shared with me was a goldmine. I replayed the part of the conversation, when she said he was from Ghana, like a favorite song. I rewound it over and over, telling myself that I was African. I belonged somewhere else, somewhere out there, through the bus window, through the twisted crowds of people, and right into the dazzling shine of the black skin that I was desperately searching for.

I wondered if my father was out there. Had I passed him on a street without either of us knowing it? Maybe he'd stood on this same bus and looked out of this same window and saw the same thing that I was seeing– a grey blur.

Don't burn your mouth, Son." Mam slid a steaming plate of pie and peas across the table. It was dinnertime and the room was a flurry of vigorous activity. Sandra had been in and out of the kitchen, unable to decide whether she wanted to eat. Mam scurried back and forth with hot food, and Dad sat complaining about the bottle of HP Sauce.

"You can never get the bloody top off, and when ya do get the top off, ya can never bloody well get the sauce out."

"Stop your complaining, George." Mam threw the dishcloth over the back of her chair and sat down at the table. "I hope I didn't overcook them peas."

"They're perfect," I said clearly, over the mumbling of Dad's persistent complaining. He continued wrestling with the bottle of sauce in what appeared to be a deeper, personal struggle.

"Well, I'm glad someone appreciates them," Mam glared at Dad, shaking her head.

"Best I've ever had, Mam. They taste better than ever, for some reason." I bit into the crust of pie and savored the richness of the minced beef.

I decided this was a good day to tell them that I'd talked with Sonia, and I knew the truth. I hadn't yet uttered a word to anyone. I wasn't sure what to say, or how to say it. But two things I did know were that it had to be said and this was the right time to say it. I gulped down a spoonful of mushy peas. It all made sense: I had to tell them.

"I went to see Sonia last week."

"That's good, Son," Mam said.

"Aye, it's good." Dad poured the sauce onto his plate. "Me and your mother were just saying it would be good if you two saw more of each other."

"I went to ask her about my father."

Mam and Dad froze for a moment, and then Dad put down the bottle of sauce and picked up his knife and fork, gripping them in both hands. He looked across the table at me. I stared back, mirroring him, gripping my knife and fork.

"Would anyone like a cup of tea?" Mam whispered.

"She said me father is from Africa...Ghana."

"Did she tell you that?" Dad said, trying to be casual.

"Yeah. That's what she said. Did you know him?"

They both looked at each other, and then Dad laid his knife and fork on the table and put his hand on my Mam's wrist.

"No."

"We never knew him, Son," Mam jumped in. The conversation transitioned from a hesitant pause to the relief of a confession. "She never told us. This is the first we heard of it. We always wondered, Son. But she never said Africa. We tried everything to get it out of her. She wouldn't talk to no one. She just kept it all inside."

I could see the anguish fill Mam's face, as if it had happened just yesterday.

"Aye, she did," Dad echoed, tapping the table with his index finger. "We couldn't get it out of her. We tried it all. Even the police couldn't do it. Twelve hours they had her, and she still wouldn't tell."

"The police?" I asked.

Dad pushed his plate to the side, clearing the way between us. "She was young."

"And she didn't tell anyone?" I asked.

"Nobody knows who he is, our Kevin." Mam said, "We just never talk about it anymore. There's been no point up until now."

Through their words, I could imagine everything. I thought of when I was arrested, and I could see Sonia as a little girl, sitting on a wooden chair, surrounded by the gray concrete walls of the police station, her lips pressed tightly together, afraid to say her name. How resilient she must have been, to never open her mouth, even under pressure from the police. I thought of how she might not ever give up her secret.

"Do you think I can find him?" I said, leaning across the table. Dad's eyes flickered and he returned a small nod of his head. I'm not sure what it meant.

"You can do whatever you want, Son." Mam looked at Dad. It was as if she were steadying him and, at the same time, making sure that he would say the right thing.

"Africa?" he said. "It won't be easy."

"Nothing that's easy is worth having, George." Mam patted the table with the palm of her hand, changing the tempo. "There's no harm in having a look."

I felt a bout of joy swell in my chest. Everything seemed to be coming together. Having the support of Mam and Dad showed I wasn't alone.

"Pass the sauce, Dad, please," I said, holding out my hand.

The office clerk stared at me from across the desk. It was her protruding lips that bothered me the most, as they spoke a whining, incessant string of words that I didn't want to hear.

"Sorry, but as I said, there's nothing on file."

"I know, but did you check for Ghana?"

"I checked. And I've checked every single time you've been here, which to my reckoning is five times in the last week. It's a good thing the university's closed on the weekends, or I'm quite sure, young man, that you'd have been here the full seven days of the week."

She took a step back as I pressed my hands against the counter. "But you must have something!"

"I told you already. There's nothing."

"But I just wanted to know if you've checked for Ghana? He was studying medicine. You can check for that too."

She waved a pencil. "We only keep records for a little while, and then they get sent away."

"Sent away?" The words pierced through me. "Are there any other African students at the university, now?"

"There very well might be."

"Who are they?"

"I'm sorry. I can't give that information out."

"But I'm looking for my Dad!" A tide churned inside me. It was the first time I'd said it out loud. It was the first time I'd told anyone, including myself. I felt ashamed and excited at the same time. And I was also confused. I had a Dad and part of me thought I was betraying him.

"Hold on. Just wait a minute." She said and placed her pencil onto the counter. Her whining voice softened. "Let me have another look for you, young man, just in case." She then walked away.

I could hear Mam's voice in my ear, "Nothing worth having is easy."

If that is the truth, then I must be close to finding my father, I told myself. The clerk walked back into the room and stood at her station, facing me from behind the desk. "Sorry, young man," she said. "I wish I could help you. There's absolutely nothing there."

Charlie ran his hand through his short, spiky brown hair and shrugged his shoulders; they were rigid with adolescent defiance.

"Boxing is better," he said, glaring at Frank and me. We looked at him and laughed as we walked down the alley, our hands in our pockets and our collars turned up toward the West End Boys Club and Boxing Gymnasium. Charlie worked with Frank, painting and decorating. Frank and I had become fast friends. He was the man who'd nudged me to find a place in line in the first kung-fu class, with his thick locks of black hair and paint-splattered overalls.

Frank chuckled, "Charlie's got a chip on his shoulder. He's always trying to prove somebody wrong. If the world was walking down a one-way street, Charlie would be pushing his way in the opposite direction."

"You won't be laughing in a minute!" Charlie pointed to a small building at the end of the lane.

"Is that it?" Frank prodded me again. "It looks like an old shed. We going to do some gardening, are we?"

"Fuck off! It was built on the site of a coal mine, actually. At least we don't train in a Quaker meeting house, like a bunch of pansies!" Charlie snapped. "And don't look at his left eye."

"What?" Frank and I questioned in unison. "Fowler's!"

"Who's Fowler?" Frank asked.

"Phil Fowler, the coach. He's got a glass eye. I think it's the left one. It might be the right. Just don't stare at it. He gets mad."

Frank and I explode into laughter.

"Fucking shut it. We're here!" Charlie pushed open the door and a wall of heat hit me in the face. A stark contrast to the cool of the evening.

"Quick, get in," Charlie ushered us inside. "Just stand here. Don't move."

I couldn't have moved if I'd wanted to. I was asphyxiated by the smell of sweat and leather. The sound of snorting nostrils, whirling ropes, and pounding of fists that were chopping, slicing, and punching into objects of all shapes and sizes. It was relentless. The clammer rolled around in the sloping roof and back down over the sweat-drenched floor to where I stood on the outskirts of the room. I looked in on the thirty or more bodies who were hard at work in the small gym.

"Wow!" I muttered to myself, staring at a boxing ring at the far end of the room. I'd seen plenty of them on television, but I'd never seen one in real life. It was arresting in an unexpected way. Its grandeur was alluring, welcoming me to try.

"Watch it!" Charlie pulled me back as an oblong-shaped, black punching bag swung past my nose. A hooded boy chased after it, swinging with both arms, burying his fists into the bag. "That's janky! Don't get in his way, for fuck's sake."

"Oh, yeah?" Frank sniggered.

"Follow me." Charlie guided us around the room and cut across the floor toward the ring. We followed, trying not to slip on the sweat.

"Keep ya hands up!" A voice like a metal file cutting through a tin can scraped through the din. "Keep ya chin down..."

"That's Fowler," Charlie pointed to the back of a bald-headed man, his stocky frame buckling the ropes as he leaned into the ring.

"Hands up for Christ's sake, unless you wanna get knocked out! Chin down! Hands up!" The two boys stood toe-to-toe, wet cotton vests clinging to them, red gloves flying back and forth. "Do it like this!" Fowler climbed into the ring and stepped between the two boys. I stood between Frank and Charlie, captivated.

"Come here!" Fowler turned to one of the boys. "Hit me!"

He opened his arms. The boy crouched and threw a punch at Fowler's melon-shaped stomach. As his hand bounced off like a rubber ball, Fowler slapped the side of his ginger-haired head. "Keep ya hands up!"

"That's Tommy Mckenzie," Charlie whispered. "Keeps getting caught. Never learns. Never learns." A bell sounded, ending the round. Fowler climbed out of the ring. My heart began to beat harder as Fowler noticed us and walked over.

"I brought me friends along to watch," Charlie said proudly. Fowler didn't pay much attention and turned away to shout across the ring to two other boys:

"Get your gloves on! I want five rounds!"

He turned back to Charlie and wiped the sweat from his wide forehead. "What?"

"I brought my friends."

Fowler squinted at us and flexed his angular jaw, as if he tasted something he wasn't sure about. "So, you wanna be boxers?"

"I just came to watch," Frank said.

"What about you?" He looked straight at me, his thick face leaning forward with an odor of salted beef. "You wanna be a boxer, do you?"

"I was thinking about it." I said, trying not to look at his left eye.

"Thinking about it? Ya either know or ya don't." He grabbed my hands and lifted them up to his face, rotated them while he stared into the knuckles. "Hmmm... Hmmm... Not bad, not bad."

I wondered what he was looking for. He examined my hands like a prospector looking for gold.

"So, if you wanna be a boxer, the club's open to ya. That's if you think you can handle it, Kid." He squinted right into my face, and then he let go of my hands. My arms fell limply to my side. Fowler turned away, climbed the steps, and shouted through the ropes at the two boys in the ring. Frank and I looked at each other, amazed.

Miss Yarm's straight, black hair fell between her wool-covered shoulder blades as she reached up and drew a thick chalk line across the blackboard.

"It was a defining moment in British history!" she said, turning to the class. She blew a lock of hair across her thin eyebrow. Her hands were chalky, and she had a dancer's posture.

"It was known as the Jarrow March. Raise your hand if you've heard of it."

"I have, Miss." Two desks to my right, Clive Burdikan's chin quivered, his hand reached up high.

"Yes?" Miss Yarm pointed to him.

"The coal miners of Newcastle walked all the way to London."

"Very good. Anyone else?" she said, ignoring Burdikan's hand as it reached up a second time.

"How about you, Nicky?"

Nicky Sherman, three desks in front of me, tucked her blonde hair behind her ear.

"Was it during the war, Miss?"

"Not quite."

Burdikan's arm reached up again and some of the boys who sat behind him sniggered.

"Quiet in the class," Miss Yarm scanned the room with authority. "I'll have none of that! Mind your manners. Now, carry on Mr. Burdikan."

"It was before the war. On October the fifth, 1936..." Burdikan went on, but I drowned out the noise of the room and looked down at the glossy pages of the book of Ghana that was hidden behind my English history book. I shouldn't have been reading it, but I couldn't help myself. I was engrossed in the photographs of slavery, and how Ghana, once known as the Gold Coast, claimed its independence from Britain in 1957. A portrait of an ebony man stared up at me from the centerfold: "Kwame Nkrumah: Ghana's first president". It felt as if he was looking directly at me.

I could hear Miss Yarms' voice fluttering over my head. She was talking about how thousands of Geordies had walked to London from Newcastle, collecting signatures along the way, because they were starving. They arrived at Parliament with 12,000 signatures.

"This is our history," she taught proudly. I turned another page and the words struck me: "Ghana" means "Warrior King".

I saw a flash of white light in my head. Bruce Lee's eyes glared at me while Fowler's voice grated in my ear: "So you wanna be a boxer?" It was all becoming clearer while the nauseating sound of Miss Yarms' chalk screeched across the black board. Warrior King.

THE DUTCHMAN

The Dutchman slapped my punch away and threw a right cross that hit my chest, then a back fist that met the side of my jaw. The referee waved his gloved hand, the crowd cheered and the tall, muscular Dutchman glided away, out of reach. He hovered in the center ring like a cobra. I charged at him, trying to disturb his composure. He moved to the side, illusive and out of reach once again, his blue eyes piercing into me,

"Watch him. He's a counter puncher!" Neville shouted from the corner. I sucked in the sweaty air of the stadium, while the crowd roared, anticipating the Dutchman's counter punch. I weaved my head under his extended arm and hurled a right cross that landed flush into the center of his muscular body. With a wince, he stepped back as the referee's arm shot into the air, like an exclamation mark.

"That's it! That's it!" Neville's voice entered the ring. The Dutchman slid back, so I went after him, pitching a solid straight jab at his head. He slapped it away, harder this time, and flung a cluster of punches, that I absorbed on my shoulders like bee stings, jostling me away to the side of the ring. The crowd was frantic. He swung another punch, racking up points.

Focus! Focus! Be alert! Be sharp! The screams sounded off inside me. *I have no time. Figure him out now.*

He flicked out his arm, baiting me. He wanted me to attack. That's his strength: to wait, to hover, to draw me in, slap down my attack and strike back. I launched a looping right cross at his head. He chopped it to the side with his palm and struck me with a stiff right in my forehead. I moved back. My face stung, and the rippling resonance of applause circled the room.

Change it up! I told myself. It was time to change strategy, but I couldn't. I was caught in the rhythm—the Dutchman's rhythm. "Move, move, move, move!" Neville roared.

I charged the Dutchman, my feet almost off the ground. I jabbed as hard I could. He swerved to the side, knocked my arm away, and punched back at me. I felt the weight of his fists as my shoulder deflected his hits. The leather smelled fresh. I was off balance, and he was a blonde shadow I couldn't pin down.

I can beat him. I'm faster! I told myself. The harder I pushed, the more relaxed he became. He blocked and struck me again, with a solid right into my chest. The crowd raged. I shook my head, as if the hit was ineffective. My mind was frantic, the seconds ticking down like a bomb eager to detonate. *Is this where it ends?*

"Keep moving, Kevin!" Neville's voice came at me. He knew me better than anyone. He was meticulous about his style of fighting, as he was about clothing: Always well groomed, hair brushed and parted, crisp white collars and polished shoes. We trained side by side for the past four years in London, working our way to be there together, at the World Championships, in Budapest.

Neville was a leading fighter in the world of sport karate. He was stubborn and physical, with long limbs and a gritty determination. He'd slap you down all day long with axe kicks and back fists. There was a healthy rivalry between us, one grounded in hard-earned respect for one and other. I began as his student, became his friend and teammate, and in due time I rose to dominate the British circuit with him in my corner.

This changed our relationship only in the way in which it increased the level of respect we shared, and the tacit agreement, that I had become his teacher as much as he was mine. Neville was strategic and direct in his approach. His voice was reassuring, a steady banter of English, laced with an intermittent flair of Jamaican patois.

"Gw'on! Gw'on! Gw'on! Tek it to him!"

I'm moving. I was moving, as fast as I could, but the Dutchman had my number. He was used to speed, he liked it. He anticipated everything.

"Move, move, move!" Neville was relentless.

The Dutchman's aim was to demoralize me. He wanted me to pursue so he could pick me off. I knew it, but still. I attacked. He moved back, parried and slapped my face with a jab. I was angry, but I smiled. I had to stay focused and ignore everything to find a way to get inside the Dutchman's head before the bell rang.

My body tightened as time closed in on me. I knew that feeling: Anticipating Mam and Dad exploding through the front door, drunk and bloody. Mam would be falling to the floor, her head ready to smash against the wall. There was nothing I could do. Nothing.

The Dutchman's fist bounced off the side of my face. The crowd's screams were muffled. I couldn't hear Neville, nor could I see him. I was alone, with only the Dutchman. It's now or never, the voice in my head exclaims. I'd waited too long for this, my dream. The five-letter word poured through my head, waking me, rousing me against the wailing crowd. *I've got to win. I must win. There is nothing else. If I can't win, I will die.*

I lunged a sidekick into the air. The Dutchman looked like he was smiling as he moved and countered with a punch. I leaned back, out of reach, and watched the tip of his glove fall short. It missed me. It missed me. His blue eyes narrowed.

"That's the way! Gw'on! Gw'on!" Neville waved his arms in the air. I caught sight of him in the distance, as my eyes followed the Dutchman hovering in center ring, waiting for me to attack. But I didn't. I moved around him, measuring him. My face was still stinging. I threw a punch. He blocked it. He threw a punch. I blocked it and countered with a right. It landed on his jaw, twisting his head to the side. The referee's white gloved hand swung into the air, marking the point.

"Thank you! Thank you! Thank you!" I shouted out, through clenched teeth, spit flying into the ring. He spun around and threw a desperate front kick at me. I stepped to the side, launching a right cross, and his knee buckled as it hit him square in the chest. The referee's hand swung up again. The Dutchman gasped and shouted out words I didn't understand. He punched back, chasing me, as I flew backwards around the ring, without slipping. *I'm out of his rhythm. I'm out of the Dutchman's rhythm.*

"Gw'on! Gw'on! On ya bike!" Neville shouted. Stiff Dutch words screamed from my opponent's corner.

I thought they were saying "Stop! Stop!" But the Dutchman couldn't stop. He was now trapped in my rhythm. I flicked my fist into his face as he muscled his way forward, each one of my punches sunk into his already flat nose, which was becoming redder as my gloves established their target. The clock ticked down. The arena was a drone.

"Ha!" I shouted, full strength powered into each punch.

The referee's hand rose into the air, as the Dutchman's mouthpiece flew across the ring. "Stop! Stop the clock!"

My ribs ached as I scanned around the room; Neville was holding his hands in the air, shouting "Twenty seconds!" The crowd was on its feet. The Dutchman's stocky coach was cramming the gum shield back into his mouth, shouting in his ear.

"Fight!" The referee waved us on. My opponent came running. I thrust out a sidekick. The Dutchman gasped as he folded forward and dropped to his knee. I thought of the Spaniard in the last round. The Dutchman hauled himself up and shook his head.

"Fight!" The referee waved on.

I moved in as the Dutchman trotted to the middle of the ring, trying to gain his composure. It was too late; my punches crashed into his face, one after another, sending him backward, stumbling toward his corner. His brow was knotted and his eyes looked empty. He'd given up.

The bell rang. The Dutchman's corner men ran out and grabbed him, and I raised my arms in the air, as I stood in the center of the ring.

I could hear the sound of Fowler's voice in the scraping of my heels against the pavement as I walked toward the old shed at the end of the alley. You can always turn back, I'd been repeating to myself since leaving the house for the twenty-minute bus ride to the West End Boys Club. I found comfort in those words, turn back, especially the way Dad had said them a day earlier, as he reclined in his armchair and slung his socked feet up onto the glass coffee table.

"I don't see any harm in it, Sally. He can always turn back."

"But I don't want him boxing, George!" Mam clasped her hands together, almost praying.

"Your mother doesn't want you to box, Kevin."

"But I want to box, Mam. And I can go on the nights I don't have kung fu!"

"No! I don't want you getting hurt!"

"I won't get hurt, Mam. I promise. Nobody gets hurt!" Mam looked at Dad and then at me. She rubbed the side of her head with her forefinger.

"Well... Well... I suppose. But if anyone lays a finger on you I'll bloody kill 'em. If you get yourself hurt, you're gonna stop! Right away! You hear me?"

"Yes! Mam! Yes, I will, I promise." I walked into the throng of the boxing gym. My eyes located Fowler standing ringside.

"End of round!" he shouted, cupping his mouth with his hands like a bullhorn. His hand dropped to the side of his hip and his bowling ball shaped head rolled to the edge of his shoulder. His chin fell and his face clenched into a tight squint, as he looked in my direction. I turned my head to see if anyone was standing behind me, then I turned back to Fowler and realized that he was looking at me.

My neck stiffened as he moved in a straight line, parting the sweaty bodies, and wading toward me like a man in deep water. The smell of beef reached me before he did. Then his nose was three inches from mine.

"What do you want?"

"I came for the boxing."

"Have a look. It's not for everybody."

"I already did. You told me to come back if I was interested."

"Did I?"

"Yeah, you did."

"Why do ya wanna be a fighter?" He stared at me as one eye veered to the left. I didn't answer. I didn't know how to tell him the emotions leading this decision spun around in me like a whirlpool, driving me downward. Despite my reticence, I knew the experience I had stepping into the boxing gym for the time. Something happened to me. The smell of sweat, the bodies struggling against one another, the tenacity to overcome ~ it all made me want to clench my fists and run right in. But how could I tell Fowler that? How could I explain that I'd felt a sliding door quietly close inside and a wall of protection go up around me when Dad told me he wasn't my real Dad. The vulnerability of that moment and the euphoria that followed when I stepped into the gym.

"I don't have all day, Kid! I asked you 'why do ya wanna be a fighter?'" Fowler's hot breath washed over my face.

"I dunno, I just like it here."

"Well, I suppose that's a reason." He slapped the tip of my chin with his fingers. "Well, what ya waiting for?" He turned, waving me to follow as the bell rang. "Terry, get here!" he bellowed across the crowded gym floor. A tall skinny kid with bushy eyebrows and small eyes ran over to us.

"Yes, Coach."

"This is—" Fowler looked at me. "What's your name?"

"Kevin."

"This is Kevin. He wants to box. Take him to get a pair of gloves." The boy raised his eyebrows and grinned.

"Follow me," the boy said. We dodged through the lines of churning ropes and rigid bodies doing press-ups. He pointed to a cardboard box that was filled with used boxing gloves.

"Take your pick." The gloves stank of old sweat, so I quickly sorted through the box. I found a pair and lifted them up like a trophy.

"Are these ones okay?"

"They'll do," Fowler's voice reached my ear before he did. "Do you have any gear? Shorts, shirt, anything?"

"No."

"How you gonna box in them clothes, Kid?"

"I dunno."

"Well, get your coat off and roll up your pants. You can box in your vest."

Fowler shook his head while he walked me to the ring. "Put your coat down there." He pointed to a small bench. A rush of blood pumped through my heart. I wondered if it wasn't too late to turn back.

"Do I have to go in the ring now? I didn't know-"

"Don't worry kid!" Fowler laughed. "There's nothing to worry about!" He stretched open the mouth of the boxing glove, and I slipped my hand inside. I was trapped. He tied the glove up, but my fingers were curious, probing the tears in the silky lining and feeling the clamminess of the damp leather.

"Now, get up there!" Fowler pointed to the ring. "Watch yourself!" he said, as I got twisted in the ropes trying to get into the ring. "It's not as easy as it looks, is it, getting in a ring?" he laughed, prying the ropes open wide enough for me to fall through them and land on my knees.

Two or three boys had already gathered at the side of the ring, their curious faces full of laughter. One belonged to Charlie, whose eyes were saying, "I told you so, boxing's better."

I'll show him that kung fu is just as good as boxing, even better. The ring seemed smaller from inside, and the lights hotter. Fowler faced me.

"Are you left or right-handed?"

"Right."

"That means you're orthodox!"

"I'm orthodox?"

"It means you lead with your left. Put your hands up, like this." Fowler raised his fists. "You're gonna lead with your left."

"But I'm right-handed."

"I know." He gently slapped my chin. "It's your left hand you want doing the work. It sets up the right hand."

I raised my arms and clenched my fists, ignoring the stench of the gloves. Fowler had me bend my knees, crouch and move around with him, slowly throwing punches at his big meaty hands.

"Easy, boy! Easy!" He tried to slow me down. I kept swinging and throwing punches but mostly missing the target.

"Calm down!" He put his hands on my shoulders, stopping me. "You trying to kill somebody?" Fowler turned and shouted across the ring, "Get up here with your gloves on."

A moment later, a boy climbed through the ropes and faced me. It was Charlie. His arms were flexed, as Fowler spoke to him. "You're gonna do the same with him now. Just hold your gloves up for him, Charlie, and let him punch at your hands for a round." Charlie looked at me, smiled and held his shiny red gloves up.

"Okay, get going!" Fowler stepped to the side of the ring, watching us closely. Charlie opened the palm of his glove and I punched into it. I'll show him, I thought, and swung my right hand as fast as I could. My wrist bent against his palm as he slapped down hard against my glove. I winced and threw another punch, trying not to show my pain.

"Easy, Charlie!" Fowler shouted. "Ease him into it!"

Charlie was still grinning, taunting me. I stayed swinging. My steady shuffle had become a frustrated stumbling dash across the ring with a pair of stinking gloves. Within minutes, our basic punching practice had turned into a full-scale slugging match. Charlie hit me in the jaw, square on the nose and on the top of my forehead. Pain surged up into my brain, and I swung blindly, slapping his head with my glove. He let out a snort, as his head snapped back.

"Easy! Easy! Calm down...calm down!" Fowler shouted. Charlie backed up. I chased him, almost tripping over myself.

"Stop! Stop!" I heard Fowler's voice as Charlie's glove bounced off my forehead, jolting my head sideways and forcing my eyes to shut for an instant. I felt Fowler's thick arm slide between us, pulling me away. "Break! Knock it off, knock it off!"

Charlie spat out his mouth guard into the palm of his glove as Fowler's index finger aligned with the tip of his nose.

"You should know better. You should'a stopped!"

"But Coach, I was just-"

"Just what?" Fowler was furious. "Now get out the ring and get your gloves off!" Charlie glanced at me and walked away. The urge to go after him was still present. Sweat stung my eyes. I panted hard from exhaustion.

"And you," Fowler turned to me with a perplexed expression. He tilted his head to the side and flexed his jaw. I was convinced he was going to throw me out of the gym.

"What am I gonna do with you, eh? You're a wild one. You're a wild one if I ever saw one." He put his hands on my shoulders as if he were holding me down and stared right into my face. "If only you can learn how to channel that, boy. Whatever's driving ya, you need to channel that."

The bell rang. He let go of my shoulders. "We'll see. We'll see what happens," he said, and then he walked away.

I stood looking into the mirror. "Can you still see the bruise?"

"What bruise, man? I never saw one in the first place," Frank answered, kneeling in the corner of his living room next to a worn-out tartan covered armchair. He flicked through a pile of albums that were stacked against the wall.

I prodded my cheekbone. For the past three days, I'd managed to hide the thumb-sized purple welt from Mam, and I wanted to be able to walk through the house again without having to obscure my face.

"Are you sure you can't see it?" I said into the mirror at Frank's reflection. "You must be blind!"

"I'm not, but Stevie is."

"Who's Stevie?"

"Stevie Wonder, and I can't find him anywhere! I could have sworn I put him in this pile."

"Stevie Wonder?"

"You don't know who Stevie is? He sings, plays the piano, and he can blow on a harmonica like you've never heard, man. And he's blind!" He pulled out an album and balanced it on the armrest of the chair. "Pink Floyd. That's a good one, as well."

"Is that why he's called Wonder? Because he's blind?"

"Fuck! I can't find anything in this place!" Frank stood up and put his hands on his head, looking around the room, taking it all in with a glare of discontent. "I need to clean this place up!"

I looked at the pile of newspapers and magazines that were strewn out on the floor. The coffee table was filled with cups and mugs that looked like they had been sitting there for days. There was a peacock-blue sofa with flowery, nylon cushions that faced a can of paint, perched on top of a small television, which sat on a pile of phone books.

"But what about the bruise? Can you see it?"

"I told you. I don't see a bruise." He turned back to his albums, flipping through them with urgency. "How did ya get bruised anyway?"

"I was in the ring, boxing."

"You what? Boxing?"

"Aye, I went back."

"So, who bruised ya?"

"Charlie."

"Charlie? Charlie couldn't punch his way out of a wet paper bag!"

"Ya should have been there to see it—" The doorbell rang, breaking my thought.

"Hang on." Frank stood up and walked out of the room. I turned back to look at my face in the mirror, but before I had a chance to re-examine my cheekbone, Frank shouted.

"Talk of the devil."

He walked back into the room with Charlie. It was the first time we'd seen each other since being in the ring together.

"I heard you two were boxing," Frank winked at me and walked over to the stack of albums.

"We just did one round," I explained.

Charlie looked at me and then across the room, pointing to the can of paint on top of the television, "Is that the one?"

"Your nose looks a bit red, Charlie! What happened? Did Kev stick one on ya?"

"Fuck off!" Charlie snapped.

"Must be the Kung-Fu that got the better of ya," Frank said. "I mean, after all, boxing only has four punches. Jab, cross, hook, and uppercut, whereas, in Kung-fu, we'll hit you with everything, thumbs, wrists, elbows, kicks, the lot."

"You're into music, aren't ya?" Charlie pointed at Frank. "You should fucking know better!"

"How do ya mean?"

"Boxing's like rock n roll music. Every song you've ever heard is built on three cords and the truth!"

"That's brilliant," Frank said. "Why didn't I think of that? But it doesn't change the fact that your nose looks a bit bent outta shape, Charlie!"

"I said, fuck off! Now, is this the paint or not?"

"Found it!" Frank stood up with an album in his hand, ignoring Charlie. "Songs in the Key of Life!"

"Is that the paint or not?" Charlie shouted, cutting into Frank's euphoria.

"Aye, that's the one. He's quick, isn't he?" Frank said.

"Who?" Charlie looked confused.

"Kev's quick." Frank slipped the black vinyl onto his palm and handed me the album sleeve. The face on the cover looked like one of the faces in the book of Ghana.

"He's not bad." Charlie folded his arms. "It's common, though. They're usually quick, blacks."

He looked at me and then at Frank, who was bent over, placing the needle onto the record. *Should I say something?* I wondered, but I kind of liked being called black.

"That's got nothing to do with it, man! It's just another coat of paint! We're all the same underneath." Frank swung around. "Now, listen to that. That's pure magic!" The sound of a harmonica blew out of a speaker in the corner of the room.

"Bruce Lee's fast, and he's not black," I said.

"Cassius Clay's black." Charlie snapped back.

"And what about me? I'm fast." Frank flicked his fingers in the air and started moving his arms, as if he were directing an orchestra.

I started laughing. *Was it true? Was the difference just a coat of paint?* "You're no Cassius Clay." Charlie looked at me. He looked angry. It was the same look on his face that he had when we were in the ring. "Now where's the rest of the paint?"

"He changed his name, you know. He's Muhammad Ali, now," Frank said.

"It's still Cassius Clay to me!" Charlie folded his arms.

"Did you know that true love asks for nothing?" Frank started miming the words to the song and shuffled towards Charlie as if he were going to hug him.

"Piss off!" Charlie stepped back and walked around the coffee table. Frank kept chasing him, while miming the words of the song. Charlie's started running backward.

"Get away. I'm not in the mood. I just want the fucking paint!"

"I'm not stopping ya!"

Frank reached for him and Charlie leaned back and tripped. He fell against the television, knocking the paint can off. It went flying towards the peacock-blue sofa.

"Watch out!" I shouted, lunging with my arms outstretched, trying to grab the paint. It was too late. "Fuck!" Frank shouted as Charlie crashed to the floor.

The can of paint bounced off the flowery cushions and tumbled down the middle of the sofa and came to a complete stop. Not one drop of paint was spilt.

"Fuck me." Frank put his hand on his forehead, and we all started laughing.

Rain hammered the tin roof and poured down the sides of the fogged windows, trapping us inside the small bus shelter. A few feet away a thick-necked, Afro-haired man stood, looking out into the dank atmosphere. It was just the two of us. I studied the angular shape of his nose and the roundness of his lips and the way the water glistened like tiny pearls atop his short Afro. I wondered how old he was. He looked close to Sonia's age, but younger. *Could he be my father?*

I nodded several times, attempting to make eye contact with him, but he ignored me. I was persistent and so was he, denying my request to invade his space. It was as if we were participating in an unspoken dialogue. Then, to my surprise, he turned and looked at me, creasing his brow.

"What?"

"What? I was just saying hello," I stammered, questioning my decision to take the bus in the first place. "I was just wondering where you're from, that's all. I didn't mean anything by it."

"So you stare. Is that it? Are you the staring man, huh? You are the staring man. Are you?"

"No... No... I was just..." A deep throb of laughter came from him. It rolled through the bus shelter like a heavy base note beneath the tapping of the rain.

"I am Nigerian. Why do you ask?"

"Just wondering. Just never seen you before," I said, riding on the smoothness of his voice and calibrating his brown skin that was not so much darker than my own. I could be closer to Africa than I had thought. Until now, every African I had seen had been a deep shade of ebony.

"And what about you, are you Indian or something?"

"No! I'm not!" I shouted against the rain, which was hammering overhead. "My father is from Ghana!"

"Ghana? Ah, he is from Africa," his face lit up, reminiscing a place that was dear to him. "What is your name, staring man?"

"My name is Kevin. What's yours?"

"Sebastian," he said as a bus pulled up several feet from the shelter. "I live at 76 Falmouth Road. Come and visit some time." He pulled his hood over his head and ran into the rain towards the bus.

I'm black, and I'm beautiful! Cassius Clay's a slave's name. My name's Muhammad Ali!" The words revolved in my head as I limped down Falmouth Road with bruises and strains from my kung fu and boxing classes. My days had become exhausting, constantly training without rest. But I was driven, so there was no stopping.

"I'm black, and I'm beautiful!" I jabbed my finger into the air mimicking Muhammad Ali. He'd said the phrase while pointing at me, the viewer, through the television screen the night before.

The camera followed him running down the street, pursued by a crowd of people. The resonance in his voice and his red sweat suit that stood out among the beige surroundings, like a dash of fresh blood, made me want to be just like him. I wanted to follow him into the TV screen and down the suburban street, following the red dash until we disappeared together into the nine o'clock news or the next round of commercials.

Over the past weeks, whenever I could, I monopolized the television, searching for black faces. American shows influenced my identity. When the final episode of Roots aired and Kunta Kinte had half of his foot chopped off for attempting to escape, I was left hopping between the only two TV channels of the BBC in desperation. On Fridays I'd find Huggy Bear, the pimp on Starsky and Hutch. On Sundays I'd get a glimpse of Summer, a black receptionist in the Executive Suite. And on Thursdays it was Isaac, the African shipmate on The Love Boat. But it wasn't enough. I wished Roots had never ended, and I wished Kunta Kinte still had his foot.

I turned onto Falmouth Road. A long line of Victorian houses stretched out before me. I limped my way to number 76 and hammered on the brass door knocker. Silence. I poised to walk away when a voice came from below, through a letterbox.

"Who goes there?"

"Does Sebastian live here?"

The letterbox slammed shut and I could hear faint laughter. Then the door swung wide open. Looking at me through a pair of large square-framed glasses that resembled a pair of ski goggles was a tall dark-skinned woman.

"Sorry about that," she said with a slight lisp that softened her thick accent. "That was my little brothers."

"That's all right," I said, taking in her braided hair, the shamrock-shaped blemish on her left cheek and her wide but small nose that struggled to hold up her glasses.

"Does Sebastian live here?" I asked again.

"And who are you?"

"I'm..." I began, wondering how to introduce myself. Then the same throb of laughter that I'd heard at the bus stop emerged from the house.

"Is that the staring man? The staring man has come." He squeezed past the lady, his bulbous shoulders exploding out of his grey vest, as he rubbed his hands on a dirty rag.

"Sebastian! Don't get oil on me again. Stop that." The lady stepped to the side as he filled the door frame.

"I'm glad you came, staring man."

"Who is this? And why do you keep calling him staring man?" she said.

"He is a friend. He is from Ghana."

I felt a jolt when he said those words. The feeling of electricity swept through my body.

"What is your name?" the lady asked.

"Kevin."

"Come inside." Sebastian threw his arms open, waving the dirty rag like a flag. "This is my sister, Virginia." I stepped into the house, inhaling a scent of spices that made me want to eat the air.

"So, you are from Ghana." Virginia closed the door behind us.

"Well, my father is."

Two boys appeared from behind Sebastian and threw their arms around his waist, trying to topple him. The boys laughed and grunted, pushing against him, as if they were trying to uproot a tree stump. He clasped their heads in his thick arms and squeezed them until their laughter muted.

"Sebastian, stop! Stop!" Virginia slapped his shoulder, and he smiled and released their heads like champagne corks popping from a bottle.

"Please! Please! We have a guest!" Virginia said, trying to control the chaos. "This is Patrick." She pointed to the taller of the two boys. "And this one is Fabian. They are our brothers. But somehow, I think it is Sebastian who is ten or eleven years old. Now, go!" Virginia clapped her hands, and they ran away laughing.

"Come." Sebastian waved the rag, and we followed, walking through a green wallpapered corridor where the boys had run and where the smell of spices grew stronger.

"So, your Daddy is from Ghana," Virginia said, as we stepped into the kitchen.

"Yes, he is." The aroma filled me. "He's from Ghana." I looked across the kitchen at the profile of a long-skirted woman with cardigan sleeves rolled up to the elbows and a combed back Afro. Her hair led me to imagine her standing in a wind tunnel, as she ripped the leaves off a cabbage and dropped them into the sink.

"Is it ready?" Sebastian sniffed as he crossed the room, passing a long wooden dining table and leaned over a pot-laden stove.

"Shoo! Shoo! Sebastian, get away." The lady dropped the cabbage into the sink, turned and slapped his arm. "Don't pick."

"All right," he stepped back. "This is Kevin."

"His Daddy is from Ghana," Virginia said, while clapping her hands together.

"Hi. I'm Rita. I am the cousin." A wide smile crossed her chocolate, dimpled cheeks. She then turned to Sebastian. "By the time you wash your hands, it will be ready."

"Your hands are always dirty, Sebastian," Virginia slapped his shoulder.

"I've been working on the car," he reasoned.

"You've been working on that car, Sebastian, all of today and all of yesterday."

"I don't want it to break down on the way back this time."

"Only you could have a car break down three times and manage to fix your it with a two pence piece." Rita said, stirring the food.

"A two pence piece can be a good screwdriver." Sebastian walked to the sink and began to soap his hands. "Kevin, come wash your hands."

"Excuse me?" I said, wondering if I had misunderstood. I looked at Rita who was stirring the pot with a big spoon and Virginia who had sat on a chair at the end of the table. I realized he was talking to me, and I had been invited to eat.

"Have you ever had Jollof rice?" Sebastian slipped the bar of soap into my hands.

"No. What is it?"

"You'll see. It's Nigerian food."

"Kevin!" Rita called out. "What is a traditional Ghanaian dish?"

"Em …" I searched for an answer, but it was nowhere inside of me, and nothing I had read in the books had taught me. "I'm not sure."

"Not sure? How can you not be sure?" she laughed. "Your mammy doesn't cook African food?"

"He's half cast!" Virginia said from her seat. "His mammy is English."

"Oh, I did not know. I thought he was light skinned, like Sebastian."

Half cast? I pondered the description. I visualized a potter casting some type of vase that was split into two parts. I wondered if it meant I was incomplete in some way. I didn't like the idea of being half of anything, so I shrugged the thought away.

"Thank you," Sebastian grabbed the soap, and I rinsed my hands under the running water, next to his. Our hands looked the same color. We were both light skinned.

"Fabian! Patrick!" Virginia shouted. "Come!" The two boys ran into the kitchen and stood side by side like soldiers. "Take Mammy ha food." She pointed to Rita who was scooping rice onto a plate.

"And hurry, unless you want to be beaten. You know she will beat you," Rita laughed and passed Patrick a tray filled with steaming food. They walked out of the kitchen. A tall young woman with elegant facial features and straight hair walked in and sat at the table. She looked like a fashion model, flicking through a magazine. The cover photograph looked like it could have been her.

"Hello. I'm Maria, the sister," she said, her eyes overtly scanning over me, and then back into her magazine.

"Hello," I answered.

"Do you like spicy food, Kevin?" Rita shouted from across the room.

"Yes." I sat down between Sebastian and Virginia.

"You missed a spot." Virginia pointed to a patch of grease on Sebastian's elbow.

"Oil is everywhere," he said. "But at least my car will carry me back to Germany."

"Sebastian is in the army." Virginia slid an empty plate in front of me. "He is stationed there."

"Royal Engineers. I go back in two months."

"That's why he can fix a car with a two-pence piece." Rita placed a pot onto the table.

"Are there many Africans in the British army?" I said, imagining him in a sea of khaki jackets and white faces, like the ones I'd seen of Dad.

"No," he said as Rita, all in one motion, passed food to Maria and him and poured two scoops of steaming rice onto the plate in front of me.

"Do you look like your Mammy or your Daddy?" Rita said as the steam wafted up into my face.

"I don't really know."

"I hope you like it," Sebastian said.

"It smells good." I looked at the heap of meat and rice.

"Is your daddy light skinned or dark skinned?" Rita said as she passed me a fork.

"Yeah, I like it hot," I said, hoping that Rita's question would get lost in the exchange of words and the passing of food. I shoveled a forkful of food into my mouth. It was so hot I almost yelled out. I reached for a glass of water.

"African food is spicy and rich." Sebastian slapped my back. "Don't choke.

"Your daddy must eat spicy food," Rita said.

"I don't know." I sat, the glass on the table. "I've never met my father." The laughter stopped, and Sebastian put his hand on my shoulder.

"Never met him?"

"No. I've never met him."

"Why?" Virginia and Maria asked at the same time.

"Dunno." I held onto the glass. "Me Mam was young—fifteen."

"A child," Rita said.

"Child," Virginia echoed.

"Here! Have some more Jollof rice." Rita dumped another serving of food on top of my full plate.

"Don't kill him, Rita," Virginia laughed. "His tongue is still burning."

M ove the feet! Move the feet!" Fowler shouted at me through the ropes. "Not bad. Don't trip over yourself this time!" His voice boomed as Billy McGregor, a lanky column of muscle with pointed kneecaps and big ears, jabbed at my head. "Move around him!" Fowler banged on the canvas with the palm of his hand, echoing the sound of Billy's glove as it landed on my nose.

He swung a looping left hook, but I bent my knees, bobbing beneath him. I felt the bristle of excitement and the hair of his armpit against my forehead, as I weaved through the arch of his swing like thread passing through the eye of a needle.

"Bull's eye!" Fowler shouted into the sound of the bell as he climbed into the ring.

"We'll make a boxer of ya yet!" He slapped my back as I spat out my gum shield into my glove.

"When can I fight?" I panted.

"Ya fighting now."

"I mean a bout. A real bout?"

Fowler laughed, "Ya not ready. Five, six months, and I'll get ya a bout."

"Five, six months? That's a long time."

"Billy! Get 'ere," Fowler shouted as he tugged at the knot on my glove. "How many bouts you had, now?" he asked Billy, who was standing behind me, breathing on my shoulder.

"Eight, Coach. Four wins, three losses and a draw."

"And did I make you wait, Billy?"

"Aye, Coach, you did."

"How long?"

"Six weeks, Coach."

"Six weeks! Is that it?" Fowler's voice strained, and he reared his head back, as if he were trying to make sense of Billy's answer.

"Aye, Coach. Ya said it was time to become a man."

"Did I?"

"Aye, ya did!"

Fowler cleared his throat and his thick ears turned a light shade of red. How could he not change his answer, after what Billy had said? I wanted to fight more than anything. It wasn't solely a need to prove myself. It was an incessant request calling me to fight.

"So, can I do it, then? I'm ready! I'm ready to do it!" I pleaded.

"No! You can't fight yet. Not yet!" He pulled off my glove. "I'll tell you when it's time," he said, while removing the other. I watched, frustrated and confused, as he walked away. *He may never let me fight.*

Kevin! Dinner's ready!" Sandra knocked on my bedroom door. I didn't answer. Since early afternoon I'd been stuck in the pages of Combat Magazine and The Boxing News, reading the ratings of professional fighters. When I finished and the back issues were piled up on the floor, I leaned back onto the headboard and buried myself into the biography of Muhammad Ali, The Greatest.

I gritted my teeth when I read that his bicycle was stolen, and he was sent to a boxing gym to vent his anger. I winced when I learned he raced the bus to school each morning while the kids made fun of him. But there was one page in the book that I had to reread multiple times. The section documented Ali throwing his Olympic gold medal into the Hudson River after being refused service in a diner because he was black.

I was convinced that it was a misprint until I continued reading: "I'm good enough to win a gold medal for America, but not good enough to eat in a white restaurant." *He really did throw it away.*

"Ya food's getting cold." Dad slurped his cup of tea when I finally sat down at the table.

"I was reading, Dad. Muhammad Ali got back from Rome and threw his gold medal away because he couldn't get a hamburger in a restaurant." Dad didn't say anything while he stared into his cup. I continued, "I think I'd keep the medal, especially if they wouldn't let me have the hamburger. At least I'd have the medal—I think."

"I got medals when I got back from the war," Dad said.

"Where are they?"

"I threw them away."

"Why did you do that?"

"They're for fools. The way I got treated when I got back—after fighting for this country."

"What do you mean?"

"I gave me life for this country! I went to war, and I didn't even know I'd ever make it back in one piece. And when I got back, what did I get? Nothing! You're treated like you're a nobody."

My mind drifted to the War veterans I'd seen over the years on television, walking to Trafalgar Square on Memorial Day, dressed in all of their regalia.

"What about the war veterans, Dad, on television. What about them?"

"They're fools. The lot of them! They can keep their tin medals. They're worth nothing!"

"I'm warming your food up in the oven, Son. Do you want some tea, while you wait?" Mam shouted from where she stood by the sink, drying her hands on a tea towel.

"Yes please," I answered, wondering if it was foolish or heroic for Dad to have thrown away his medals. I couldn't make up my mind, so I pushed that thought away, and told myself that I could decide at another time. "Dad, what do you think of the name Marvis?"

"What ya talking about? Who's Marvis?"

"He's a boxer from Philadelphia. I like the sound of it. Marvis," I rolled his name off my tongue. "I could change my name. Marvis Brewerton."

Dad didn't say a word. His eye probed me from over the rim of his cup. It wasn't the first time I had mentioned changing my name or adopting a different abbreviation. A week earlier I had declared that I wanted to use the last three letters of my name when being referred to, instead of the first three. But after two days of careful consideration, I changed my mind. "Vin" sounded more Italian than African. Dad didn't say anything then, except for the same probing eye over the rim of his cup.

"Marvin's a canny name." Mam walked toward Dad with a teapot.

"It's Marvis, Mam. Not Marvin."

"That's canny, as well. Who's he then, when he's at home?"

"I was just wondering what it would be like to have a name like Marvis."

"Kevin's a lovely name. It's better than Marvin."

"Marvis, Mam. I said 'Marvis'."

"Marvis, Marvy, Marvin...whatever his bloody name is," she laughed. "It's a tongue twister. Here you are, son. It's hot." She placed a plate of pie and peas in front of me.

"Mam, is there anything else?"

"But it's your favorite, pie and pea supper," her eyebrows arched.

"I feel like having rice."

"Rice!" Dad put down his cup. I could sense that he was on alert and looking for potential trouble. It would be easy to irritate him, which I didn't want to do.

"Well, you've never asked for rice before," Mam said. "What's wrong with pie and pea supper?"

"I just feel like a change."

"Well, your mother took the time to cook that. So, you'll eat it," Dad demanded.

"But I'm not really hungry. I just feel like something else."

Mam filled his cup with tea. "Never mind, George, never mind. Everyone's entitled to a change."

I walked into the Kung-fu class and I could feel something was different. There was an unusual buzz in the air as I walked into the Crudas Park Community Centre. Perhaps the venue was the reason for this peculiar feeling I had. After all, we had switched our locations from the Quaker meeting house to this room with a vaulted ceiling, wooden floors and enormous glass windows that overlooked the council estate. This was our new dojo. It was a much better location by far, given the size of the space and the quality of the furniture in the lobby.

"Get ready, lads. He'll be here in a minute," Ian Walker shouted across the room. We lined up in our usual places, ready to begin class. But when the doors swung open, it wasn't Mr. Tin who walked into the room, but a black man with a smooth swagger.

"My name is Steve Babbs," he said. "I will be teaching the class from now on."

His Afro was perfectly rounded, and his body looked muscular and powerful. *Where was Mr. Tin. Will he return?* I asked myself, with a certain sadness that my teacher wasn't there. Babbs, who was standing in his Chinese kung-fu uniform, with a black sash hanging by his side, looked like an amalgamation of Bruce Lee and Muhammad Ali.

"Some people call me Babbsy," he said, just before we bowed to begin class. His voice was soft, but direct and clear. "Let's start with sparring!" he said.

There were at least fifty of us made up of boys and men, spread out in the room, sparring with one another. Each was eager and ready to impress our new instructor. Unlike Fowler, Babbsy sparred with us. He moved like nothing I'd seen. He was everything, a perfect fusion of grace and power, precision and timing. It was magical.

"Fucking hell!" someone said out loud, as Babbsy threw a spinning kick, which glanced across Jimmy Hague's forehead, at precisely the right angle to ward him off without hurting him. Hague's shirtless body was rippling with muscle and his fists were rolled up into tight, iron balls. He was the hard man who'd helped me in my first class, watching over me with a fatherly presence. Babbsy was smooth and elegant, dancing around him and choosing exactly where and when to hit.

"He's the real deal," I heard someone whisper. "He makes it look easy." The fighting went on and on, and each of us was fueled by this new energy Babbsy had brought.

By the end of class I was both exhilarated and exhausted. I looked around the room; everyone seemed different.

D o it like this," Sebastian flicked a long silver-toothed comb through his hair at rapid speed until his Afro was a flawless curve.

"It looks like a halo," I said, amazed at how his three-inch Afro had expanded to twice its original size. I thought about Babbsy's Afro, and how flawless it had looked while he was sparring. I was still enthralled at how smoothly he moved in a linear plane of motion. He had a rhythm that was completely different than anyone else I'd seen. He would move and then, while in motion, somehow pause for a split second before changing direction. He controlled the space between him and his opponent. And all along, his Afro remained unwavering.

"Your turn," Sebastian said. "Just do what I did."

He handed me the comb and walked to the opposite end of his attic bedroom, leaving me standing in front of the door mirror. The roots of my hair pulled as I dragged the comb upward through the curly knots. I smiled, whimpering and wincing in pain.

"Ha," Sebastian laughed. "I can see that you never used an Afro comb before?"

He sat on his bed, which was a single mattress wedged into the corner of the room where the ceiling sloped toward the roof. A short stack of green army shirts, pressed and folded, sat next to a shiny pair of black army boots.

"It's working!" I turned to him.

"Of course, it's working. Why wouldn't a comb work?" Sebastian pulled out a guitar from under his bed.

"No! I mean my hair's working," I reacted in awe of the tufts of hair that had sprung out of my head with the flick of a comb.

"I don't believe you've never used an Afro comb before."

"Neither do I." I dug the comb into my hair, flicking the strands upward with great enthusiasm, while Sebastian plucked the strings of his guitar. "I've never had a reason to use an Afro comb until now."

"What did you comb your hair with before?"

"A normal comb."

"That wouldn't be good for me. But for you, I suppose. You have white hair."

"White hair?" I answered, disliking his observation and wondering what exactly he meant.

"I mean, it's just not as thick," Sebastian laughed. "Don't worry."

"What about this? This is not white hair" I dragged the comb through my hair one more time and stared at myself in the mirror. A twisted, two-inch halo of frizz, lumpy and thin at best, sat on top of my head. It wasn't the dense weave of Sebastian's exotic rug, but at least it was there.

"It's an Afro!" I shouted.

The door flew open and Patrick and Fabian rushed in. "Get him!" They ran past me toward Sebastian.

"Go away!" he shouted as the boys jumped onto him, wrapping themselves around his neck and shoulders. "Get off." He stood up, still strumming his guitar, the boys holding onto him.

"Boys! Boys! Stop!" A spicy fragrance wafted into the room with Rita, as she pursued the boys. She stopped and stood in the doorway, arms folded, with a stern jaw.

"Get out of the room, now!"

"Help us! Help us!" The boys struggled, ignoring Rita, while giggling and trying to hold onto Sebastian.

"You are weak. You are too weak!" he sang, still strumming.

"Mammy wants you both, now!" Rita said, and with those words the boys released themselves from Sebastian's shoulders, and ran past Rita out of the room.

"Kevin," Rita said, her eyebrows arched with curiosity. "You look different today."

"I do?"

"Yes, you are looking more and more like Sebastian to me every time I see you." She winked at me and pulled the door shut as she left. I took in my reflection in the mirror.

What do you think of Bill Wallace and Joe Lewis?" he says.
"What? You know who they are?" I answer, surprised by his question. I'm impressed he knows of these fighters. In the early days, the sport of martial arts was not typically acknowledged in the mainstream. Even in my era, mainstream publicity has been limited. I'm one of the few fighters to ever break down those boundaries and gain mainstream attention.

"Of course, I've heard of them," he says. "Boxing is a martial art, as well, you know."

"Of course. It is, of course," I nod my head. I'd never really looked at it that way. Although I successfully merged the styles of boxing and kung-fu and karate into one cohesive form, I'd still seen them as two separate entities in my mind. "Those guys are kickboxing pioneers," I continue. "You'd have to be a fan to know who they are."

"Cus D'amato made us study all types of fighters. He grew up fighting on the streets, lost an eye."

"One eye?" I respond. "I had a coach who had only one eye." Fowler's face flashes through my mind.

"Really?" he's surprised.

"Yeah. Funny how someone can see so much in you with just one eye." We both laugh.

And then, out of nowhere, he quotes, "F. Scott Fitzgerald said, 'Show me a hero, and I'll write you a tragedy.'"

The words echo within me. There's a profound truth there. I feel it in my bones, and as firmly as his sentiment grips me, the question arises in my mind: *Is it my tragedies that made me a champion?* The answer swells up in every part of me. But rather than dwelling on the things that have caused me suffering, I reflect on Fitzgerald's observation. I wonder what tragedy must have fallen upon him.

"You read a lot?" I ask.

"Sometimes," he answers. I'm surprised at how agile his mind is and how comprehensively we are able to span our conversation. There doesn't seem to be a subject in which he's not been educated. He has a thirst for knowledge. Either he is a relentless reader, or he watches documentaries frequently.

"Did you ever read Norman Mailer's, The Fight?" I ask. "He loved boxing and he knew how to write about it."

"Yes! He used to come to Cus's house. He had this big house. All the fighters were there. We had to do chores and sweep the floors. When people like Ali, or other champions came, we had to show them respect. If we were called over to talk to them, we had to address them by their last name. Mr. Mailer came many times," he recalls.

"I remember a Mailer quote I once read," I say. "It was something like, 'There was that law of life, so cruel and so just, that one must grow or else pay more for remaining the same.'

"That's deep, man," he acknowledges, shaking his head and looking down.

"It is deep. What was he like?" I ask, curiously.

"He was always very polite and respectful."

I envision Mailer walking into the house bowing as he enters, with an ardent reverence.

"I was once in Tolstoy's house," he reflects.

"The Russian writer?"

"Yes, I was a guest. They took me to his house, where he did most of his writing."

"How was it?"

"It was a small house. Ceilings were low. Books everywhere."

"That must have been interesting," I comment, imagining a small brick house, with endless shelves of books. "I was once married to a Russian," I continue. "Kema. I met her in London, right after I had recovered from a ruptured Achilles tendon. We had a lot of similarities. She was mixed race, born in Rostov ~ on the river Don, which is like Newcastle ~ on the RiverTyne. Her grandparents raised her, just like mine did for me. Her mother was Russian, and her father, whom she lost to Idi Amin's political regime at the age of eight, was from Uganda. He went missing and was never seen again. His name was Soul Muyingo."

"Man, that's tragic," he says.

"Yes, in so many ways," I reply. "It devastated the family. He left behind a wife and four children."

"Do you have any children, Kevin?"

"Yes," I answer. "How about you?"

"Yeah. I'm a Dad, too. How old are your kids?"

"Kema and I have a daughter. Her name is Kaivalya. She's thirteen. I also have a son, Kolby, from an earlier relationship. I was twenty, living in London, making my way up as a fighter. I met his mom, Linda, in a nightclub. She was in the U.S. Navy, stationed in London. We never married and when her service was over, she moved back to the U.S. For the first number of years, he would come and spend the summers with me. He eventually lived with me in England. Despite the distance, we've been able to create a strong bond over the years. Our relationship is a little different from the one I have with my daughter, who I've raised by my side, never missing a day. But I've always remained aware of the father-son dynamic. I sometimes wonder if he feels like he might have missed anything during the times I wasn't physically with him. Was there something critical that didn't pass on or a gap that needs to be filled? I always try to make sure that he knows I'm there. And then again, maybe all of those thoughts are what I'm feeling. What is it that I've missed out on? Have I been a good enough father? I have to remind myself, 'yes'. Isn't it just crazy how our childhood affects our entire life?"

"A person can be stunted all throughout their life by a vision in childhood," he says.

"Where did you hear that?" I ask.

"That was Carl Jung."

We pause and sit back into stillness. Only the faint buzzing of a lawnmower somewhere out in the grounds of the property, is heard. While inside, a rush of warmth runs through me with a love for Newcastle that I've never felt before.

"Did you know that the Russian poet, Pushkin, was mixed race?" he says, breaking the silence.

"Really?"

"Yeah. His great-grandfather was African. Can you believe that? Some say he's the father of Russian literature. And he's black."

We laugh.

"It's fascinating," I say. "Writers put on the paper what we put into words in the ring."

Sandra screamed the moment I walked through the front door. "Kevin! What have you done to your hair?"

"Quiet!" I waved my hand at her face, hoping that she wouldn't alarm the rest of the house. But just as I closed the front door behind me, the living room door swung open.

Mam flew out with her arms wide. "What's a matter?" She looked at me without blinking and then at Sandra, who was bent over in hysterical laughter. "What is it? What's so funny?"

"My hair. She's laughing at my Afro," I said.

"Your what?"

"My Afro. I've got an Afro," I grinned and pointed to my head.

Sandra stopped laughing when we heard the jingle of keys and the front door opening. It was Dad returning home from work.

"What's going on? I could hear you lot from across the Leazes Park!" Dad walked into the house, jacket caked with dry mud and blades of grass.

"Nothing. We're just having a laugh," Mam said.

"Having a laugh?" His eyebrows contorted as he noticed my hair.

"That's his new hair style," Sandra suppressed her giggling.

"It's nice," Mam said.

"And what's that you're holding?" Dad looked down at my hand.

"That's my Afro comb," I said and flicked it through my hair.

Dad shrugged his coat off his shoulders as if it were made of lead. The sudden tension burdened all of us. Mam looked worried. *Was Dad about to get angry and say something about my hair?*

"I've had a hard day, and I'm hungry. What's for dinner?" He stared at my Afro comb, as I held it in my hand, and then turned and walked into the kitchen.

"Lamb chops, and they're nearly ready." Mam followed him, exhaling a sigh of relief, leaving Sandra and I standing in the hallway.

"Your hair looks like ya electrocuted yourself. Does it hurt?" Sandra said.

"No! Don't be stupid."

"Can I touch it?" She reached toward my head.

"Get off!" I slapped her hand away and headed to my room.

I raced the bus as it rambled down the Old Coast Road, stopping and starting in slow moving traffic. My backpack was slung over my shoulder and my teeth were clenched. I wanted to show a crowded bus of startled passengers my determined canter– the same way Ali had. The only difference was that I was racing the bus from school, and the few passengers who I could make out through the frosted windows were nowhere near noticing how fast I ran or the way I defied the icy wind. So I didn't care when the bus sped off, hurling a cloud of black smoke at me. And neither did they.

I imagined I was Ali, running through the streets of Louisville, deciding which route to take home. As I emerged from beneath the dip of Jesmond Bridge, I was pulled north to Doreen's house.

It was the deeper shade of brown in my cousins' skin and the strands of my new Afro, resembling theirs, that kept me running. I ran and ran, up the Great North Road, circling the giant roundabout at Kenton Bar. I ignored Sonia and my shiny, straight-haired siblings who were only streets away.

"Our Kevin's here!" Doreen shouted while the dog barked from the backyard. She wasted no time ushering me into the lush, orange and cream living room.

"We haven't seen you in weeks, our Kevin. Look how much you've grown. Where you been?"

"Oh, I've been boxing," I said.

"Never in the world. Boxing?"

"And kung-fu."

"Well, I never. Our Kevin, who would have thought?" She looked straight at me, tapping the tip of her nose. "I can't put me finger on it, but there's something different about you."

She hasn't noticed? I thought. It was my Afro that I wanted her to notice, but her eyes surveyed everything but my hair. When I began to ask her what she thought of my Afro, my cousin Mark blew into the room on a skateboard and came to a halt next to me. He was wearing lime green pajamas, and his Afro was the size of a large watermelon.

"Mark! I've told you about that bloody skateboard! No riding it in the house," Doreen shouted.

"I just wanted to say hello to Kev," he smiled at me.

"He's getting tall, isn't he?" Doreen said.

"We're the same height," Mark said.

"That's because you're standing on the bloody skateboard. Now get off!" Doreen leaned against a cabinet where a red lava lamp sat glowing. "I should get your father to take you to Trinidad one of these days, teach you some culture."

"I'd love to go there!" I said, noticing how Mark had picked up his skateboard and was cradling it like a baby.

"Yes, I bet you'd love it, Kevin."

"I wouldn't go to Trinidad if you paid me. I'd rather go to Mad Dog Bowl—best skateboard park in the country."

Doreen kissed her teeth. She had all of the traits of a black woman, even though she was white. Being married to a Trinidadian with four kids had steeped her soul in West Indian tradition.

"You have no sense of culture," she said. "I don't see why you're not more interested in your roots. You should be more like our Kevin. I bet he'd go to Trinidad."

"Yeah, I would. I'd go right now if I was given the chance." I stood in the middle of the room. Mark may have no sense of culture, but his Afro was much bigger than mine.

"It's too far and too primitive," Mark said.

"Hopeless," Doreen said as the lamp glowed, twisting and turning behind her. "I never had those chances when I was growing up. Well, you could always go to London for the Notting Hill Carnival. It's closer. There are hundreds of thousands of people in the streets every year—best steel bands in the world."

She waved the dog leash and tossed out words that made me wish I were there with the hundreds of thousands. I wondered how Mark could so easily pass up the chance to go to Trinidad with his father.

"I'll go to London," Mark said.

"Good, I'm glad you've got some sense, Son," Doreen smiled.

"But not for Carnival, for Mad Dog Bowl." Mark dropped his skateboard onto the floor and stepped on it, raising his arms in the air.

"Mark, Mark, Mark, off the bloody carpet!" Doreen lunged, waving the dog leash. Mark picked up his board and flew out of the room before she had a chance to catch him.

"No sense of culture, none whatsoever." She closed the door. "I've been meaning to ask you, our Kevin." Doreen put her hand on my shoulder, and her voice hushed into the mellow tones of the orange room. "Did Sonia tell you?"

"Yeah," I said, thrown by the unexpected. I was eager to follow her question in the same hushed tones. "His name is Addo, and just like you said, he's from Ghana."

"And wasn't he studying medicine, or something?"

"He was studying medicine. A doctor. Do you know anything else about him?" I asked.

"No, that's all I know. But I do want to tell you something, Kevin." She gazed at me, I could see a hesitation, and then she leaned her head closer. "Did you know that I don't know my real father, either?"

I stood there shocked. "What! Dad's not your Dad?"

"No, he isn't. It's a long story. But my father was someone that me Mam met when Dad was away fighting in the war"

"No. You're kidding me," I said, trying to calibrate the impossibility of that equation.

"It's a known fact. The kids know, everybody knows. The whole family's privy, but no one talks about it. It was a secret for years, but we all just leave it alone. It is what it is, our Kevin. All I know is that he was a Greek sailor, and his name was Sandy."

I stood looking back into Doreen's fluttering eyelashes. Then I heard Dad's voice shouting the name Sandy over and over in his tormented rage. I'd heard that name. I'd heard it many times when Dad was beating up Mam or smashing furniture in the house.

"I was in an orphanage for a few years," Doreen continued. "Me dad wanted nothing to do with me. I was a lot like you. Did you know that when you were born, me dad didn't want you either? He wanted to send you straight to an orphanage as well, but me mother wouldn't have that. She brought you home from the hospital against his wishes, but when he saw you, he fell in love with you. I've never seen him love anyone as much as he loves you."

I thought of all of those moments with Dad, when we would walk through the Dene together. I'd show him how I could swing from the hanging tree branches and jump off the rocks, landing safely on the embankment without falling into the river. He would watch me for hours and never get tired. How could he not be Doreen's dad? How could that have happened? I wanted to push her words away from me. I needed distance. And yet, I felt closer to Doreen than ever before.

"Maybe I shouldn't have said anything. But I just thought I should tell you, our Kevin. Enough of all of these secrets."

"I'm really glad you did."

"That's what's different about you." Doreen's voice became louder, as she shook herself out of the trance-like state she was in. "You're wearing a school blazer! And I'm not used to seeing you in a blazer. It suits you."

"Oh, yes. Thanks," I said, wondering why she still hadn't noticed my hair. She must've been just as caught up in telling me about her dad as I was about mine.

The African's head snapped to the side, as my fist connected with his thick jaw. Sweat shot from his short spongy hair, spraying the referee's shirt, while he lifted his hand, marking my point. The African was undaunted. He kept coming forward, bulky and fast with bloodshot eyes and glistening black skin.

"Keep moving!" Neville shouted through the dense noise. The volume of the crowd increased, but I tuned it out. All my focus was on my opponent. He swung, missed, and swung again. I blocked his punch and moved to my left, sweeping past his corner, where his coach churned out French words in a heavy, African accent.

He launched a kick. I blocked it and countered with a combination of two punches that landed drilled into him. His head snapped back again. The crowd roared, the referee raised his hand and the African continued swinging, not letting me slow down for a second.

"Keep moving!" Neville insisted. "Jab, jab, jab, jab, jab, jab!" He shouted, as my fist crashed into the African's face.

I've found my form. I've found it, I assured myself. But the African was fighting for his life, swinging and pressing forward without pause. His jab hit my shoulder and another grazed my glove and yet another took me by surprise. It twisted my jaw and turned my head sideways toward the crowd. I exhaled, absorbing the weight of his heavy hand as he grunted and stepped forward, inspired. The referee marked his points. The African threw a round kick, his thick leg powering through the air in an arc. I leaned back, letting the kick fly past. As his foot touched down, my right fist crashed into his wide chest. It left him snorting and flailing his arms in frustration.

Harsh French screams vomited from his corner. The African tightened his jaw and smiled at me, fueled. He ran at me, his head bobbing from side to side. His long, thick arms extended as if to measure the space between us. I stepped to the side and threw a jab. His head stopped bobbing as my glove slammed into his face, yet again. More points escalated on the scorecard.

His next advance was weak. He couldn't match me, but anguish propelled him in an awkward motion of looping punches and straight-arm thrusts. *Is his goal simply to keep me away?* He stumbled toward me.

The African could not touch me. My skill and experience outweighed his. When I moved to London at seventeen, I spent most weekends traveling around the country, fighting in tournaments, amassing hundreds of bouts under my belt. It all served to refine my craft.

I went to college to become a student, with the intention of getting a scholarship and having more time for myself to train and ultimately follow my career in martial arts. I worked part-time jobs, selling furniture in Clapham or shoes in Selfridges. I hustled in every way possible, became a martial arts teacher at 18, while intensifying my own training regime. I remained single-minded, with one goal: to become a world champion.

I trained in Kung fu in the evenings, and you'd find me boxing in the mornings, at the world famous, Thomas-A-Becket, pro-boxing gym on the Old Kent Road in South East London. Everyone was there. All of the past, present and future British and World boxing champions. From Henry Cooper and every contemporary champion of his day to America's greatest: Ali, Frazier and Sugar Ray Leonard, this gym housed the best. They trained there during the early days whenever they fought in England. I presented myself as if I, too, carried on the tradition of being an American fighter in this Mecca of boxing. And yet, I was unique from the standpoint that I was the only kickboxer at the gym. There, my past was irrelevant. All that mattered was whether or not you could fight. The only way to earn respect was through ability.

On many training days, Frank Maloney, who managed an up-and- coming heavyweight named Lennox Lewis, would frequently ask me to turn pro boxer.

"I'll manage you and make you rich," he'd say.

"Let me think about it," I'd answer each time. I never fully agreed. Lennox Lewis later won the World Heavyweight title. I wondered if I would have taken his offer, would I have found the enormous amounts of fame and fortune that I craved. Still, I never looked back. I knew I was on the right path. I could feel it in my gut.

"That's the way!" Neville shouted. And I slid back, out of reach, leaving the African to struggle with my speed. Applause rippled around the room. The African thrust out a kick that hit my shoulder. I deflected it, shaking my head. The African steamed in with a swinging hook that landed on my glove. He swung again, I leaned away, out of the trajectory of his fist, letting it glide past me. I thrived in my element.

"Break!" The referee ran towards us as the African wrapped his arm around me, buying time. His breath was hot and his heavy head pressed against the side of my face. I smelled a musky, cocoa odor. It reminded me of Sebastian, and how I'd run through Newcastle, desperate to be embraced by my African friends.

"Break! Break!" the referee shouted.

I pushed my opponent away. He stumbled back, staring at me with wide eyes. He's still dangerous. He was as deceptive as his black skin, so dark it's tinted blue. Exhausted, he gasped for air. His pink, gaping mouth an open wound.

He continued to charge forward. I couldn't help but recognize his frustration as he tried to get close enough to land his cumbersome blows. Superiority flowed through me. I moved around the ring dominating him. Gone were the desperate days of chasing the African. Now, the African was desperately chasing me. I threw a jab into his face. The referee marked the point.

I danced around the African. I danced. I danced. He swung harder, wilder, spurred by the cheering crowd, his corner, and the dying seconds that breathed life into his attempt to win.

I shoved his arm away and hurled a right cross. He buckled to the side, as his rib cage bent against my fist. The African grunted and heaved his arm through the air. The referee shouted in Hungarian as the punch skimmed his shoulder and forced him out of our way. I kept moving, zigzagging my way into the final seconds. I felt it; the clock running out. He could not beat me. He swung and missed.

The African slowed. He glanced to his corner. I sensed his useless cry for help. He was alone. I've been there. He ran at me and lobbed a punch past my face and into the thick muggy air. The bell rang.

"Aarghhh," he moaned, trying not to cry.

Ghana! Ghana!" I chanted to myself as I punched the heavy bag that hung in the corner of the gym. "Ghana. I want to go to Ghana!"

The words pounded in my head.

"Bang! Bang! Bang! Combinations! Punch in combinations," Fowler shouted into my ear. "Don't throw them all at once. Take your time!"

I could hear what Fowler was screaming, but my arms wouldn't slow down. The more I punched, the more I wanted to punch. The more he screamed at me, the louder the word echoed in my head. *Ghana!* I didn't care that my wrist was swollen or that my knuckles felt raw. It didn't matter that my lungs were burning, and the sweat was stinging my eyes. They were small problems that would end when the bell sounded for the one-minute rest. There was only one question that bothered me more than anything, including the smell of raw meat from Fowler's breathing over my shoulder: *How would I find my father?*

It wasn't fair that Mark knew his father and that he could go to Trinidad to see his family as easily as gliding into the living room on his 70 mm green Kryptonics skateboard. It wasn't fair that he didn't care about any of that, and it wasn't fair that his Afro was bigger than mine.

A tacit bond formed between Doreen and I since she had shared her story. Although I was curious, I didn't want to ask why or how Doreen had a Greek sailor for a father. It just seemed too ridiculous a thought. All I wanted to do was to find my own father, so I tried to blank out that part of the family history and keep fighting for what made the most sense to me.

I grew tired of running out into the ring, swinging at the sound of the bell but finding nothing to hit. There weren't any signs. No traces, no odor in the air of a stinking armpit or a bloody nose, nor the stale marks of leftover vomit on the canvas. There was nothing but a black barrier, as immovable as the heavy bag I slammed my fists into.

"Combinations," Fowler shouted. "Are you deaf or what? Throw Combinations!"

My heartbeat accelerated, the light hands of a boxer's flurry. It was the same flurry I felt each time I walked out of the office of the university empty handed.

"Bang! Bang! Bang!" Fowler's voice kept coming. I kept punching, trying to drown him out of my head.

I'll dig. I'll dig into it, I thought. I'll break through that barrier, that black wall, that endless tunnel. I don't care how long it takes.

Did he leave me behind? Or did he really not know that I was born? I kept punching. My knuckles burned. *Did Sonia tell me the truth? Did she really not know where I could find him?*

Fowler put his hand on my shoulder and jerked me away from the bag. "Whoa! Stop for a minute!" He leaned his face into mine. "What's the matter, Kid? Why you crying?"

"I'm not crying!" I spat out.

"Well, that must be sweat coming out of your eyeballs. You've got the fire, Kid. You've got the fire. But ya ears aren't working. Ya gotta listen. Now, it's all about timing. You hear me!"

I looked over his shoulder at the bag. I wanted to keep punching away at it. I wanted to punch until it fell from the ceiling and crashed to the floor.

"Do you hear me?" Fowler grabbed my shoulders.

"I'm listening," I answered.

"What did I say?" He shook me by the shoulders. "If you're listening, what did I say?"

"Timing. You said it's all about timing."

Sebastian sat on the edge of his bed, pulled a jacket out of his backpack and threw it at me. We had spent most of the past hour looking for items of his clothing that I could wear to look older.

"Why do I need to wear this?" I said, catching the green canvas army jacket with one hand. "Don't you think I look old enough?"

"You're supposed to be seventeen and you're short a couple of years."

The bedroom door swung open. Virginia stood wearing bangles in her ears and high heels. "What's taking so long? Don't you know, I could have walked there by now?"

"We are ready!" Sebastian tucked his shirt into his pants. "I had to help Kevin with the correct clothing."

"What do you think?" I stretched my arms out, feeling swamped by Sebastian's jacket.

Virginia lowered her forehead and looked over the rim of her glasses. "Sebastian, we are going to a club. We are not going to war!"

"It makes him look older," Sebastian insisted.

"What is taking so long?" Rita appeared. "You look cute, Kevin, but I am confused. Aren't we going out?"

"Yes," Sebastian interjected. "It's to make him look older."

"Oh, I see," Rita laughed as we all descended the four flights of stairs. We slipped through the front door, straight into the back seat of Sebastian's two-door Opal Manta. There was a small refrigerator in the front seat, so I sat wedged between the two women in the back.

"What's this place called again, that we're going to?" I asked as the car pulled off.

"You'll see." Virginia elbowed my arm as she raised a small mirror to her face and started tracing the shape of her mouth with a cherry-scented lipstick.

"Sebastian," Rita raised her voice above the grind of the engine. "It would have been nice if you had removed that refrigerator from the passenger seat before we got into the car!"

"Sorry, I did not have time." The car swerved onto Shields Road, making its way towards the city center. I didn't care where we were going. I enjoyed the smell of cherries and the fact that I was wearing Sebastian's jacket that had his African name, Otigbah, sewn on the breast pocket.

"Watch out!" Virginia shouted, pointing to the fridge that was leaning sideways as we turned onto Pilgrim Street.

"We're almost there!" Sebastian turned another corner and came to an abrupt halt. "We're here," Sebastian said, looking at me. "And just remember, if they ask, you're seventeen."

"No one will bother him. They never do." Rita patted my shoulder as we climbed out of the car.

We hustled up the street, past a row of shop fronts and boarded up windows. A ragged, blue awning leaned over the entrance of an old brick building. The neon sign on the wall read, PLAYGROUND.

"Stick together." Sebastian pushed open the door, and a sea of music poured out.

We stepped inside. I'd never seen anything like it. I'd been to The Kings Arms, The Rat and Ferret, and the Newcastle Working Men's Social Club, with the rows of slicked back, bee-hived and permed bingo players bidding for a fifty-pound jackpot or tickets to Scarborough Fair. I'd seen the pint- glass filled tables and the inebriated faces, wistful as the night burned on. I'd even seen Dad punching into the air and stomping his steel-toed Chelsea boots to a good local band while Mam, trying to control her slurred voice, shouted "I'mmmm getting the next round in." She'd lean across the table, spilling all of her change on the floor. I'd seen all that before, but never anything close to the Playground.

The giant speakers that hung above my head boomed "Boogie Wonderland" while I stood in the doorway. And there it was, everything that I had been searching for: Black culture. Everyone was black, or at least they looked it in the dim light. How did this happen? Which part of town had they all come from to be here on a Sunday night when the rest of Newcastle was recovering from a weekend of drinking and gearing up for work on Monday morning?

I inhaled the smell of sweet sweat and took in the meld of bodies bumping and grinding, swerving and screaming. It made every cell in my body erupt, like a string of fireworks that had just been lit.

"How old are you?" I felt a hand on my shoulder, and a trench-coated tower looked down at me.

"Excuse me?" I said, timidly.

"How old are ya!"

"He's old enough!" Sebastian cut in.

"Yes, we are all together," Virginia smiled and kept walking, seductively, into the club. Rita followed, leaving the doorman focused on following the shape of her body.

Sebastian winked at me, "Come."

My heart raced as I followed him past the crowded bar toward the throbbing dance floor. A cheer went up as I stepped closer, bodies twisting and stomping. I jogged, trying to keep up with Sebastian who had already slipped into the maze of Afros. He disappeared as quickly as the words, "Wait for me," left my mouth and dissolved into the music.

I heard his voice and felt his hand on my shoulder, dragging me backwards through the dance floor until we were standing at the opposite end of the room.

"There they are." He pointed to a table where Rita and Virginia were seated amongst a group of people.

"Sit next to me!" Rita waved when she saw me, and I sat down between her, Virginia and a girl with porcelain skin and blonde hair.

"This is Robert!" Virginia pointed to a stout-necked, short-haired man with jet-black skin. "And this is Roger." She pointed to a young Indian man who looked my age. "He is our next-door neighbor."

"Hello," he said. "Are you in the army?"

"No," Rita laughed. "This is Kevin."

"Kevin, this is Christine." Sebastian sat down at that moment, put his arm around her and kissed her on the cheek.

"I'm buying the drinks!" Sebastian dug into his pocket and pulled out a handful of crumpled pound notes.

"I'll have any beer," Rita said, and everyone else shouted for beers.

"And what will you have, Kevin?" Sebastian said.

"I'll have a Coca Cola. Thanks."

"Coca Cola?" He laughed. "Have a beer!"

"No!" Rita shouted. "He is too young to drink beer."

"Oh, come on. One beer won't hurt!" Sebastian insisted.

I was about to reject the offer a second time when Virginia howled out loud with laughter.

"Ooohhh! It is not true! It is not true!" Virginia leaned toward us trying to control her laughter. "Robert said that he heard if a white man sleeps with a black woman, he will eventually turn black himself!"

"It's nonsense!" Sebastian sprang to his feet, athletically. "I'm going to get everyone beers."

"What do you think, Kevin? Is it crazy?" Rita turned to me, while laughter surrounded us.

"I don't know," I said, wondering if the woman would have to be really dark skinned for it to happen.

Rita grabbed my arm.

"Come," she said, pulling me towards the dance floor.

I had already broken a sweat by the time she dragged me into the middle of the floor.

"Why don't you take off that jacket?" she shouted as she rolled her shoulders in front of me. "You must be hot!"

"No, I'm okay!"

Rita moved back and forth, pressing her body against mine. I tried to follow. It felt both natural and awkward, but the freedom of everyone doing their own thing and not caring how they looked made me feel at ease. It was amazing the way we all just moved together. We danced until Rita threw her arms in the air, "My song has finished." And then she grabbed my hand and led me back through the crowd.

"Look who I found!" Sebastian waved as we approached the table. His hands were clasping beer bottles and his arm was slung around a slim-necked ebony man with square-rimmed glasses. His hair looked like it had been pressed down with an iron.

"Kweku!" Rita shouted excitedly.

"Can you believe it?" Sebastian said. "It's been so long."

"I have been locked away, studying like a madman." He held up his hand and laughed into his palm.

That's odd, I thought, looking at his acne-scarred cheek and wondering why he had such a strong upper-class English accent. He sounded like Winston Churchill.

"It is my first night out in months," he said.

"And what a night it is!" Sebastian raised his beer. "Cheers to all." "Cheers." Everyone raised their bottles and threw their heads back, swigging. I picked up a bottle of beer and took a mouthful. As the bitter taste washed over my tongue, I wondered how Mam and Dad were able to drink pints and pints of Brown Ale.

"Kweku!" Rita put her hand on my shoulder. "This is Kevin. His Daddy is from Ghana!"

Kweku reached out to shake my hand. "It is good to see a fellow Ghanaian."

"Kweku," Rita said carefully, "is studying medicine at the university."

"It was perfect timing that I ran into him at the bar. I needed help carrying the drinks!" Sebastian shouted across the table as the sound of a bell rang in my head.

There it is, I reasoned as I extended my arm, the clue I'd been looking for. I grabbed it in my palm as I shook his hand with fervor.

"Nice to meet you. It is very nice to meet you!" My voice quivered over the music. There had to be a link between him and what I was looking for. Somewhere between Ghana and the medical books of the university, there had to be an answer.

"That's a fine handshake you have there, Kevin!" Kweku said, wriggling his hand free of my grip.

Rita interjected, "Kevin's daddy also studied medicine at the university!"

"Oh, really?" Kweku's ears twitched and his head centered, as if he were posing for a portrait. He was an intellectual in every sense of the word.

"Yeah, he did!" I said, as Sebastian and Robert argued about who could drink more beer.

"When did he graduate?" Kweku raised his eyebrow.

"I don't know."

"You don't know?"

"He doesn't know!" Rita said, leaning toward us.

"Why don't you know?" Kweku said.

"Because I've never met my dad."

"Excuse me. What did you say?" He cupped his ear, trying to block out the music.

"I said, I don't know who my dad is!" I shouted, toppling the bottle of beer as I leaned further across the table. I rushed to stand the bottle upright and wiped the frothy spill from the table with the edge of my hand. Everyone was in deep conversation and didn't seem to care that the beer was dripping from the table.

"You don't know your father?" Kweku said.

"No, he doesn't," Rita leaned closer.

Kweku looked at her. "I am talking to Kevin, not you."

"Sorry!" she sat back and smiled at me.

"I've never met him," I said.

"How do you know he studied medicine?"

"My mother told me!" I forced the words through the music. "I just know his name is Addo and that he is from Ghana."

"Addo?" Kweku smiled as if he was recalling someone's face.

"Do you know him?" I rose up in my seat as Kweku raised his bottle and swigged a mouthful of beer.

Kweku emptied his bottle and looked straight into my eyes. "No! I don't know him. But I do know the name. It's a family name—fairly common in Ghana."

"Can you help me?" I asked.

"I don't think I can help you," Kweku burped into his palm. "I wouldn't know how to begin."

"Yes, you would! You've already started," Rita poked his shoulder.

"I suppose you're right," he said.

"Maybe you can just ask around, see if anyone remembers him," I said, imagining a white-bearded professor, as old as the school, who knew everyone who had passed through the halls.

"All right then," Kweku leaned back as if he were being carried away with the thought of it. "All right then. I'll investigate."

Rita clapped her hands and stood up. "Now let's go and dance!"

Women weaken the legs!" Fowler hung over the top rope of the ring, shouting down at us as we sat on the floor of the gym like elementary school children being chastised.

"I don't like having to stop the clock, but we've got a boxing match coming up in less than two months—and I can smell it. I can smell it when there's too much distraction!"

I sat behind Charlie, looking over his shoulder as my mind cascaded like a waterfall with the feelings I had had on the dance floor the night before, and the promise of Kweku.

"Now get on ya feet and get cracking! I want six rounds out of ya!" Fowler shouted.

"Come on," Terry nudged me and raised his bushy eyebrows. "I'll work on the bag with you!"

"Okay," I sprang to my feet. "I'll hit first, and you hold the bag," I said, shuffling on my toes and rolling my shoulders like Rita had when we danced.

"You're in a good mood, Kev. What's a matter with ya?" Terry handed me a boxing glove.

"I'm just feeling fast tonight, and I'm feeling good!" I started punching the bag, light flicks, quick and easy. "Float like a butterfly!"

"You've gotten much better, you have!" Terry yelled, as he braced the bag.

"He's not that good!" Charlie shouted as he walked past us towards the I smiled and threw six more punches hard and fast.

"Start digging into it, everybody! Dig in! Dig! Last minute of the round!" Fowler clapped his hands.

"It's the kung fu!" I snorted, while punching into the bag. "Secret weapon!"

"You must be crazy, doing kung fu and boxing at the same time. You must be a glutton for punishment. It's pure madness!" Terry snorted back, his head peeking out from behind the bag. "Is it really a secret weapon?"

"I can't tell you because it's a secret!"

"Ha, is that supposed to be funny?"

"I'm just feeling good!" I punched harder, thinking of Kweku and visualizing myself on the dance floor, moving from side to side with Rita's rear end pressed against me. The bell rang.

"That's the round!" Fowler climbed down the steps of the ring and walked across the gym floor. "Kevin and Terry, I want you two sparring next."

"Aye, coach!" Terry wiped the sweat from his narrow forehead with the sleeve of his sweatshirt. "Do you know who I'm fighting at the next bout, Coach?"

"Yeah." Fowler rubbed his chin with the tip of his thumb. "I'm getting ya a rematch with the kid that beat ya last time!"

"What about me, Coach? When can I fight?" I said.

"You're not ready," he started to say, before one of the kids shouted from across the gym.

"Coach. There's someone here to see ya!"

Fowler squinted, "Who is it?"

"Don't know, Coach," the kid shouted.

"Tell him to come over here!"

"I'm ready, Coach. I can fight," I tapped my gloves together, trying to get Fowler's attention. I was determined to change his mind.

"Listen," Fowler scratched his neck. "The match is in seven weeks. Ya need a bit more seasoning, Kid."

"But I'm feeling good," I said as someone placed a hand on Fowler's shoulder.

"Micky Burns, I don't believe it!" Fowler turned to face the square- framed figure of a man with cropped hair and lamb-chop sideburns. "What ya doing here, kid? I haven't seen you in a few years."

"I was just passing through. I'm turning professional next month!" His angular face looked like it was chiseled out of granite, and I wondered if he found it hard to breathe through his flat nose that lay flush against his high cheekbones.

"You're turning pro?" Fowler said.

"Aye, I'm getting on. I'm twenty-four, and I've had nearly a hundred fights. It's time."

A *hundred fights!* I thought, noticing his thick hands.

"I was wondering if I could do a couple of rounds with some of ya boys? For old times," he said.

"I'll spar with him!" I jumped in, raising my gloves. "I'm ready."

"Maybe at the end of the night," Fowler said as the bell rang.

"But I'm ready!"

"If he wants to spar, Coach, I'll go easy with him. No problem," Micky rubbed his nose.

Fowler looked at me with hesitation, and then he said, "All right then."

"Yeah. No problem, Coach, no problem," I said.

"Okay!" Micky smiled and grabbed a pair of gloves.

I spat into the bucket that hung in the corner of the ropes, and Mickey Burns climbed into the ring.

"All right, Kevin, you ready?" Fowler tapped my shoulder and slid the plastic gum shield into my mouth.

"I'm ready," I muttered and moved toward Mickey as the bell rang. The first jab I threw caught him on the side of the head. Then a launched straight cross to his jaw, forcing him to sidestep, like a man trying to rush through a closing elevator door. I could see his green eyes widen as he threw a left hook at me. Before it could reach its mark, I was already dancing around him, flicking my jab and tapping at his forehead. The wind whistled through my gum shield as I blew out.

"That's it, Kevin! That's the way," Fowler's voice grew loud with excitement.

I buzzed around Mickey Burns' wide shoulders like a fly. I threw another right cross that hit his glove and made him snort in a way that said, "I didn't expect this."

Wow! I'm feeling good. Wow! Wow! I didn't expect this, either.

I glided around him with the feeling of hot air shooting up from my stomach and filling my chest like a balloon. *I'm in! I'm in,* I told myself. *I'm in here with Mickey Burns, a grown man, about to turn pro, and I'm holding my own!*

I worked hard. I stayed alert, punching and deflecting Mickey's punches.

I'm in here with a man who's had a hundred fights and has the nose to prove it, and I am holding my own!

"That's it, Kevin!" Fowler clapped his hands.

Mickey started veering away from the instructions that Fowler had given him to take it easy, and he started unloading heavy shots. I could feel the weight of his bone cracking punches and the strength of a grown man who had decided to teach a young kid a lesson. I could sense that the entire gym had come to a halt, watching us exchanging punches. We were a spectacle. I was on the ropes with no one to help me.

I had to fight with everything I had, so I punched back with full conviction. Some of my punches landed on his head and stung him slightly but not enough. He sent some hard uppercuts into my chin. I felt his fist crush my cheek. I staggered, trying not to show that I was hurt. Time barely moved, as I lay against the ropes, unyielding. I absorbed all of the heavy blows reverberating through my body.

"Watch him, Kevin! He's got experience! Watch him!" Fowler kept shouting.

I got off the ropes and started shuffling around him into the open space of the ring, flicking more jabs at him. My senses returned, and I started to get the spring back in my legs. *You can't beat me!* I thought, throwing punches at him with speed fueled by anger. Then, in the bat of an eyelid, I saw the red flash of Mickey's glove as his fist flattened my nose and snapped my head back. I bit down, tasting the dirty leather in my mouth as the wordless voice of Fowler rumbled in my head. I fell back into blackness.

"Wake up! Kevin!" I cracked open an eyelid, trying to block out the daylight. *Why is Sandra's voice in my head?* I opened my eyes wider, noticing I was in bed and that she was screaming through my bedroom door.

"Breakfast is nearly ready!"

"Breakfast?" I could taste the leather in my mouth. It triggered the flash of red. It was painful to get out of bed. I held my head as I dragged myself up. Bruce Lee smiled at me from the poster that hung on the wall in front of me.

How did I get home? I asked myself as I walked to the mirror, struggling to breathe through my left nostril. My nose was so tender, I wondered if it was broken. My jaw felt shattered, stuck. I tried to open my mouth and pain seared up through the side of my face.

"Kevin! Come down and get ya breakfast. Hurry up!" Sandra banged on the door. I heard her feet clattering downstairs, and I see Fowler's veering eye looking down at me as I lay on the canvas.

"Do you know where you are, Kid? Do you know where you are?" Fowler threw the wet towel over the back of my neck. "See if ya can stand up Kid! See if you can get on ya feet!"

I walked downstairs into the sizzle of frying food. It smelt delicious, but I had no appetite. I was careful not to be seen as I passed the kitchen. I couldn't let Mam see that I was hurt. I slipped out of the front door, closing it quietly behind me, and trod down the road before anyone would realize I skipped breakfast.

Destination in mind, I strolled past the neighbors and down the stairs without looking back. The icy air bit into my face and filled my lungs, as I stepped out onto the street. I prodded my nose. It was tender. Something inside of me felt broken.

"That's the spirit!" Fowler's voice whispered in my head. Crossing the busy road, I remembered his car door swinging open and my foot stepping out onto the pavement.

"That's the spirit!" he said, standing by the car. He watched me stumble toward the house. Last night's events became clearer, little by little. My family hadn't noticed my return at all. I nudged my bedroom door open, tossing my clothes in a pile and collapsing onto my bed without even brushing my teeth. That's how I got home.

I followed the path past the swings, and then along the straight strip of concrete that spanned an open field. *Maybe fighting's not for me.* In the distance, where the grass disappeared into Grangeville Road and a line of lampposts stood like tall matchsticks, I could see the outline of brown buildings. *Is that the place? If I keep going, maybe I'll forget about the night before.* I stretched my stride, ignoring the leather that lingered on my tongue.

"Excuse me! Do you know where the dormitories are?" I waved at a woman who glided past on her bicycle, her red scarf flapping behind her.

"No!" she shouted. I kept walking until I reached the brown building. Gravel crunched under my feet, as I stepped through an arch that led me into a small courtyard. The arrowed sign on the wall read: DORMITORIES. I searched my memory for the dorm number. I pushed open a door at the side of the building and stared down a long fluorescent corridor. I stopped at number twelve and rang the bell. The door slowly opened, revealing Kweku, standing barefooted, wearing a plain white T-shirt and pale blue pajama pants.

"Kevin, hello."

"Hello," I answered.

"Come inside." Kweku, excited to see me, pushed the door open wider and waved me into the room. "Excuse the mess," he said, pointing to a heap of clothes that were strewn across a single bed to one side of the cube-like room. "I'm just doing my laundry."

"No problem."

I took in the three stacks of books at the foot of his bed, the book cluttered desk, the view of the frosted Town Moor through a curtain-less window, and the smell of raw onion.

"It's easy to get lost here," he said, as he closed the door behind us and walked to the pile of clothes.

"Yeah, I'm lucky I found you." I stared at a map of Africa that hung above his desk.

"I didn't expect any visitors this morning." He unraveled a pair of striped briefs from the heap of clothes and began folding. "But I am pleased you came."

"I'm pleased, too. Did you find anything?" I asked, while prodding my jawbone. It felt brittle.

"As a matter of fact," he said, holding up a sock. "Possibly."

"What happened? Please tell me."

"Well, there aren't any promises." He sat on the bed. "But there is currently a student at the university who might be of help."

"Who is he?" I sat on the edge of the bed looking at Kweku, the pile of laundry between us.

"His name is Edgar Nwosu."

"Edgar?" A dull pain throbbed in my jaw.

"Yes, he is Nigerian." Kweku began sifting through the pile of clothes. "And his father, it just so happens, has a brother."

"A brother? So? So, what about the brother?"

"His brother was studying medicine at the university at around the time that your father would have been studying here."

"That's good. That's great."

"It's so easy to lose clothes." Kweku pulled another sock from the pile.

"Can he help me find him?" I asked.

"Yes. I think so." Kweku draped the single sock over his shoulder, looked at me, and raised his eyebrow. "What on earth happened to your nose?"

"Nothing. Why?"

"It looks red and swollen," Kweku pointed.

"Oh, it's just cold outside, that's all," I explained. I didn't want him to know that I'd been knocked out. I wanted to forget that it had ever happened. "How do you think that he can help me?"

"He is going to ask his father to ask his brother if he remembers anyone who fits the description. And the best part is," Kweku said, standing up and pulling a shirt out of the pile, "his brother is currently living in Ghana."

I rose up, denying all of the pain in my body. "He's in Ghana?!"

"Yes, he is, but nothing is certain. So don't get your hopes built up. We'll see where this takes us."

I knew a fella by the name of Nwosu when I was living in Nigeria." Rita sat on the edge of Sebastian's bed. She was braiding Sebastian's hair while he sat at her feet.

"Ouch! Don't pull so hard," Sebastian winced.

"You asked me to plait your hair," she said, her fingers weaving the strands of his hair into rope-like knots. "So don't be a baby. I'm almost finished." Rita kissed her teeth and pushed his head down. "Anyway, we are talking about Kevin," she transitioned, "and I think it's wonderful that Kweku has already found someone to help."

"It's great! I couldn't believe it when he told me." I looked at Sebastian's head. "Does that really hurt?" I leaned back into the small wooden chair, facing him from the opposite side of the room. I twinged at the way Rita forced Sebastian's hair in all directions and sliced the steel afro comb through his hair.

"No, it doesn't," Rita said, twisting his hair to a new extreme.

"Ouch! Speak for yourself," Sebastian grouched.

"There! It is done." Rita released her hands from his head. She leaned back and took a deep breath, as if she had just completed a marathon. Sebastian stretched his neck from side to side, relieved.

"Wow. That's great," I commented, in awe of the rows of hair braided across his head.

"It is good for the Afro. Makes it grow." Sebastian stood up.

"Would you like me to plait your hair, Kevin?" Rita picked up a towel from the floor and wiped her hands.

"Who? Me?"

"Yes, you. Come to me."

"He may not want to." Sebastian picked up his guitar.

"I do. I do, I want to." I rocked forward in the chair.

"Then, come." Rita clapped her hands together. "Sit here. It is still warm from Sebastian." She pointed to the floor. I eagerly sat between her legs at the foot of the bed.

"Will it take long?"

"No, I am very fast."

"Unless she decides to pull out all of your hair!" Sebastian sniggered.

"Stop it, Sebastian. You are going to scare the boy." Rita grabbed my hair. "You are both like babies." She parted my curls like a tornado ripping through a cornfield. I didn't mind the feeling of my scalp being stretched as her fingers tugged and weaved away.

I sat, cradled between her legs, while Sebastian strummed his guitar. The smell of her coconut-buttered hands and the gentle ripple of her fingers down my neck brought a soulful satisfaction. I'd experienced moments of it before. Befriending the Yeungs, a Chinese family, offered that similar sense of belonging. They'd taught me how to cook egg fried rice in the kitchen of their restaurant. I felt that same gentle flutter in my stomach when Jimmy threw his arm around my shoulder for the first time.

Moments like these proved as fleeting as they were sensational. It was the feeling of safety, and pure happiness that intrinsically weaved through my being, on those rare Saturday nights in the Dene. Mom and Dad would, after much deliberation, have a night in and watch television with me and Sandra. We'd pass chocolates and crisps between us while we laughed at Morcombe and Wise, The Two Ronnie's, or any number of those other Quintessential British comedies. Mam was the loudest, pointing at the television, jovially mocking the cockiest of the performers.

"He does love himself, doesn't he? He loves himself. Boy, he really loves himself!" We'd laugh together.

"It's done! What do you think?" Rita said. "Look in the mirror."

"Now you really do look like me," Sebastian brimmed.

"It looks weird." I gazed in the mirror at the small braided pigtails springing out of my scalp like bean shoots. "It looks different."

"You look African," Rita giggled

"I feel like my head's been tied in a knot."

"It has," Sebastian's deep laugh filled the room

"It is getting late." Rita stood up and walked toward the door.

"It is only eight o'clock," Sebastian reasoned.

"Eight o'clock," I said, still stuck on my reflection. "I told me mam I'd be home for dinner nearly two hours ago."

"I am making Jollof rice tomorrow," Rita said, as she brushed past me and disappeared out of the room.

"Okay. See you tomorrow," I waved at Sebastian.

"Yes. Tomorrow, then."

Sebastian strummed his guitar, and I descended the staircase and left through the front door. I chuckled as I walked through the streets of Heaton, touching my hair as I went and making sure none of my plaits had come loose. The tighter the better.

There were few people at the bus stop and even fewer riding as it rattled across Byker Bridge. With the exception of the occasional glance from a passenger and the blatant stare of the driver as I boarded the bus, no one seemed to notice my hair.

The short trip brought me home quickly. I jumped off the bus and ran up the stairs of Queens Court. I was fully prepared to hear Sandra laugh. I didn't care.

I turned the key and stepped into the house, the smell of baked potato overcoming me. The living room door opened and Mam stepped out.

"Ya dinner—" she began and stopped before she could say another word. Her mouth froze and her eyes widened.

"Sally, bring some biscuits, will ya? I feel like a biscuit with me tea!" Dad's voice resonated from the living room. Mam tried to smile as she inhaled through her mouth.

"I've had your dinner in the oven. I hope it's not ruined."

"Was that our Kevin at the door?" Dad shouted.

"Aye, it was." Mam walked into the kitchen. Dad was sitting in his armchair, slurping a cup of tea, when I walked into the room.

"Hi, Dad."

He looked at me, his brows clenching as he stood up, struggling to swallow.

"What the bloody hell is that!"

"You mean me plaits?" My throat tightened.

"What do you think you're playing at, Kevin?" His cup and saucer trembled in his hands, tea spilled over the edges. "You're making your mother ill!"

"Here's your biscuits, George!" Mam ran into the room holding a plate in her hand.

"Lots of African people do it! It's normal," I said.

"You're not bloody African! It looks ridiculous." He threw the cup across the room. Tea and broken china splattered against the wall.

"Stop it, George!" Mam reached toward him, but he slapped her hand away.

"Get them out of your hair now!"

"I am African! I've got every right to wear my hair like this!"

"That's enough! Stop it now," Mam cried as Dad stepped forward, his eyes wild.

"Get 'em out!"

"That's enough, for God's sake!" Mam dropped the plate of biscuits.

"Stop it! Stop it! You're gonna kill her! You're gonna kill her this time!" Sandra ran into the room shrieking, terrified that Dad was attacking Mam.

"Sandra, sit down! Sit down. I'm all right!"

"Get 'em out!" Dad's neck bulged. His eyeballs strained.

I stepped forward, and a rush of heat blazed up my spine. Maybe it was all of those times that I'd stood powerless, unable to stop the violence, that fathered my rage. I could no longer remain silent and allow terror to flood my mind and my home. I refused to watch her drag across the floor or hear her scream for him to stop. I was resolute; fear would not paralyze me.

"I hate you. I hate you! I can't wait to leave this house! I'm African!" I tipped forward onto my toes, and he tipped back on his heels, my words bashing him square in the face. His eyes flickered, as if something had collapsed inside of him.

Mam cried and Sandra screamed, "Where ya going, Kevin? Where ya going?"

"I'm African, I'm African." My only words, sufficient. I ran out of the room and slammed the front door behind me.

I didn't run for cover when drops of rain began falling on me. I just kept walking down the narrow path toward the boxing gym. I'll get there when I get there, I told myself, wondering what everyone must bethinking of me after getting knocked out.

The rain exacerbated as I reached the entrance. I stood outside with my hands in my pockets, listening to Fowler's voice and the faint sound of punching. Maybe everyone forgot about my Mickey Burns' beating, I motivated myself to step inside. The break bell rang the moment I walked in. All heads turned. Fowler stood in the ring as if he were at the helm of a ship, grasping at the top rope.

"You've got one minute to rest. Make the most of it!" he shouted.

Terry's jaw dropped, and Charlie grinned when he saw me. I couldn't tell if it was because my head was braided or because of the knockout.

"You. Kid! Get over here, now!" Fowler's stiff-arm pointed at me from across the room. "Where ya been? Haven't seen you in a week." He waved me over and climbed down from the ring, as I crossed the gym floor. The glare of a gym full of eyes seared my neck.

"I'm giving ya six weeks, Kid." He put his hands on his hips and scanned my face with his eyes.

My chest tightened. I wished I'd stayed out in the rain.

"Is that how long I've got to get better, before you kick me out?" Fowler threw his head back, erupting into laughter.

"No! I mean six weeks before your first fight, kid! Anybody that goes after Micky Burns the way you did deserves to fight. You're ready!"

"I'm ready?" I responded, confused.

"Yes!" Fowler said, and someone whistled behind me.

"I'm ready!"

"All right now! Let's get some work done!" Fowler shouted. The sound of punching resumed in the gym, filling me with fear and excitement.

When Cus was sick, I told him that he should go to the hospital and fight the cancer. All he said was, 'Don't worry 'bout me. Worry 'bout yourself. You've been getting hit a lot, lately. Move your head more! You should be thinking bout that.'"

"It sounds like he was always thinking about the fight," I say with Dad in mind. "It's been almost seventeen years since I'd returned to London after competing in New York and Mam gave me the news.

"Her voice was calm, but tense. 'Your dad had a stroke,' she said. 'He was just standing there in the living room, drinking a cup of tea, and then he fell and smashed right through the glass coffee table.'

"I flew to Newcastle to see him in the hospital. He laid there, his mouth drooling and his face frozen. He mumbled, forcing the words out of his mouth, 'I'm proud a ya, Son,' he said. 'Look after ya mother.'

"He survived the stroke and eventually moved home, but he was bound to a wheelchair, never the same. Whenever I would visit him, he'd sob. 'Come here,' he once said, urging me to put my ear close to his mouth. 'I had a dream last night,' he slurred, 'I was free, Kevin. I was running through a field. I was free. And then I woke up.'

"Milton used to always say, 'My job as a teacher is to wake up the student.'"

"Yeah, sounds just like, Cus. He tells me, 'If you stop fighting, I'm gonna come back and haunt you.' That's what he told me. He'd come back and haunt me."

"Cus was like a father to you," I state, knowingly.

"Yeah. Cus was a tough guy. If I won a fight, we didn't celebrate. He just felt like you were supposed to win, anyway. Why would you celebrate, if you were supposed to win?"

"There's some truth in that," I acknowledge, trying to imagine a win without a celebration. "Milton, he used to always expect a celebration after a win. In fact, he encouraged it, and if you didn't want to, he'd insist that you do it."

We look at each other. I can see his intrigue.

"I guess there's no right or wrong way." He smiles at me. "If you're winning, you're winning."

"How did you wind up here, in L.A.?" he asks.

"I was visiting Los Angeles, early in my fighting career. I had flown into San Diego and I was driving up to L.A. on the freeway. It just seemed magical. I remember admiring the mountains and the ocean for the first time. It was the same feeling that I had when I first went to London. I felt like I belonged there. You could live here, I thought.

"When the time finally came, I moved here with my wife and daughter. I had always wanted to be an actor, so when I stopped competing, I told myself that I would direct all of that energy into the arts. My intention was that it would feel like I never stopped fighting. I'd be the same fighter, but in a new arena. That's how it started. I rented a room in Los Feliz, and the person who rented the room to me was an actor, Chris Callen. She said, 'I got a feeling you should check out this school that I go to. There's this guy called Katselas. I don't know why, but something tells me you should go.'

"So, I walked in through the back door of the Skylight Theatre, ushered in by Milton's assistant, Allen Barton. It was like a dojo. I had that same feeling in my gut when I first started martial arts. I learned about the craft of acting, which I found is similar to fighting. Iton led me to other aspects of art. You ever hear that story about the musician, Sting? He was looking for a new pianist, and there was this one guy who was supposed to be highly acclaimed. Apparently Sting called this guy up and offered him the opportunity to join him. Well, the guy said he was leaving the next day to fly to Tibet or somewhere to become a Buddhist monk. I guess he had to make a choice."

"What did he end up doing?" he asks.

"He went with Sting. Just when you think you're about to get what you want, one way, the universe turns it around and says, 'You want spirituality, or whatever else it is you're looking for? Sure, you can have it, but you're going to get it in another way. We have a different plan for you.' I kind of feel like that happened to me, somehow."

"Bruce Lee was an artist! He drew. Basquait painted boxers," he encourages.

"I'm not surprised," I answer. "I like Basquait, and how about Salvator Rosa? He was a seventeenth century Baroque painter. It's not what he painted that makes me like him, but who he was. He was a painter, writer, actor, musician, and a freedom fighter! How about that? A freedom fighter!"

"Ali was a freedom fighter," he says. "That's why he was the greatest. He was fighting for the little guys. He fought for the Black people, the bum on the street, the people who didn't know how to fight for themselves."

My heart hammered against my chest as I sprinted down Richardson Road, yelling out my made-up mantra, "The road to Marrakeshis long and hard, the tasks are many and difficult, but the reward is greatness." It came from a dream I'd had. In it, a voice directed I go to Marrakesh where a golden crown was lowered onto my head. It seemed like a good thought to hold onto, so I did. I ran with that image at the front of my mind and the positive words to bolster my resolve.

I looked like an orange streak in the workman's overalls I had taken from a pile of clothing Dad never wore. The inside tag read: PROPERTY OF NEWCASTLE PARKS AND RECREATION. On the outside, splayed across the back of my shoulders, were the words I'd written with a thick black marker, BREWERTON. NUMBER 1 CONTENDER.

Sweat saturated me, and the overalls clung to my body. The wind whistled past me, freezing my face. I liked the words on my back. I felt silly the first time I'd worn the orange suit, but those thoughts disappeared under the pounding of my heels the moment I ran down the street. Contender. I'd taken the word from a list of fighters in Boxing News magazine, and it made me feel that I was somehow aligning myself with my future.

My chest burned, as the sun began to rise, turning the empty street into a smoky blue vortex. I was rejuvenated. Micky Burns might have been the best thing that happened to me. I'd always trained diligently, but getting hit so hard that night inspired a conviction. *That'll never happen to me again.*

I'd been up and out for almost an hour. I'd left five minutes after Mam walked downstairs to the kitchen and two minutes after Dad ventured on hisstroll to work through Leazes Park. I had planned it well. The less interaction, the better, and there had been very little over the last three days. We'd see each other in passing, nod or glance. Dad might offer the occasional mutter beneath his bulging frow line. Mam scrubbed down the kitchen each day as she'd never scrubbed it before. Sandra was the exception. She'd walk through the house having a full-blown conversation with herself.

I flew past the final lamppost, head back and nostrils flared, tripping through my last strides. I crashed onto the pavement, palms first. I rolled onto my back like a flipped pancake, too tired to move and too hot to ignore the cold pavement against my back. I took a deep breath and watched the steam rise from my mouth, dissolving into the gray sky. I was happy for another completed morning training.

I sat up and climbed to my feet, feeling my heart drop its tempo. I swallowed the cold air and looked across the street to the brown building of Kweku's dormitory. Crossing the road, I jogged into the courtyard and up the dormitory stairs along the fluorescent-lit corridor.

"Who is that?" Kweku groaned through the door.

"It's me, Kevin."

"Who?" The door cracked open.

"It's me," I said.

He opened the door wider, standing in his blue flannel pajamas. "Goodness gracious." He rubbed his eyes. "What on earth have you done to yourself?"

"My braids? Do you like them?"

"Your braids are fine. It's the rest of you. You're dripping wet!"

"I'm in training."

"Come in." He turned and walked into the darkened room. "You're a bit bright for this hour of the day."

"I was up early," I beamed.

"Here." He picked up a towel from his bed and handed it to me. "Please sit down."

"Thanks." I took the towel with both hands and sat on the edge of his bed, noticing for the first time that his pajamas had tiny bears on them. "Any news, yet?"

"News?" He pulled the wooden chair out from his desk and sat on it, facing me.

"News from Africa?" I continued.

"Oh, from Edgar." He picked up his glasses from the desk. "Not as yet. It's only been a week."

"Nine days," I corrected.

"What are you training for?" He slid his glasses up the bridge of his nose and leaned back into the chair.

"Training for a fight." I wiped my chin with the towel. "How long do you think it will take?"

"Well, it can take the Royal Mail several weeks to reach Africa. If it goes by air, it can be as soon as two weeks."

"Two weeks!"

"Be patient, Kevin. Who on earth are you going to fight?"

"I'm going to have a boxing match," I said, visualizing a Royal Mail plane touching down on an African runway.

"I didn't know that you did boxing."

"I do kung fu, as well."

"Good heavens."

"First fight is in less than six weeks."

"Oh my God, I just remembered! I have a biology lesson in less than an hour!" He plucked his glasses from his nose and rubbed the lenses with the sleeve of his pajamas. "Don't you have school?"

"Yeah, it won't take me long to run home and get changed."

"I suppose I have a little time, too," he said, reassuring himself.

"What's it like in Ghana?" I asked, looking at the map of Africa that hung on the wall above his desk.

"Ghana, well, it's very green."

"Green," I repeated, remembering the bright pictures in the book I'd read. "Are there lots of people?"

"In Accra, the capital, there are many." He stood up and walked to the window.

"Is that where you're from?" I looked at him, trying to create a city in my mind as he yawned into the windowpane, fogging up the glass.

"Yes, there are many people there."

"Do you miss it?"

"Yes, I miss it. But when I graduate in three months, I shall return home."

I felt a ripple in my stomach, jealous that he had Ghana waiting for him. "That's good." I wiped my hands in the towel. "I wish I could go."

"I hope that one day you will. And you will meet many people," he laughed. "The world is full of people."

"If you could meet anybody in the world, who would you meet?" I inquired. He reached under his desk and grabbed a backpack.

"Well, I've never really thought of it, but if I had to choose someone, I suppose it would be Alexander Fleming, for discovering penicillin. Who would you meet?"

Watching Kweku pick up a book from the desk and put it into his backpack, I didn't want to say that it would be my African father. That would sound too obvious, or too depressing. I leaned back against the wall and tipped my head up toward the ceiling fan.

"Muhammad Ali. I'd want to meet Muhammad Ali!"

"That's a good one." He threw another book into his backpack. "That would be incredible!" I said, imagining Ali rubbing the top of my head and shuffling around me. "Yeah, I'd box with him. He'd love that, I bet." I stood up, and Kweku chuckled, as I punched into the air.

"I've seen him taking his jacket off in the street and boxing with the kids," I continued.

"Terrific. That would be something to see." Kweku zipped up his backpack.

"That would be marvelous."

Get your bloody hands up!" Fowler shouted at me through the ropes as Terry threw punches at my head. His lanky arms were like windmill sails. I grunted, holding my arms higher, and biting into my gum shield as I leaned back onto the ropes. My arms were tired from the one hundred press- ups and jumping kicks that Babbsy had made us struggle through the night before.

He'd told us he was putting a team together to fight in a tournament. He had just won the European Kickboxing Championship, beating Dominic Valera, a Frenchman, who was renowned in the sport. He had defeated Valera on his own turf, in France, and returned to his students with added vigor. I was determined to prove myself to Babbsy. I wanted to show him that I was good enough. I had to show the same to Fowler, removing any reason for him to change his mind about letting me fight. So, I kept working to keep my gloves from slipping below my chin.

"Don't drop 'em. Keep 'em up!" he shouted, as my shoulders sagged over the top rope. I leaned further away from Terry's swinging arms. "It's all about defense. Boxing is about defense!" Fowler walked around the edge of the ring until he was standing behind me, leaning over the ropes. "A little lesson for ya. Now, stay on the ropes and work your defense!"

I was trapped between the two of them, having to dodge Terry's fists while Fowler's breath raised the hairs on my neck.

"Bob and weave! Bob and weave, for crying out loud, bob and weave." I moved my head from side to side while trying to avert my opponent's punches or deflect them with my shoulders or gloves. It wasn't going very

well. I was exhausted further than the physical battle of this third round or the rigorous training I'd been doing. I'd grown weary from my desperate escapes at home.

Day one and two had gone quite well. I had been able to coordinate my entrances and exits with ease, like a traffic officer on a quiet, two-lane street. By day three and four tension escalated, and our home had become a crowded four-lane junction. There was little or no place to go without bearing the weight of vexation. I had no idea what to say to either of my parents.

"Get out the bloody way, Kevin!" Fowler pulled on the top rope. Terry squinted and let out a grunt as his glove hit my shoulder. "Keep ya feet planted and move without moving"

Move without moving? I pondered, digging my heels into the canvas. It sounded more like something Bruce Lee would have said. Is that what being trapped on the ropes is all about, looking for the smallest of gaps to escape through without moving my feet?

"Thirty seconds to go." Fowler clapped his hands together.

I walked past Dad, straight out of the kitchen, holding my plate of sardines. No eye contact and not a word was spoken. As I climbed the stairs and walked into my bedroom, I wondered how long eating dinners in my room would continue.

"Seconds to go. You're letting your paws down!" Fowler wailed and Terry's glove bounced off my forehead, as the bell sounded. Fowler slapped my shoulder. "Okay, that's the round."

I opened my eyes to a sky of soot billowing past my bedroom window. My arms felt like lead as I climbed out of bed. I looked in the mirror, realizing it wasn't only my arms that had taken a beating from Terry's punches; my plaits had unraveled, and my head looked like a frayed cotton ball. I had managed to keep my braids reasonably intact for almost a week. I combed my hands over my head, trying to flatten it all down and wondering if it'd be better to go downstairs for breakfast or stay in my room until Dad left for work.

Go downstairs. The thought turned in my head. It was Saturday morning, and Dad wouldn't be leaving for work. I snatched my blue cotton T-shirt and pulled it over my head, determined not to back down this time.

I descended the stairs in silence and walked into the kitchen. No one was there. I took a bowl from the counter, opened the fridge, grabbed a bottle of milk and poured it into a bowl of Cornflakes. I walked out of the kitchen, shoveling the cereal into my mouth. When I elbowed open the door of the living room, I froze. Dad was standing, looking out of the window.

"Morning, Son," Mam said, sitting wrapped in a nylon gown with her legs crossed and stubbing out the butt of a cigarette in the glass ashtray that rested on the arm of her chair.

"Morning." I walked into the room, heading for the caramel-colored couch. Dad's hunched shoulders hadn't moved as he leaned against the windowsill. I wondered what he was looking at and what Mam was thinking as she stared at the blank TV screen while lighting up another cigarette.

I swallowed a mouthful of Cornflakes. "It looks like rain," Dad's voice made me jump. "Cats and dogs. It's gonna come down cats and dogs." He turned to me. His eyes had the same glazed look that they always had whenever he reflected on the war.

I leaned back onto the headrest, holding my spoon. "Me and ya mother had a talk." Dad sat down.

"Aye, we have, Son." Mam stubbed her cigarette butt into the ashtray. Dad looked at Mam and slapped his thigh, as if he were breaking through something. Then he looked at me and rubbed his neck.

"You can do your hair any way you want to. You've got every right, Son."

"Aye, you've got every right," Mam echoed, standing up and pulling the belt of her gown tighter.

"Really?" I sat up, startled at what Dad had said. *Had they noticed that my hair was in disarray?* "Okay." I nodded, trying to stay calm but contrarily standing up with exuberance. I was so excited that I could not hold back my feelings.

"I might be able to find my dad," I said. "I know someone who knows someone and that person who knows someone is in Africa and—" I stopped in my tracks, noticing that Mam and Dad seemed to be lost in my words. Their eyes reached out to me and their smiles were paralyzed. I knew that they would do anything for me, but we were in a place that none of us had ever been before. It didn't feel right to say anymore, so I sat back down. "Thank you."

I could see Doreen's front door from where I stood at the end of the cul- de-sac. "Get here as quick as you can, as quick as you can!" Mark's muffled voice had pleaded to me, over and over, through the telephone. Before I had a chance to tell him that I was on my way to school, he had hung up, leaving me with the receiver pressed against my ear, puzzled.

Throughout the school day, I'd wondered what it was that was so urgent. When the bell rang at the end of the day, I ran toward Haggerston Crescent. I'd never heard Mark's voice sound the way it had that morning, and there were no clues in his exasperated breath. In fact, as I investigated his tone I heard panic in how he'd spilled out the words. Kingsley barked and pushed his nose through the letterbox before I reached the door. When I rang the bell, his bark turned into a howl.

"Back. Back. Sit, boy, sit!" a voice struggled from inside the house.

The barking faded away, the door swung open, and Mark stood before me, his skateboard in hand, eyes wide. "Kev!"

"What is it?"

"I need to talk to you. You won't believe it. You just won't."

"Well, why don't you try me," I said as we stepped into the living room and sat on the leather couch.

"Okay. Okay." He dropped his skateboard onto the white rug, and as he put his hand on my shoulder, the door swung open and Doreen walked into the room in a cascading, red-checkered dress that fell to her ankles.

"Hello, our Kevin. Did Mark tell you the news?"

"He was just about to."

"Mark," she pointed. "Get that bloody skateboard off the carpet. Now!"

"What's the news?" I looked at Doreen. She turned her glare from Mark and smiled at me.

"Well, the London carnival is six months away."

"What's the London Carnival?" I asked.

"It's one of the biggest Afro Caribbean festivals in the world. I won't be able to go this year, but I told Mark," she paused, watching him rest the skateboard on his knees. "I told him he could go if he does as he's told. That reminds me," she paused, folded her arms, and stared at Mark. "Your friends have been over every night this week, Mark. Is there something going on that I should know?"

"No." Mark forced a fake cough and glanced at me from the corner of his eye.

"I'm gonna let him go to London for the carnival, our Kevin, and I wanted to know if you would like to go with him?"

"Me?"

"Yes!" Mark spun the wheels on his skateboard.

"Really? I don't believe it," I said. "To go to the carnival would be a dream!"

"Mad Dawg Bowl," Mark grinned.

"You better get permission first, our Kevin, just to be certain," Doreen walked out of the room.

"I'm going to Mad Dawg Bowl!" Mark stood up. "I don't care about the carnival."

"I can't believe it. No wonder you wouldn't tell me on the phone. That's great news."

Mark's voice dropped into a whisper, "That's not the news. That's not what I was gonna tell you."

"What do ya mean?" I said. The door opened and an ebony-skinned girl walked into the room like a dancer moving across a stage.

"Mark, have you seen my blue cardigan anywhere?" she said.

"No," he replied, straightening his shoulders, "but have you met my cousin, Kevin?"

"Hello, Kevin," she said with a smooth voice and flashed a smile at me. "I'm Mandy. It's nice to meet you."

"It's nice to meet you, too," I said, feeling my back ripple as we shook hands. *How have I never seen her before?*

"So, Mark, if you find my cardigan, let me know." She whisked herself around and my eyes followed the curves of her body out of the door.

"Who was that?" I asked.

"That's what I wanted to tell you. She's been staying with us for two weeks. A friend of the family, parents are from Barbados. She's the news, not the carnival!"

"Hold this," he put the skateboard in my hands and grabbed the lapels of my jacket. "I had sex with her. You can't tell anyone."

"You what?" I dropped the skateboard on the floor.

"I did! I did!" Mark sniggered.

"No way. You're only thirteen."

"I did. And so did Al Morton, Baza, and even Lat Almond," he grinned and I pictured Baza, the red-headed neighbor's skinny legs and freckled face.

"Baza? That's nuts!"

"It is." Mark picked up the skateboard. "If he can do it, anyone can."

"Is that why your friends have been over all week?"

"Yeah. And I bet you could have sex with her, too."

Sebastian let out a deep, raspy laugh and leaned over the bonnet of his car. "It's true. It really is!" I stood staring, as Sebastian's laugh echoed through the small, box-like garage of his house.

"And you say he is thirteen years old?" he said, catching his breath and looking at me with watery eyes.

"Yes!" I stomped my foot on the concrete floor, jealous that my little cousin, Mark, had done it before me.

"Look!" Sebastian dried his eyes with the back of his hand to stop himself from laughing. "He might have done it with her, but I am certain he did not know what to do. How old is she?"

"She's nineteen," I folded my arms.

"Nineteen, she is. Nineteen, ha! Maybe she showed him what to do!" He roared again, and I joined him, holding my ribs. I felt a small consolation, unsure of whether or not I would know what to do in that situation.

"Come, pass me that." Sebastian, still laughing, pointed to a toolbox that lay on the floor. "Give me the small spanner, please."

"Here," I dropped the spanner into his palm. "How old were you when you first did it?"

Sebastian chuckled, "I was fifteen. It was a girl in Nigeria."

"What was it like?"

I stepped up to the car as Sebastian reached down into the engine. "You want to know what it was like?"

"Yeah. I wanna know."

Sebastian pulled his arm out from the engine and turned to face me, holding the spanner as if he were shading us with an invisible umbrella. "It. Was. Fucking incredible," he whispered. Then he turned and dived back into the engine.

"Wow! Fucking incredible," I said.

"I saw her many years later, but it was never the same."

"Why's that?"

"Damn. It is stuck. Pass me the hammer, please," he said without looking up.

"Tell me why." I dropped the hammer into his hand.

"Because, my young friend, it was like a dream come true." He stood and looked at me. "You will remember the first time for the rest of your life because it is when you touch the golden nectar, and when you touch it, you are changed forever. Your gwaiwa will drop."

"My what?" I said.

"Your balls!" he interjected, with a raised forefinger that carefully stressed every syllable. "Now listen to me and never forget what I am telling you. It is like stepping into the River Niger for the first time and becoming a man!"

"Where is the River Niger?" I asked

"It is the great river! The great river that runs through Africa."

I'll walk out with you, Son," Dad emerged from the living room. He buttoned up his jacket.

"Okay," I said.

"It's a nippy one this morning, Kev." The cold air rushed at us as we stepped outside.

"It is cold." I rubbed my hands together, looking down from the balcony at the empty street, wishing I were still curled up in bed. I could feel Dad trying to get closer to me. It was always a clue whenever he called me "Kev."

On mornings like this one, particularly after I told him I was going to have a boxing match, he had taken to knocking on my bedroom door or turning on the stereo ~ which was wired to a speaker in my bedroom, ready to play Ali Boom Aye, the Muhammad Ali war cry ~ to wake me up. As I ran, somehow, he'd make it to the bridge at the end of the Great North Road to stand as a silhouette, watching me disappear across the open moor. I couldn't help the feeling that I had to break away. As hard as I fought against the north wind, to run through its natural barrier, I could feel Dad fighting just as hard to hold onto me. I would run for miles, an orange blip on the horizon, running and running and running. When I felt like I couldn't run any further, the vision of Africa or the red flash of Micky Burns' glove and the taste of leather impelled me. Past the moor, through the town center, over Byker Bridge, down Shields Road, to the dockside, and past the old castle. Newcastle was getting smaller and smaller.

"It was freezing like this in the desert." Dad closed the door behind us. "Hot as hell in the day and freezing at night."

"It doesn't make sense that the desert can be so cold," I said as we walked down the corridor towards the lift.

"The years are flying by, Son. You're getting taller, and you're getting some muscle on ya. You're overtaking me."

I looked at the height of our shoulders as we walked, noticing that I was becoming taller and that I didn't have to lift my head to look in his eyes anymore. "Was it really as cold as this in the desert?"

"Aye, we were relieved when the Germans captured us and took us as prisoners."

"Why?"

"We got a chance to rest." Dad pressed the button, and the lift door opened. "Make sure you're fit for the fight, Son. It's the battle of the fittest out there."

"You're right," I said, imagining Dad in the desert, surrounded by the Germans. As we stepped into the metal box, I tried to ignore the reek of disinfectant. There was only the creaking of the lift cables, as we stood, side-by-side, staring at the metal door.

Dad broke the silence and said, "Did you know that Jamaicans talk like Geordies? Similar words, like 'Aye'."

"What, Dad?" I said, noticing that he was still staring at the door.

"Nothing." He didn't move.

The smell of disinfectant was making me feel sick, and I wondered why Dad had mentioned Jamaica. Maybe I'll ask him some other time. But I already knew. He was trying to bridge the gap between our colors and find the common ground, so I wouldn't lose sight of him. We walked to the end of the path, and Dad turned right and walked down Barrack Road. I turned left and ran toward the moor.

I was still drenched in sweat as I sat next to Mark at the dining room table opposite his teenage sisters, Cheryl, Alison and Debbie. They were three years apart in age but looked like twins with caramel-coloredskin, braided Afros and silver hoop earrings. Mandy, who looked more beautiful than ever to me, sat between the three girls, slurping a spoonful of soup.

"Our Kevin, I'm glad you made it just in time for dinner." Doreen walked across the kitchen and placed a steaming bowl in front of me. "Watch it. It's hot. And I don't just mean hot. I mean it's spicy."

"Huh," Mark sniggered, nudging my arm with his elbow.

"What are you laughing at, Mark?" Debbie said, reaching to the middle of the table for a bread roll. "You can't handle spicy food, either."

"Well, it is called spicy stew for a reason," Doreen said. "And our Kevin, you do look hot. Are you alright?"

"I just ran here from the gym. That's probably why Mark's laughing," I said, trying to cover for his innuendo. An hour earlier, he'd called to tell me that when he had walked into Mandy's room, she asked him if he "liked it spicy."

Looking at her it was hard to believe she could have had sex with Mark. Maybe he had made the whole thing up. These thoughts, coupled with Mandy's pouting lips that navigated the rim of her steaming spoon, were all consuming. *I'm positive he'd made the whole thing up,* I assured.

"Mandy, would you like some more?" Doreen walked to the table with the pot of stew, while Cheryl and Debbie fought to raise their bowls in the air. "Where are your manners? Guests first."

"They don't have any," Mark said.

"Quiet!" Doreen shouted back across the table, and then I shouted.

"It's delicious," the words erupted from my mouth, hushing the room.

"It is delicious," Mandy repeated, looking right at me from across the table. The room seemed to pause. All I could do was stare back into Mandy's playful eyes, while trying to look unbothered by a chunk of lamb that was burning the roof of my mouth.

"Our Kevin, are you all right, there? Are you sure it's not too hot?" Doreen laughed, and everyone laughed with her.

"I'm finished." Mark nudged me, stood up, put his plate into the sink and grinned at Cheryl as he walked out of the kitchen.

"See! He just did it again. Why does he always get to leave the table first?" Cheryl snapped.

"Cheryl! Calm down and eat your food," Doreen said and then looked at me. "Your bowl is empty, Kevin. Would you like more?"

"No, thank you. I'm full. I think I'll go and find Mark now." I glanced at Mandy, but her eyes frisked her bowl instead as she mopped the remaining stew with a piece of bread.

"It's true, Kevin. It's true. If you don't believe me, go down and see for yourself," Mark said sitting on the floor of his bedroom before an army of miniature soldiers that were spread out on the carpet.

"It's not that I don't believe you. It's just that it seems impossible."

We had been sitting in his bedroom for the past three hours, since leaving the kitchen table. It hadn't seemed like three hours had passed while we played war games, battling each other with his toy infantry. The game had been absorbing while the taste of stew and the image of Mandy wiping her bowl clean lingered in my mind.

"Just go downstairs," Mark yawned and rubbed his eyes. "She'll be in her bedroom. Everybody's in bed now, sleeping."

"What?"

"You heard me. And next time, I'll immobilize your tank division." He yawned again and jumped into his bed. "Goodnight. Say hi to Mandy for me."

"What do you mean?" I replied, but he was already snoring. I looked at his gaping mouth and his chest rising up and down, like that of a pigeon. I wanted to shake him and wake him up, but I just sat there wondering how he had been able to fall asleep so quickly.

"Hello. Hello." A soft voice came with a tap on the door.

"Who is it?"

"It's me, Mandy," she said and pushed the door open.

I stood up as she walked into the room, her chocolate skin glowed. Her hair was in a bun, and she wore fluffy cotton pajamas that were covered in strawberries as if she was fresh from a shower.

"He's out cold," I said. "Was it important? Should I wake him up?"

"No," she stepped over the soldiers, careful not to tread on them, and stood next to me. "I just felt like having a chat before I went to sleep."

I wanted to say, "I'll keep you company," but instead I clasped my hands together and said, "Yeah, it's getting late. I should really be going home. I've gotta get up early tomorrow and go running."

"Tomorrow's Sunday," she said. "It's a church day."

"I don't really go. Training is a little bit like my church. I run every day."

"Come with me, so we don't wake up Mark." She flipped the light off, leaving us in the shadows, and we stepped out into the hallway. The floorboards creaked when we passed Doreen's bedroom and descended the staircase towards the second floor of the house. We stopped at the guest room.

"This is my bedroom," Mandy said.

"Really?" I felt clumsy, and I wanted to run away. I also wanted to kiss her and see if Mark was right about her. *Maybe I could kiss her right now,* I thought. Don't be stupid. You'll make a fool of yourself, Kevin! And so, I leaned to the side, patted her strawberry-patterned arm and said, "Goodnight."

I walked away, and I heard her say, "Goodnight."

I thought I had made a fool of myself. I turned the handle of the front door, hesitating. *What would she do if I went back up there now?* I heard Mark's laughter in my ears, "She said, 'Do you like it spicy?'"

I turned back and walked up the stairs. There was no response when I tapped on her door, so I twisted the knob and stepped inside the room.

"Hello," I whispered, inching my way across the soft carpet until I could see the outline of her body lying on the bed in the darkness.

"You took your time," she giggled. I wasn't sure if that was a good thing. I didn't like the idea of being slow, so I slipped off my plimsolls and sat on the edge of the bed.

She grabbed my arm and pulled me on top of her, lifting my shirt and spreading her fingers across my back. I wanted her to think I knew what I was doing. I kissed the top of her spongy Afro. I inhaled cautiously, stealing the jolting scent of her body: cucumber and pickle. She kicked off her pajama bottoms with a coy giggle and guided my hand until it settled on her inner thigh. The soft bristles of her hair on the back of my fingers brought the unusual memory of waking with my foot between Sonia's legs when she'd sometimes sleep in my bed.

"Go on," Mandy whispered. "It won't bite you."

The blur of the red glove rushed at me, scorching past my head. I jolted back, staring up at my opponent: a six-foot-seven Hungarian beast. We fell into a pattern, circling each other at speed, like the hands of a clock, sweeping the ring. Two voices struggle against each other in my head: *There's no time! He's impossible to beat,* discouraged one. The other, a ceaseless demand, *Stay focused. Work your way inside then smash him!*

The crowd roared when the Hungarian flung out his fist, as if he were tossing a coin across the room. His reach was long. He had arms like poles. I tasted the leather of his glove as it stung my cheek. I shook my head at him, saying, "You're wasting your time!"

The crowd rose to their feet. We both knew what was at stake: the winner would go forth to fight for the world title. It's all a state of mind. I had to beat him psychologically. But I knew that in order to conquer him, I need first to conquer myself: *Fight hard, but stay relaxed. Be willing to die, but make it a game. Envision the outcome. I must win.*

The Hungarian spit on the floor, marking his space. The crowd applauded him. "Hoogary. Hoogary!" spilled across the room, like a giant wave of energy that crashed into my face accompanied with another of his jabs.

Come on! Come on! I screamed in my head, as the referee's hand flew into the air. Another point for Hungary.

"Hoogary! Hoogary!" the arena was relentless. I smiled back at him, as if to say, "It's not enough. Give me more. I can take anything you got!" I wanted him to think I was not intimidated. I would not let him see that my body was aching and my legs felt heavy and that my ribs were sore from The African, the Spaniard, the Dutchman. They'd each left a mark somewhere.

He flicked out his arm again. I stepped to the side, blocking it with my open palm. "Gw'on, gw'on," Neville shouted.

The Hungarian swung again. I moved under his arm, and rushed inside, punching into his body. He grunted, my head in his armpit. He smelled of oil and tasted of metal. I didn't care. I dug my forehead into his body and squeezed my arms around his waist, almost tripping him over. We stumbled across the ring, like a couple of drunks, but I was in control. I disturbed him, threw him off his game, took him out of his comfort zone.

"Brik!" the accented referee screamed for us to break apart.

I ignored him, staying inside, where I was safe. Inside, where his reach was worthless and his arms became a tangled liability. That was my strategy. "Brik! Brik! Brik!" The referee's hands struggled to unravel us, as I held on, pushing the lanky giant backwards across the ring. He was left with no choice but to embrace me, we were forged together. He snorted through his nose and his neck writhed from side to side.

"Brik! Brik!" The referee eventually pried us apart, making sure he pushed me further away, while pointing a stub of a finger into my face. "Brik!" he exhausted, chastising me. But I ignored him. I still tasted the bitterness of my opponent, but the voice in my head promised if I won this, then the world title would be mine. And then I could rest. I could rest.

"Fight!" The referee waved us on. The Hungarian shook his shoulders, as if he was shrugging himself into composure. He looked like a man wearing a jacket that he couldn't quite fit — and he was frustrated

Good. Fucking good. I've rattled him, I told myself as I crouched my way towards him, looking for an entry point. It was the same way as it had always been; nothing new. The little boy again, standing at the gates of the university, locked out, trying to find Dad, trying to find a way in.

"That's it!" Neville shouted, his voice barely pushing through the noise. The Hungarian launched a right cross. It landed on my chin. Everything slowed down and blurred. Applause rippled around the room as the impact rippled through my body. The thought of losing crept deeper. Lonely, I searched for Neville's voice.

"Gw'on." I thought I heard. I couldn't see Neville, but I imagined him the same way I'd imagine Dad, standing on the bridge behind me, a silhouette in the distance, as I ran across the Town Moor, struggling against the wind.

The Hungarian spit as he threw his jab. I bent, and his arm swung over my head. The balls of my feet were blistered, my legs were tired, but I pushed inside. My fist slammed against his chest. I felt the bone of his sternum. He swung again. His sweat lashed my face as I dipped under his punch. Again, my head was wedged in his stinking armpit. I could not breathe. His arm was wrapped around my neck, and my arms were around his body. We staggered around the ring and I held onto him, knowing that the referee would be pulling me away. I could feel the Hungarian tiring, as he struggled to break free.

"Brik!" Brik!" The referee pushed us apart.

I didn't waste time holding onto the Hungarian. There was only time to preserve my energy and look for ways to break down the freak. *I'm doing it, little by little,* I assured myself. I stared into his eyes, which looked softer, vulnerable, and unsure. The voice in my head that begged me to stay focused rose with arrogance, *Sharp. Sharp. Fuck him up!*

The crowd became louder, sending another wave crashing into the ring. The Hungarian rode the momentum and lunged a side kick at me. Instead of waiting, I slammed my right fist into his body. I reached up and swung a left hook from the tip of my toes. He shut his eyes just as my fist connected. His neck and forehead were a mass of bulging blue veins, as his head torqued, taking the full impact.

"Gw'on! Gw'on!" I heard Neville shout, as the Hungarian fell to one knee. I was taller than him for the first time. *Fucking right, you're taller than him now!* The voice in my head persisted. *I told you. I told you. Stay focused!* The Hungarian's corner was wild with screaming mouths and waving arms. They were buying him recovery time. But he was already broken, I could see it. His eyes were soft and his shoulders slumped. *You've taken his confidence. You have him. Finish him. Finish him.*

"Fight!" the referee signaled. As I moved towards the Hungarian, something was different. The crowd had become quiet.

"Work him!" Neville shouted. His voice was crystal clear.

The Hungarian moved around the ring, as if he were trying not to step on something. He'd become timid. The crowd started to chant again, and behind the Hungarian, a wall of red flags swayed from side to side. I inched my way forward. Inside of me, the last seconds burned away. *Stay focused! Stay focused.* I threw a jab that flew over his shoulder, and a short right that hit his chest. He stepped to the side, trying to swing his hook at me, but his arm was labored with fatigue, and his mouth twisted. 'I've had enough,' it said. The bell rang, as his fist swept over my head into the moan of the audience.

Women weaken the legs!" I heard Fowler's voice in my head as I ran down Falmouth Road. I flew towards Sebastian's house. I wasn't just flying. I was skipping, bounding through the wet streets like a helium-filled balloon.

When I had snuck out of Mark's house the night before, I was filled. *I did it. I had sex!* The voice rejoiced inside me as I closed the door and ran across the moonlit moors like a man with rockets on his boots. Upon reaching Barrack Road, I turned back and ran four more laps, ruminating on the way Mandy had parted her legs so naturally. It was the smell of cucumber that baffled me the most. And the way she squeezed her legs around me, moaning like a boxer receiving a punch.

"Oh my god! I can't believe I fell asleep," Mark had said, when I told him that morning over the phone. I was now en route to Sebastian's house to tell him that I had stepped into the great river. When I arrived, the door swung open and Patrick stood with his head down and his hands in his pockets.

"Patrick, come here. Come here, now!" Virginia appeared from behind him. "Kevin, hello there," she said, pushing her glasses up the bridge of her nose. Patrick turned, brushed past her and disappeared into the house.

"Come in," Virginia said.

"What's wrong with him? He looks sad." I stepped inside, inhaling the usual smell of rich spices. But there was a tension that I hadn't felt in the house before.

Michael, the younger brother, ran through the hallway, zipping past us, stomping his feet, as he ascended the stairs, grief- stricken. His head hung low. "He said he'd take me to the movies today! I hate it. I hate it," he shouted.

"What's wrong with Michael? Why's everyone so upset?" I looked down the hallway to see if Sebastian was in the kitchen.

"Sebastian left," Virginia said, folding her arms, as if she was holding her body together.

"Okay," I replied, "No problem. What time will he be back?"

"No. You don't understand," she replied "He left, and he's not coming back."

"What?"

"They called him back to Germany. He overstayed his leave. They came to get him. He left last night."

Ten days to go!" Fowler shouted down from ringside. I stood stifled, at the back of the packed room. I was still out of breath from the last five rounds of punching the heavy bag, and as I watched Fowler's mouth twisting and turning as if he was eating something bitter, I found myself wishing that I could have told Sebastian about the great river.

It had been only two days since I'd learned he was gone. We'd grown accustomed to seeing him go back and forth to his post in Germany, but this time was different. Virginia's words repeated in my head, "they came to get him." Her voice, ascending in shock, manifested in the form of a dignified shrill. I felt an emptiness, longing to have seen him before he left. It accompanied the acknowledgment that I'd been able to avoid much of the pain. I sustained my cycle of stuffing all of those feelings deep down inside of me. Oddly enough, within Virginia's shrill of misery I could hear Mandy's shrill of ecstasy. I wondered if I would be able to see her again.

"Ten days isn't long," Fowler grunted, "and each one of ya better be focused! I want a hundred percent." He climbed down from the ring. "Boxing's about discipline," he said, weaving his way through the room. "Discipline. It's about discipline!"

I heard Fowler loud and clear but couldn't stop wondering if they would let Sebastian come home. Knowing that I wouldn't be able to run to see Sebastian after school brought an internal displacement. *I can always just visit the house and get my dose of Africa,* I told myself, aware that it wouldn't be the same. At least I still had Kweku. And at any moment, I could receive news from Ghana.

"No fooling around! I don't want any fooling around! Ya, bloody mind's gotta be on one thing and one thing only! And what's that one thing? What is it? Eh?" Fowler's voice boomed across the gym floor. My eyes were fixed on Terry, who was standing up front. A pool of sweat was gathering at his feet.

"What is that one thing?" Fowler's volume increased, becoming unbearably tolerable, and I realized he was standing next to me, breathing hot air onto the side of my face. "What's that one thing ya mind's gotta be on? What is it?" He stepped in front of me, his left eye pulsating. "What's it gotta be on?"

"The fight," I shouted. "It's gotta be on the fight."

Forgiveness is not for the weak.' That's a quote from Gandhi," he says.

"Really?" I'm intrigued, "That's a very interesting way to put it."

"Adversity makes the weak weaker, and the strong stronger," he continues.

"I believe that," I reply, while wondering. Shouldn't adversity also make the weak stronger? Perhaps weakness is a choice. I'm pretty sure, somewhere in the annals of history I've been told that the weakest of the weak rose up to become the all-mighty.

"When I went to jail," he reminisces, "there was this guy who had the elephant disease. You know the one that disfigures you?"

"Yes, I've heard of it," I answer, noticing how open he is with me.

"Well, he had this disease," he repeats. "He never made contact with anyone. Everyone left him alone. All I wanted to do was go up and hug him and tell him that his disease is how I feel inside."

"That's powerful," I say. My voice is hoarse, barely audible, but my words hang in the air. They drift through the cavernous room, like that bell beginning the round, or ending it. I'm unsure of what else to say. I can only picture some type of grotesque figure, hiding behind bars in the shadows of his cell. Somewhere in that monstrous form I imagine myself, still hiding, still running away. In the pit of my gut I sense the opening of an old wound that has been scarred over and hardened. It's aching to be cut open.

We lean back in our chairs, and I divert my gaze out to the horizon. My mind is turning, curious about his thoughts as we glance at each other without making direct eye contact. It's as if we're starting the first round of a title fight again. We're feeling each other out. I can't help but think of Ali when he fought Joe Frazier to the death. How much love they had for each other?

When Dad died, I walked into the funeral parlor. A slight, dank smell filled the empty room, and soft morning light shone through a bay window. I walked across the brown carpet in a black suit towards his open coffin. Gone was the contorted look of struggle on his afflicted face from the past eight years, since his stroke. From the neck down, a sky blue, silk tunic covered his entire body. I reached into my pocket, took out my gold medal and hung it around his neck, placing the golden circle on his chest. It completed him, the shining gold contrasting the blue, emanating from his heart center. His pallid face had been shaped into a gentle smile. He looked like a king at rest, and the thought that he could be at peace comforted me. I kissed his cold, hard forehead and the bitter taste of formaldehyde seized the warmth from my lips, abruptly reminding me that beneath the beautiful silky, sky blue tunic, lay a twisted body that was filled with years of pain.

There was a hidden pain, like a thread, that seemed to stretch through my entire existence. Every inch of it was tied together in a string of circumstances that filled me with anguish.

Fifteen years later, after Dad's death, Milton suddenly died of a heart attack. And the dark tide came crashing down again, overwhelming me with pain and confusion. I realized then, I had made Milton a father figure, and once again, all of those losses came tumbling back in on me. A giant ball of hay rolling down a hill, building momentum, as it gathered the most speed and size upon impact.

I'd gone alone to Milton's art studio, searching for him in the things he'd left behind. I'd found a small book, tucked away on a shelf: Mandala Symbolism, Carl Jung. A page was marked and a paragraph underlined: the yogi shall become inwardly aware of the deity. Through contemplation, he recognizes himself as God again, and thus returns from the illusion of individual existence into the universal totality of the divine state.

I cared nothing about yogis or totality. I was angry. None of it made any sense to me. The one thing I wanted was to see Milton alive again, in flesh and blood, not in the pages of a book spouting some ethereal formula to an ultimate state of being.

"Keep punching, Kid. Keep punching! Dig deep!" Fowler's voice echoed in my head, as I drove back from Malibu. I could almost feel his wet, clammy forehead pressed up against mine. His stale breath of salted beef washing over my face.

He'd forced me to reach deep down inside of myself. The idea of forgiveness requiring strength led me on that inward search on my drive home. Call Sonia, your mother, and tell her that you love her. I picked up my cell phone and dialed the number. As the phone rang, I could see the Ferris wheel on the Santa Monica Pier turning in the distance. This is it, I told myself, inspired to talk to her to break through the barrier once and for all. It was time to build a bridge. But the phone went to voicemail and before I had a chance to leave a message, flashing red and blue lights filled my rear-view mirror. I was pulled over by the police and given a ticket for being on the phone.

What? There's still no news? It's been nearly two months!" I threw my arms up in the air and looked at Kweku, who was sitting at his desk, holding a cup of black coffee.

"Well, sometimes things can go rather slow in Africa."

"It's too slow," I protested, folding my arms.

"Good Lord, that's strong." He looked into his cup.

"It's been a long time. We should have heard something by now!"

"Patience, Kevin."

"Patience?" I stared at the steam rising from his coffee mug. I could hear Mam's voice in my ear, "Patience is a virtue, Son." And then Fowler's voice followed right behind, "Patience, Kevin, be patient! Don't throw all your bloody punches at once. Wait for the gaps to appear."

"I'm trying. I'm trying to be patient." I looked at Kweku, pleading. "Don't you think it's taking a long time?"

"Well, it depends on how you look at it." He raised his cup.

"Why are your eyes so red?" I noted, Kweku's eyes appearing bloodshot.

"I've been up all night, studying for an anatomy test." He shook his head. "Thank God for coffee. Would you like a cup?"

"No, thanks. I don't know how you can drink that stuff."

"Neither do I," he chuckled.

"But seriously. Do you think we'll hear anything?"

"One can only hope."

"I just wish things could go faster." I looked at the pile of books at the foot of Kweku's bed. "I've got my fight coming up in a few days. Maybe I'm just a bit nervous."

"Oh, yes! Oh, yes!" Kweku shook his head. Mam had shaken her head a day earlier, shouting the opposite.

"But it's my first fight, Mam."

"I wish you wouldn't fight, our Kevin!" She stood up in the living room, wringing her hands together. "Do you really have to fight? Do you really?"

"It's alright, Sally," Dad butted in and leaned back in his chair. "It'll be alright. It'll make a man of him."

"What's it like, fighting?" Kweku swallowed a gulp of coffee and looked up at me.

"I don't know, really. It's hard to describe," I said, trying to visualize Kweku wearing a pair of boxing gloves. We were from two different worlds. "Ha," I laughed. "Could you ever see yourself boxing?"

"I don't think I could," he shuddered as if he were shaking free from the very thought of it. "I think I'd die."

"That's how I feel sometimes," I admitted. I thought of telling him about the first time I dipped my hand into a boxing glove, but instead I said, "Did you know that Sebastian went back to Germany?"

"Did he?"

"Yeah, he had to go back." I wondered if I should tell Kweku about Mandy.

"That's really too bad." He looked into his cup again, contemplating something. "Well, he might be back. One never knows. It's a curious profession, being a soldier."

"Kweku, have you ever heard of the great river?"

"Which one are you referring to? The River Tyne, here in Newcastle?"

"No!" I sat down on the edge of his bed. "The one in Africa, the Niger."

"Yes, of course. I know that river. It's a big river. What about it?" He stirred his coffee.

"Oh, nothing," I laughed, deciding not to talk about Mandy, while Fowler's voice whisked through my head, "Keep your mind on the fight."

"What is it? Why are you asking?"

"I was just curious."

No one said a word while I sat in the back seat of Fowler's car, between Terry and my old friend Sean Finneran, who I'd introduced to the boxing gym. He'd been incessantly bullied, but since then, no one had laid a finger on him. We wound our way through dark streets. My body felt numb, and my mind was racing in all directions, trying to escape the feeling of being trapped. I wanted to jump out of the car and run as fast as I could to get away, but it was too late. All I could do was sit, trying to brace myself in the black leather seat of Fowler's four-door Cortina.

"Nearly there," Fowler broke the silence as we turned another corner. I should have listened to Mam, I thought. I should have stayed away from boxing altogether. I looked out the window at the blurry headlights of passing cars. When Fowler pulled over, I could dash away. But where would I go? I couldn't even tell which part of Newcastle we were in. It all looked unfamiliar, and I didn't have any change in my pocket to pay for a bus ride. So I sat hoping it would all be okay.

"Here we go," Fowler said. We turned into a car park. NORTH EAST SOCIAL CLUB, the white neon sign read on the side of the red-brick building. "Just follow me."

Fowler opened the back door of the car to let us out, and the gravel crunched under my feet. The cold air hit us as we headed for the back entrance of the building. I realized how unusually quiet Fowler had been.

"The other lads should be inside," he said as we neared our entrance. "It should be a good night. We've got nine fighters on the cards, so stick together."

I nodded in agreement and stepped through the doors. Staggering, I inhaled the burning smell of liniment ~ my first boxing match. *There's no turning back!*

"Shit!" I scanned the room of pensive fighters who were warming up. I wonder which one is Neil Far– Fare? No. Farquar, that's it. Farquar. That's all I'd been told: Neil Farquar. What kind of name was Farquar, anyway?

"A novice," Fowler had grunted. "He's a novice from the Coxlodge and Fawdon Boys Club. He's got a good jab, and he's handy on the footwork." That's all he had told me. The word novice had given me comfort, and I hoped he wouldn't be as awkward to fight as the pronunciation of his last name.

"Follow me." Fowler cut through the middle of the carpeted room.

"Howdy, Phil!" An old man with a flat cap and no teeth walked through the crowd. "Good to see you, again. Your lads are over at the far end."

"Good to see you as well, Arthur," Fowler nodded as the old man disappeared into the crowd.

"Come on," he waved his hand at us, pulling us through the room. "There they are. Now go on, get over there and get changed."

"Righty-o, Coach," Terry cheered as we joined the cluster.

"Evening gents," Steve Jacobs flicked his stringy arm into the air, while Charlie stared at me, silently.

I threw my bag onto the table, sat down, and pulled out my necessities: gum shield, gloves, boots and the new boxing shorts I had begged Dad to buy me. They were white with a black stripe, just like Muhammad Ali's.

"Are you lot ready?" Fowler gathered us closer. "The first match just started, so be ready when I call your name—there it goes!" Fowler cupped his ear as the sound of an applauding crowd drifted into the room. "There could be a knockout coming, so make sure you're ready at any time. It could be an early night."

I wondered if Dad was there among the cheers. I wondered if Mam had changed her mind and come to the fight with him.

"I'm not going! I can't go and watch anybody put their hands on you, son. I can't. I just can't do it! I'd bloody kill them," she had stressed to me.

"Come on!" Fowler put his hand on Steve Jacob's boney shoulder. "Remember, you're fighting a Southpaw, but he's got a glass jaw." They walked across the room and disappeared through the big black door.

"I'm glad I'm not fighting a southpaw tonight, glass jaw or no glass jaw." Terry bent over and began lacing up his boots.

"It doesn't matter who it is," Charlie said as he passed the two of us, punching the palm of his hand. "Just do the fucking business—no matter what!"

I could hear the muffled, cheering mob from the dressing room. Spurts of applause, shrill laughter, and spontaneous shouts of anger. Stay focused, I demanded myself. Keep your mind on Farq— Furq— Farquar. That's it, Farquar.

The crowd let out a roar. Seconds later, Fowler entered the room with a tight entourage of fighters. Steve Jacobs was in center, holding an ice pack to the side of his face. "Sit down, you'll be alright," Fowler soothed.

"He got knocked out," someone explained as Fowler directed him to a chair.

"You'll have him next time, Stevie. He was fighting dirty, the bastard," Fowler said. He pointed to Terry. "Come on, Son. You're next."

More muted cries came from the crowd. The big black doors at the end of the room kept swinging open, as fighters came and went. Some of them had their hands lifted in triumph, and others were in tears, their heads held low. Terry returned with bruised cheekbones and a broken lip. His fight had gone the distance and ended in a draw. Charlie came back beaming after winning by a knockout in the first round. Then Fowler stood in front of me, towel over his shoulder and sleeves rolled up.

"You ready, Kevin?"

"Yeah, I think so."

"You better know so," he said as we walked through the big black doors. A blanket of cigarette smoke and the smell of Brown Ale choked me. I followed Fowler through the rows of chairs, shouts from the crowd increasing.

"This one looks quick!"

"Darks are usually quick."

"Go on, Kid. Give 'em hell!"

I glanced across the room, looking for Dad, but all I could see were the faces of strangers.

"Come on. Up you go!" Fowler pried the ropes open with his foot. A spattered applause and screams echoed in the room, making me feel like I was being jeered. I stood in the corner of the ring, the hot, white lights glaring down on me. Fowler rubbed my eyebrows with Vaseline. I pictured myself as Muhammad Ali.

A big cheer went up as Farquar paraded into the room with his coach. "Don't listen to that," Fowler said. "Keep your eyes on me." He slapped the tip of my chin with his palm. "Stay alert, look at me. You'll have plenty of time to eyeball him when he gets in the ring!"

A voice crackled through a speaker, "In the red corner, from the West End Boys Club, Kevin Brewerton!"

Relax. I held onto Fowler with my eyes. My heart was thumping faster and faster within my chest, and my mind was spiraling. *What if I get knocked out? What if he's faster than me? What if I can't land a punch? What if I have a glass jaw?*

"In the blue corner, from the Coxlodge and Fawdon Club, Neil Farquar!" A loud cheer went up and echoed around the room.

"Now you can look," Fowler permitted.

I turned around. There he was, standing in his corner, green shorts with a black stripe, long arms hanging by his sides, cropped red hair, firm wide shoulders. He was chewing on his gum shield, his eyes fixed on me.

"Come here, boys." The referee glided to the center of the ring, folding down the collar of his white shirt and pulling on his black bow tie.

Farquar's glare intensified the closer I got to him. By the time we were standing toe to toe I could see the red, thread-like veins stretching around the whites of his bulging eyeballs.

"I want a nice, clean fight." The referee wiped his forehead with the back of his hand. "If I say 'break', you break. And if you knock your opponent down, go straight to a neutral corner. Now, touch gloves."

I took a deep breath and sweat poured out of me as I jogged back to the corner.

"Alright, keep it sharp! Move around. Lots of footwork," Fowler grabbed my shoulder and squeezed the gum shield into my mouth. "Here we go," he acclaimed as the bell rang. "You've got this! It's easy. It's easy for ya, Kid!" Something in the way he said that last sentence impelled me to wink at him as I turned to start the round. For a moment, as I circled Farquar, I felt like a king the whole world was watching. It's easy for ya, Kid! I repeated to myself. Then Farquar's left jab lanced me square in the face, snapping my head back.

"Get on ya toes!" Fowler shouted. I had already had that thought the moment his glove slammed into my nose. The memory of Mickey Burns' putrid glove in my mouth spurred me to punch back with a vengeance. The problem was, we were only seconds into the first round, and I was flinging my arms as fast as my shoulders could carry them.

"You'll punch yourself out! Slow down. Slow down," Fowler urged, but I couldn't stop. I was fighting for my survival. The mere thought of slowing down scared me to death.

"Slow it down, slow down!" Fowler barked as Farquar's right hand hit the side of my head and his left hand hit me square in the mouth. He was swinging as fast as I was, but harder, and at odd angles. His glaring eyeballs were locked on me.

As Fowler shouted as fast as he could, trying to slow me down, the drone of the crowd echoed in my head like a swarm of bees. It sounded as if my name was being called from someone underwater.

I was out of fuel. My body began to slow down like a wind-up toy grinding to a halt. I bounced against the ropes and lay there, trying to keep my arms up as Farquar's heavy hands pelted me. The bell rang.

"Get over here! Quick!" Fowler demanded. I wobbled to the waiting stool that Fowler was holding out for me. "Sit down here"

"I can't breathe! I can't breathe!" I panted.

"Quiet! You're wasting energy." He pulled out my gum shield.

"But I can't breathe... too much smoke!"

"Just breathe." He threw a sponge on the top of my head and wiped it down my face. He worked fast, like a surgeon trying to revive a patient after a heart attack. I wanted to stop the fight. I couldn't imagine mustering up the strength to go into another round. I looked down to see blood on my white shorts.

"You're doing good. Just move around and keep away from his right hand." Fowler didn't care that I was tired. He must have seen this a million times. He squeezed the mouth guard into my mouth.

The bell rang. I stood up and looked across the ring at Farquar. He was already stepping out of his corner with his hands held high, looking fresh. I questioned if Mandy had weakened my legs. I bit into my gum shield and moved around in a circle, throwing jabs at him.

"That's nice. That's nice!" Fowler grunted as my punches landed on Farquar's face and gloves, stunning him and making him reel back on his heels for a moment. "That's it. Press him now, Kevin! Now!"

I pushed forward, getting underneath his long reach and throwing punches at his body, but when I came up, his fist came down and clobbered my eye socket like a sledgehammer. I wanted to throw up.

The hum of the crowd deepened as he hit me with a body punch. I winced, hearing the same underwater voice shouting my name, pressing me to fight back. I did, until the bell ended round two.

"You need the next round to win!" Fowler threw the sponge in my face.

"Stop the fight. Stop it, I can't go any more."

"Just one more round." Fowler, ignoring my plea, grabbed my face in his palms. For the first time, I didn't care that his breath reeked of meat or that his eye crossed to the left. I longed to stay in his stinking breath, hiding in it for as long as permitted.

"Just one more round, Kid!" he demanded. The bell rang for round three. Farquar rushed at me, throwing punches. I swerved around him and countered with fast hooks to his head. He stumbled back, so I chased. I could barely reach him to follow through. Just as I was about to throw a jab at him, he hit me with an uppercut that twisted my jaw and sent me falling backwards toward the canvas. The ropes broke my fall, and I managed to stay upright. Our bodies were tangled as we tried to swing at each other.

"Get off the ropes!" Fowler shouted. Everything moved in slow motion, the muffled holler of my name continued. As we remained clinched with our arms wrapped around each other and our heads side by side, I glanced over Farquar's shoulder. I thought I saw Dad through the ropes, throwing wild punches in the air like a mad man, with all of his fury, spurring me on. My spirit was sinking, but

I heard Farquar panting like an out-of-breath dog inspired me. He's just as tired as I am.

"Break it up!" The referee's arms slid between us, prying us apart like two pieces of wet clay. When the referee stepped away, leaving room to punch, I started swinging with the sound of Farquar's gasping breath in my ear, propelling me. *Don't stop! Don't stop! Don't stop!* My head pounded as we stood toe to toe. I was digging in and punching from the bottom up, from the soles of my feet, every fiber and cell, every part of me thrusting forward.

"That's it! It's over," the referee screamed with the bell, throwing his body between us. I dropped my arms, and the room spun around me. The crowd was deafening, and I craved to fall onto the canvas.

"This way!" Fowler put his arm around me. "You're walking to the wrong corner!" he said, pulling the gum shield out of my mouth and guiding me to our corner. I couldn't speak as Fowler sat me on the stool and started unlacing my gloves. My hands were on fire. *Get them off!* I pleaded internally, *Get it all off. I'm on fire. Everything's on fire!* I kept hearing my name, but I couldn't turn my head to look for Dad.

"You did great, Kid!" Fowler grabbed my face between his hands and pressed his forehead against mine. "You did just great, Kid! Just great!"

"Did I... Did I win?"

"It was a close one, kid. Ya did yourself proud."

"But did I—"

"Get over there! He's gonna read the score cards."

Fowler pointed to the center of the ring where the referee was standing. Farquar was already on his feet with a towel around his neck, as if he were anticipating a prize. The referee grabbed my wrist and stood between us. His black bowtie was twisted. I squinted through the ropes, looking for Dad in the hazy white light. Did I win? I tried to imagine the thrill of my heavy arm being lifted into the air and announced as the winner. I strained to visualize the crowd raising their drinks and cheering, but I just couldn't see it. I was too tired to dream.

"And the winner, by a majority decision," I held my breath as the crackle of the microphone paused. "In the red corner, Kevin Brewerton!"

You should have seen him last night, Sally!" Dad sat up in his chair and slapped his palm on the breakfast table. "He threw everything at him but the kitchen sink."

"Well, I'm glad I wasn't there because I probably would have fainted." Mam slid a hot plate in front of me.

"Thanks," I said, ignoring the ache in the back of my neck and focusing on the plastic trophy of a boxer set on the table, next to the ketchup instead. "But I'm over the moon that you won, Son." Mam put her hand on my shoulder and laughed through a sigh of relief.

"You stuck it out, Son!" Dad sprinkled salt onto his eggs. "You've got guts, you know that?"

"Our Kevin! Our Kevin!" Sandra burst into the kitchen, her long black hair whirling from her head.

"Calm down, Sandra. Let him eat his breakfast in peace," Mam said.

"He's the champ." Dad stuffed a piece of bread in his mouth.

"Tell me again how you beat him, Kevin! Tell me. Tell me." Sandra tamed her hair behind her ears with both hands.

"Do you want some more sausages, Kevin?" Mam walked over to the cooker.

"Yes, please."

"Is it real gold?" Sandra grabbed hold of the trophy, lifted it up and started shaking it. "It's not very heavy."

"Stop it. You're gonna drop it," I scolded.

"Is it real gold?" she repeated, lifting the prize above her head.

"Give it to me, now!" I demanded, now standing up.

"Sandra, stop messing around!" Mam shouted from the other side of the kitchen.

"I thought he had ya for a minute there." Dad, still engrossed in the fight, slapped the table again.

I reached out to Sandra. "You're gonna break it."

"Sandra, give it to him," Mam shouted.

"But you didn't give up. Ya just kept at him. You kept at him," Dad smirked proudly, reliving every moment of the fight.

"What kind of gold is it?" Sandra turned the trophy upside down and shook it.

"Give me it!" I pulled the trophy out of Sandra's hands. "It's not real gold."

"You deserve gold," Dad beamed. "You bloody deserve gold."

"You cheeky devil, you can keep your trophy. I don't want it anyway." Sandra stood, rubbing her hands together.

"Here, there's some sausage for ya, Sandra." Mam dropped two links onto her plate. "Now sit down, the two of ya, and eat your breakfast."

"It should be solid gold, if you ask me," Dad said.

"But at least it looks real." I placed the trophy back onto the table, next to the ketchup.

I 've got good news and bad news," Mark said as I walked into his bedroom. "That doesn't sound good. Where's Mandy?" I looked around. "Is she here? I didn't see her when I came in. I was hoping she'd be here." I leaned against the window ledge, the wall heater warming the back of my back.

"I bet you were hoping," Mark sneered.

"I want to see her. Where is she?"

"Well, that's part of the good news, bad news."

"What happened?"

"She's gone."

"No way." I felt a sadness creep through me, but I immediately shut it off with a nonchalant reply. I reminded myself, *it's no big deal.*

"Why did she leave?"

"She left yesterday," he bounded across the room and peaked out the door.

"Mark, what are you doing?"

"Making sure no one's listening." He closed the door and walked toward me. "I almost got caught, man."

"What?"

"Me mam found out everything."

"Everything?" I grabbed the lapels of his jacket, in desperation and fear.

"She found out that Mandy was sleeping with everyone."

"Everyone? How?"

"Don't worry. I don't think she knows about you. She might be suspicious," Mark tapped the side of his head, "but I don't think she knows."

"That was close." I let go of his jacket and took a slow, full breath. I felt like I'd escaped, but I was curious. *How many people had she slept with?* I yearned for her legs to be wrapped around me.

"Me mam burst into my room, seven o'clock this morning," Mark recounted the morning's events, depicting the key moments, pointing to his bunk bed. "I pretended I was sleeping. 'Mark, Mark,' she rushed, 'Did Mandy ever touch you? Did she ever put a hand on ya?'"

"All I did was crack open my eyes and moan. 'Huh? What, ma? What ya talking about?' I think that convinced her, because she tucked me in and said, 'go back to sleep,'" Mark chuckled.

"Too close for comfort!" I said, shaking my head. "I hope she doesn't find out."

"Me too, or else she won't be letting us go to London next month."

"London?" I replied.

"Oh, yeah." Mark clapped his hands together. "That's the good news. It's official. London's gonna happen."

"Serious?" I pushed Mark's shoulder. "I don't believe it."

"Yeah. We got a place to stay at Isaac's house," Mark smiled.

"Who's Isaac?"

"Friend of the family." Mark picked up his skateboard, thrusting it above his head like a trophy. "And he lives close to the Mad Dog Bowl. It's the best skatepark in London."

"That's just great!" I shouted, hoping Mandy would be at the carnival. I wondered if Dad would let me go.

No! You can't go to bloody London!" Dad rocked forward in his armchair.
"Why?" I stood in front of him with my hands on my hips. He slammed
his fist on the glass coffee table.

"Because you can't."

"George, don't. You're gonna break the table," Mam said, gripping the sides
of her chair. "Your dad does have a point, Son. Leave it alone."

"But I'll be going with Mark," I said, prayerfully.

"That's the bloody problem." Dad stood up and glared at me. "Just the two
of ya, and he's only thirteen, isn't he?"

"So? I'm nearly sixteen now."

"Well, when you're sixteen, come back and talk to me. But until then the
answer is NO!"

"What difference does a few weeks make?" I pleaded.

"That's true, George. He's nearly sixteen, you know." Mam looked me up
and down as if she were evaluating me, whimsically. "Can ya believe it? He's nearly
sixteen. How time flies."

"You're a fine one to talk, Sally. You didn't want him to do boxing, and now
you want him talking about London."

"I still don't. But I'd rather see him go to London than see him in a boxing
ring."

Dad's eyes pulsed. I could see his urge to rush over and slap Mam. Instead,
he looked at me, stuffed his hands into his trouser pockets, and turned to look
out of the window. "You're spending too much time over there, anyhow."

"Over where?" I looked at Dad, who was framed in the window of white
cotton clouds.

"Doreen and them. You're spending a lot of time over there."

"George, don't." Mam sat forward in her chair.

"Well, it's true, isn't it?" Dad said.

"We're cousins." I searched Dad's clenched jaw and Mam's flushed face, her
eyelashes fluttered, and I remembered what Doreen had told me.

"I'd sooner see you spending more time with Sonia, getting to know that side
of the family." Dad turned around and leaned against the windowsill, holding
onto it with both hands. *Was he bracing for an anticipated explosion?*

"Don't, George. Please," Mam pressed her hands together. She looked at me and stood up out of her chair. She put her finger to her lips, her eyes begging me to stop.

"Why should I?" I looked at Dad. "It's more fun at Doreen's house. It's a lot more fun there," I repeated. I only intended to punch my point home, but I could taste disdain in the words as they launched off my tongue. I was angry with Sonia for leaving me behind. "It's a lot more fun there!" I rose up on my toes, allowing the anger to swell in me. Dad moaned, and the clouds behind him shifted.

I heard Mam whisper defeat, "You won't let me forget it, will ya, George?"

"I just don't want you keeping the wrong company," Dad explained.

"Wrong company? What do you mean, the wrong company?" I questioned.

"I didn't mean that. But Sally, you tell him. Tell him what I'm trying to say!" His forehead was creased.

"Why can't you tell me? I'm asking you!" I said. I looked at Mam and noticed her wipe tears from her cheek with the sleeve of her dress. "What's the matter, Mam?"

"I've had it, George. All these years, and I can't take it anymore." Mam's voice teetered.

"Tell him, Sally, tell him!" Dad boomed.

"George ~" Mam began to say, but he cut her off like a butcher's knife, slicing through her words and silencing the room.

"Tell him about Doreen!"

Mam looked straight at him, and then her eyes dropped. In a firm tone, as if she were talking to the floor, she said, "He can go wherever he wants to, George. He's nearly sixteen."

I felt warmth cast over me like a fisherman's net, catching me off guard. I wanted to smile at her and thank her, but Dad had already spun around with hunched shoulders and a clenched jaw, growling, "What?"

"You're a bastard, George. You're a dirty rotten bastard, I've left ya before and I'll do it again if I have to. I've had enough of it! I'm finished with you, George. I've had it!" Mam flinched as Dad stepped forward threatening to launch himself at her.

"I'm not going to Sonia's!" I stepped in front of Dad, cutting him off. "I don't care about Sonia. I don't care. I don't care if I ever see her again!"

"Kevin!" Mam reached out, and as she grabbed at my arm, the doorbell rang.

"Who the effing hell is that?" Dad's eyes narrowed, and Mam's hand squeezed my shoulder. The bell rang again.

"I better get that." Mam said, exiting the room.

The stubbornness in Dad's eyes revealed he'd never let Mam forget the past. I was certain he wanted her to tell me that Doreen was not his child.

"Who's this?" Dad stepped forward with a look of shock. I turned around and froze.

"Kevin, there's someone here to see you, Son." Mam walked in with Kweku behind her. I opened my mouth intending to say "Stop! Don't come in. You can't come in," but the words wouldn't come fast enough. I watched Kweku pass across the pastel colors of the living room like a shadow. The awkwardness of two worlds being flung together. I stood in the middle, bracing myself against the impact. I was pulled in both directions.

"Kweku!" I said, and he laughed. His black face, so black that it was purple, seemed to shine brighter than ever against the flowery pink wallpaper and Mam's pallid cheeks.

"I thought I would surprise you."

"Who is this?" Dad grunted.

"Well, I'm surprised, all right. Very surprised," I said, trying to draw Kweku's attention away from Dad.

"I said who is this?" Dad pushed his voice forward. Beads of sweat ran down the sides of his face.

"This is my friend, Kweku. He's from Africa."

"Hello, sir," Kweku said, but Dad didn't answer, opting to stand with his eyebrows arched.

"It's nice to meet our Kevin's friends!" Mam stepped between Dad and Kweku. "Can I get you a cup of tea, pet?" She said in the same tone that she always used the morning after a big fight, when we carried on as if nothing had ever happened.

"Yes, please. I would love a cup of tea, if it's not too much trouble?"

"Of course not," Mam smiled at Kweku and then looked at Dad. "George," she said, raising her voice into the arch of his name. "Do you want a cup of tea?"

Dad's lips were pressed together. It looked like a hailstorm of words were about to explode out of him. He opened his mouth and said, in a whisper, "No. I couldn't stomach a cup of tea now."

Mam didn't move and raised her voice a notch higher. "George, go on. Have a nice cup of tea."

"All right." Dad blinked, and behind him the clouds seemed to have spiraled into the shape of a giant bird.

"Do you want a cup, Son?" Mam walked to the kitchen.

"No, thank you."

The room fell silent. As I stood looking at Kweku, I wondered if he could sense the string that was being stretched inside me. An avalanche of thoughts pelted me as the room turned upside down like an empty jar. *Will Dad make a scene? Could he smash the glass coffee table, or Kweku, or Mam, if she ran in to stop him? Would he hit Mam in front of Kweku? Or is it me he would hit?* "Here's the tea!" Mam walked into the room, balancing three cups and saucers on a wooden tray.

"Thank you." Kweku took his cup with both hands.

"George, here's yours." She walked over to Dad and held up the tray while twisting her neck in my direction. "Why don't you give your guest a seat, our Kevin?"

"I think we'll go up to my room," I said, watching Dad, who was refusing to pick up the cup.

"George, please take your tea!" Mam's voice rattled with the cups and saucers as she raised the tray higher. I looked at Kweku, wondering if he noticed our family feud.

"It tastes very nice, Mrs. Brewerton."

"I'm glad you like it," Mam said.

Kweku slurped his tea as we walked out of the room. We climbed the stairs, and I heard Mam say, "What a gentleman that young man is."

I imagined the glass coffee table being smashed into pieces and Dad shouting at the top of his lungs. But it remained silent.

"I had an idea where you lived. I just couldn't remember the number. Glad I found it," Kweku said.

"Well, what a shock," I pushed open my bedroom door.

"Good Lord!" Kweku shook his head as we stepped into the room. "Good Lord! There are posters everywhere!" He pointed to the trophy that I'd put on the table next to my bed. "What is this?"

"The fight. I won the fight." I sat on my bed, noticing how Kweku blended into my room.

"Good heavens. You really are a fighter, aren't you?"

"I can't believe you're here in my house." I leaned back against the wall as Kweku sipped his tea and sat facing me on the bed.

"Well I've got news for you, young man."

"What news?"

"I received word from Ghana."

"You gotta be kidding!" I sprang forward and slapped his arm.

"Careful," he said, the tea dripping over the sides of his cup. "My uncle's cousin will be traveling to see a doctor who studied at the university during the time that your father might have been here."

"He's my father? You're telling me he's my father?"

"No! No! I'm not implying that, although he could be. Anything is possible. All I am saying is that, if nothing else, he may know something about your father."

"Really?"

"Yes, but it could still take some time."

"I don't care, I'll take it!" I stood up. "I'll take it! I've waited this long."

"There is no guarantee." Kweku stood up with his cup in hand.

"I've got a good feeling about this." I walked across the room and leaned against the windowsill, laughing with my forehead pressed against the cold glass. "This is grand! It's just grand."

YES!" I hollered into the cold air as I ran up Barrack Road throwing punches into the dusk. I'd been running for almost an hour, taking the long route to the boxing gym, and I was hardly out of breath. It all felt so easy, as I ran across the cobbled streets, launching jabs everywhere while pivoting, crouching, and lunging into the yellow haze of the streetlamps. Then I was off again, at a full sprint, past the corner shop and down onto Sutherland Avenue.

I was holding onto the winner's title. I'd gone over the fight a thousand times in my mind, reliving each second until the recollection made me dizzy. People looked at me differently when I walked into the gym, including Fowler. His proud grin made me feel like a king. I was unstoppable ~ in the ring and at home. The news from Kweku made Africa more tangible than ever. Things were finally going my way.

I won't ever be stopped again, I told myself. I slowed down as I neared the gym and walked the final fifty yards in a confident stride, composing myself. I pushed open the door of the gym and raised my hand to let everyone know I had arrived. But the gym seemed different; it had a certain euphoric bliss in the atmosphere. Terry walked up to me, "Where were you last night?"

"What do you mean?" I answered. "The gym is closed on Tuesday nights, why would I be here?"

I felt a slap on my shoulder. It was Charlie, grinning at me as he walked by. "Hi, Charlie." I waved, confused to be on the opposite side of his smile.

"Where were ya?" Terry repeated insistently. "You should have been here! You missed it."

"I missed what?" I laughed at Terry, wondering what type of joke this was.

"Muhammad Ali was here!"

"Muhammad Ali!" I smirked. "Of course, he was here. Why wouldn't he be?"

"No, he was, really!" Terry continued.

"Sure, he was." I laughed. I scanned his ecstatic pale blue eyes in the same way that I'd looked into Cookie's eyes, when he told me that he knew who my father was. *How could Muhammad Ali have been here in this tiny little gym in Newcastle? It's impossible.* I refused to believe what he was telling me, so I pushed him away with a forced, emphatic laughter.

"Sure, he was here. You should be an actor." As I shook my head, I heard the door swing open behind me, and Fowler's voice filled the room.

"I want everybody ready in five minutes!" Fowler slapped me on the back. "Where were you last night, Kid? I thought you'd be here," he said as he walked past me.

"Do you believe me now?" Terry folded his arms. "Hello, are you listening to me? Do you believe me now?" I was lost for words, my mind collapsing like the tallest building.

"I can hear you, Terry," I whispered. "I can hear you."

Fowler's voice emerged, as he came into view, standing behind Terry. "Shame you missed it last night, Kid!"

"How come no one told me?" I asked, trying to look undisturbed. I didn't want anyone to see the helplessness I felt inside. Sebastian and Mandy were nothing compared to this. It was the same betrayed feeling that I had when I was told that Sonia was my mother, and that everyone knew.

"Everybody knew, Kid! I thought you knew," Fowler threw a towel over his shoulder, and casually walked away. I felt my body constricting with anger. No one deserved to have met Ali more than me. *It should have been me!*

Terry explained, "Muhammad Ali was touring the North East, promoting the boxing clubs. He said he loves Newcastle. He said he's never been loved anywhere like he was loved here."

"Really?"

"Aye, It was incredible! It was absolutely unbelievable! He got in the ring and sparred with me and Steve and Charlie. He was bloody amazing. It was fantastic!"

I tried to fathom how I could have missed this, while my spirit plummeted to immeasurable depths. Terry's voice rose like a Ferris wheel as he tried to take me on a wonderful ride. I had already crashed into darkness.

Sandra shouted through my bedroom door, "Ya haven't been eating anything. Mam's worried about ya."

"I'm not hungry! Go away!" I shouted, leaning against the window, my forehead pressed against the glass. For the last few days, I'd done little else, imagining Ali plucking me from the crowd and the two of us sparring in the ring. I could see myself laughing as he did the shuffle. I'd wrap my arms around him in the clinch and hold onto him as hard as I could.

"Are ya coming down for dinner, or what?" Sandra pleaded, as if somehow my eating dinner would satisfy her craving. I didn't answer and left her to whine until she grew tired and ran downstairs. "Alright, I'm gonna eat without you!"

I wondered what Ali would have said to me as I looked out of the window. I envisioned him standing with his hand on my shoulder, surrounded by a sea of people who had crammed themselves into the little gym. The thought of it made me numb.

There was always more to the fear, the possibility of disappointment. *What if Kweku couldn't find what I was looking for? Would I ever see my father?* My wish to go back in time and meet Ali mirrored the experience I had each time I'd traced my footsteps along the path of the university, knowing that my father had once walked there. *Was that as close as I'd ever get to him?* I scoured the outlines of my imagination the way that I'd traced the footprints of Muhammad on the sweaty floor of a boxing gym.

"Kevin! What's the matter?" Dad knocked on the bedroom door.

"Nothing! I'm fine. Just not hungry!"

"Can I come in?" he said. I turned around to say no, but he was already opening the door. He was wearing his working jacket. The smell of freshly cut grass entered the room with him. "What's going on?" He looked around as if he was seeing my room for the first time.

"Nothing. I'm fine." I folded my arms, persistent.

"Your mother's worried about ya."

"I'm not trying to worry anybody." I looked at Dad standing in his old worn-out grassy jacket. Behind him, a full-size close-up of Ali's face smiled at me.

"So, what's the matter? You've been locked up in your room for two days straight."

I looked at Dad, deciding whether or not I should tell him. I hadn't wanted to tell anyone because I was too upset, and I didn't really know what to say. It seemed a lost cause. The further away I could get from my feelings of despair was my only secure way of dealing with the pain.

"You really want to know?" I said.

"Spit it out, Kid," he replied.

"Okay then. Muhammad Ali was at my gym and I missed it," I said, holding back my anguish.

"Ya, what? Muhammad Ali, at your gym?"

"Yes! Nobody told me!"

"How come?"

"I don't know. Nobody told me!"

"Well, I'll be damned." He shook his head and took a deep breath, as if he was inhaling something rancid. "I'm sorry to hear that, Son. I know how much that would have meant to ya."

"I didn't want to tell ya," I said.

"You can come to me anytime you want, you know that. You're my son."

"I was hurting, Dad."

"I know. I could see it. It was written all over ya face."

"I don't know how it happened."

"You'll get over it, Son."

"I'm fine, Dad," I said.

"Don't worry about it. You might get another chance. Life's sometimes funny like that."

"You never know," I said, though I didn't believe that one bit. "When we escaped the prisoner of war camp," Dad kept talking, "I got Beriberi disease. It's caused by not getting the right food. Ya feet swell up. It's very painful. Well, I had a bad case of it. I couldn't walk. I thought I was going to be left behind, but the lads didn't give up on me. They picked me up and carried me all the way over the Alps until we were safe. They carried me for weeks."

Dad coughed as if he was clearing his throat to say more, but he stopped. I was left lingering in the space between us, ruminating on his words. I liked the thought of being lifted, and I wondered if one day I would get another chance. It made me feel lighter and it eased the pain. Dad sat down on my bed and rested his clenched fists on his thighs. I opened my mouth to ask him how long it took to climb over the Alps, but before I could speak, he continued.

"I know what it's like," he said. "I know what it's like to want something." His face was still and he looked like he was traveling through time. "When I was a prisoner of war, all I wanted to do was get home. But I learned you don't have to be in a prison to be in a prison—the bastards."

I wondered what he meant. I wondered if he knew what he meant. "What's that, Dad?"

"Nothing." He splayed his thick fingers across his thighs and shook his head, as if he were trying to pull his thoughts in a different direction. "Look, all I'm saying is, you'll get over it, and you'll forget all about it by the time you get to London."

"London? But you said I couldn't go to London."

"You're nearly sixteen. Now, don't ask me again, before I change me mind." He didn't look at me, but rather in the opposite direction. From my perspective it looked like he and Ali were staring at each other.

I felt my shoulders arch back, and I wondered why he'd changed his mind. I wanted to run into his arms and smell the fresh-cut grass on his old jacket. I wanted to say, "I hope I haven't hurt you, looking for my dad, Dad. But I need to find him, Dad, and I hope you know what I mean, Dad." It was too awkward a thing to say. I was still in the clinch, holding onto Ali with both arms as hard as I could. I waited until he stood up and walked toward the door, and then I said, "What's for dinner?"

Fowler laced my glove up. "You ready, Kid? It's a packed house tonight."
"I'm ready!"

"Of course, you are," he laughed as we stood in a crammed dressing room, surrounded by fighters and trainers. "Let's do it, then." Fowler turned, and I followed, and the room parted like a wave as we cut through the mass.

I felt different this time. Maybe it was the fact that I'd changed my white shorts with a black stripe to black shorts with a white stripe. Maybe it was just the budding familiarity with the arena. The blanket of cigarette smoke and staring faces didn't bother me as much as before.

"Just remember, he's a southpaw. So don't go walking into his left hand." Fowler parted the middle ropes, so I slid between them and danced into the empty ring. A spatter of applause circled the room.

I felt confident standing in the corner as Fowler smeared grease across my cheekbones. "I've never mentioned this before, but you might just be the quickest I've ever seen," his raspy voice encouraged. A flash of fire rushed through me.

"I feel good, Coach," I said as the crowd cheered, and a small pack of bodies hustled across the room toward the ring.

"Here he comes," Fowler said. "Now, just stick to the plan, and you'll have him." I raised my eyebrows. Sullivan was thick-necked; his skin was pallid and muscular. Fowler must have sensed my fear because he clamped his hand on the side of my neck and said, "Don't worry. Forget the fact that he's a so-called 'knockout specialist'. He's just an awkward bastard because he's a southpaw. You're too fast for him, and that's all there is to it!"

"In the blue corner, from the West End Boxing Club, Kevin Brewerton!" My heart pumped as my name poured through the speaker. "And in the red corner, from The Fawdon Boxing Club, Gary Sullivan!"

"Go on!" Fowler said. I turned and advanced to the center of the ring waiting for the referee to bark out the rules. I looked into the green slits and blonde eyebrows of Sullivan, who seemed to be floating above me. He was tall. I averted my eyes to his protruding larynx, which made him look like an anaconda swallowing its prey whole. His collarbone stretched wide across his shoulders like a shotgun ready to launch its missiles in the air and explode into the skull of anything that came near.

"If you knock your opponent out, go to a neutral corner until I reach the count of ten. Now let's see a good, clean fight, gentlemen." The referee blew his nose into a handkerchief as we walked back to our corners.

"Speed and footwork, Kid. Speed and footwork." Fowler crammed the gum shield into my mouth. I turned as the bell rang and felt Fowler's hand release my shoulder, launching me off like a ship. I left with loneliness in the pit of my stomach. Sullivan ran toward me at full speed from across the ring, his red boots bouncing off the canvas and his matching gloves tapping away in applause for himself.

"Move," Fowler shouted, but I was flat-footed and shocked at my opponent's speed. Before his command could reach my motor neuron system, Sullivan's left fist was crashing down onto the side of my head.

"On your toes," Fowler screamed as my head jolted sideways. I felt another heavy blow on my forehead, and then another to the side of my face. It felt like a hard slap, and it made me gasp as I reeled back onto the ropes. *How can he slap so hard?* I wasn't quick enough to stop the piercing jab to my chest that made the wind squeak out of me.

What's wrong with me? I thought as I glanced at another red blur looping its way to the one side of my head that had not yet been hit. *Fight! Fight!* The words welled up inside me. As his fists scorched my head, throwing me against the ropes, I felt the same humiliation I had felt when Jimmy had smashed the heel of his boot into the top of my foot and slammed me against the wall.

Fowler was yelling an inaudible stream of garble, and Sullivan was winding up another slingshot. *How much can I take?* I dipped my head under his swinging arm, managing to squeeze myself off of the ropes in an awkward, clumsy stumble. I didn't care what I looked like to the crowd. I had found enough room to start fighting back. Jab, jab, jab. All of my punches hit his gloves, but Fowler shouted, "Yes, that's it! That's it." His voice became clearer as I flared my nostrils, filling my lungs with hot air and shrugging my shoulders like an escape artist.

Sullivan grinned, tapping his gloves together. I could feel him coiling his shoulders and planting his red boot into the canvas, ready to drive his fists forward. I didn't wait. Jab, jab, jab. Three more hit his gloves. Then a fourth grazed his chin and a fifth squared him in the nose. I hear him grunt, his eyes narrowed. How'd you like that? I taunted, as I moved around him and punched my right cross into the side of his head.

"Go on, Kevin! Go on!" Fowler's voice cut through the din as Sullivan kept swinging his arms, forcing me backwards into my own corner. His punches fell short. I circled, leaving him in an empty corner. Fowler was banging on the canvas with his fist.

The room engulfed me in a whirling roar. My head was clearing, and I told myself, *I'm too fast. I'm too fast for you, you awkward bastard.* Sullivan turned around and came running out of my corner with twice his initial speed. Before I could pivot into my impulse and throw a hook into his body, he jabbed his glove into my mouth, presenting me with the taste of leather, the memory of Mickey Burns, and the motivation to stand toe to toe and slug it out. *I am good enough. I am, I am, I am.* The words in my mind pumped with adrenaline.

I dug my heels into the canvas and sent my knotted fist, like a heat- guided missile, towards Sullivan's pointed chin. My fist reached its target, and I felt a jolt travel to the soles of my feet. The room became a carousel of white light, but all sound ceased, as if muted by a greater, spectating force. Time slowed, and I was in an alternate universe ~ a dream.

Everything seemed normal, and yet everything before me was disarranged. I looked around, wondering why the office clerk from the university was looking down on me through her penny-rimmed spectacles. *Why was she smiling and pointing her finger at me? Whose red balloons could I see in the distance? Have you seen my father?* I wanted to ask, but I pushed the thought away and focused on my breath, hard and fast. A frantic voice ruptured my eardrum as the referee screamed, "Four!"

I exploded into real-time. I'd been hit, and I was sitting on the floor of the ring. Those red balloons that I could see in the distance were Sullivan's boots as he stood in the neutral corner.

"Five!"

I tipped onto my hands and knees and thought of Mr. Tin leaping onto the stage like a cat.

"Six!"

I saw Fowler, but I couldn't hear the words that were gushing from his distorted mouth. Instead, I heard Sebastian gloating in my head, "The great river, the great river..."

"Seven!"

My heart was pounding, and in Sullivan's corner were flashes of laughter. I saw Saif's blinding smile, as he looked up at me, thrilled to be my little brother.

"Eight!"

I stumbled to my feet with the quickness of mind to tell myself, Smile, until your body catches up. I heard Frank Shields shout from the crowd as he stood on his chair, waving his arms in the air. *Is that Frank*, I thought, *or is it Miss Yarm wiping the blackboard and telling me that the coal miners marched three hundred miles to Parliament?*

"Nine!"

Mam would be crying if she could see me now, and Dad will be disappointed if I lose by a knockout. *Is that Dad in the crowd?*

"Do you know where you are, Lad?" The referee's probing eyes looked into mine.

"Ya...Ya," I stared back at him, wondering if I'd fooled him. He grabbed my wrists and wiped the tip of my gloves on his white shirt.

"Let's get on with it, then!" He pointed at Sullivan and whirled his hand in the air as if he were winding a clock. Before Sullivan could leap across the ring to get at me, the bell rang, and Fowler had already jumped through the ropes like a fireman leaping into a burning building. He wrapped his arm around me and pushed me to the waiting stool.

"Breathe. Breathe. Pull yourself together." He threw cold water in my face. "What ya trying to prove? What do ya think ya doing out there? I told ya, don't go toe-to-toe. Are ya mad? Do you wanna get knocked out? It's a mugs game. It's a mugs game, it is! Get on ya bike and use the ring. Use the bloody ring!"

The bell rang as he shoved the gum shield back into my mouth. I didn't want to go out for the second round, but Fowler had snatched the stool from under me forcing me to stand on my aching legs. If all else fails, I thought, I might find enough strength to hold up my arms and hide behind my gloves. Whack! A heavy fist brushed my neck, sending me sideways in an attempt to loop around the ring. Fowler shouted, "Get on ya bloody bike!"

But Sullivan cut me off, forcing me to change direction. Before I had a chance to carve my way around the ring in a big circle, looking for an opening, Sullivan had already stopped me in my tracks and pressed my back against the ropes.

"On ya bike!" Fowler refused to relent. Sullivan grunted while his fists came at me from all angles. "Come on," Fowler begged. "Come on!"

I slid off the ropes. Jab, jab. Two punches on his forehead, and the crowd screamed. Sullivan smiled taunting for more, but I was back on the ropes with a fountain of images springing up in my mind: Sonia's pink-feather duster, Rita's round hips on the dance floor, Mam crying in the kitchen, Babbsy throwing a spinning kick. They all swept through me while Sullivan pounded me straight into the corner, stuffing me down a giant funnel. There was no escape, I was destined to be in that corner.

The referee watched with an eagle eye, ready to step in and stop it all or start counting to ten if I hit the deck. I stared into the slits of Sullivan's eyes. He grunted harder, trying to finish me off, annihilate me. But the weight of his punches lightened, and his breathing deepened. We locked eyes, and something quicker and harder than any punch landed on us both at the same time. He couldn't finish me off no matter how hard he tried. He had given me his all. Now he was punched out and I was still standing. I stared back at him, filled with determination. I've taken your worst, and I've survived it. *You can't beat me.*

It was the most rejuvenating feeling that I had ever had. The great weight of an unknown burden lifted off of me. I felt lighter and everything that had tied me down, was suddenly gone. An unconquerable spirit began to lift me.

I threw two crisp uppercuts that landed on Sullivan's chin. The room became deafening. His eyes were wide open as he backed up. Mine remained half-closed as I chased after him, tripping over myself and whirling my arms like a windmill. In a breath, flashes of life, once again, streaked through my mind: Mandy's legs spreading, Dad's silhouette on the bridge, Kweku turning his back and walking away.

I had Sullivan on the ropes, so I kept punching. My fist landed on Sullivan's fleshy cheek, and the referee jumped in front of me with rough hands, pushing me away. He waved his arms in the air as if I'd done something wrong. Sullivan was on his knees and elbows, and someone shouted, "It's over!"

I looked around. The ring seemed to turn upside down. *Do I need you? Do I really need to find you, Father?*

I felt myself being hoisted up. Fowler was lifting me back to my corner. I kept staring at Sullivan, expecting him to spring to his feet and the referee to wave me back to fight. But he didn't. Fowler dropped my exhausted body onto the stool and pulled off my gloves one by one. "Ya had him. Ya took his morale. And a man with no morale has no heart." He splashed cold water over my face. "Now get over there and pay your respects."

Sullivan's back faced me as I walked towards his corner, and Mam's voice whispered, "Be a gentleman, Son." Sullivan turned to face me, his eyes were soft circles. I was taken aback.

"Well done, Kid. Good fight." His coach slapped my arm. I wanted to reach up and swing my arms around Sullivan. I wanted to hoist him up onto my shoulders. Anyone who fought that hard didn't deserve to lose.

I wanted to say, "I wish there was a way that you could have won." But I didn't. We bowed our heads in a sign of respect, and our shoulders brushed as we turned away from each other. As I walked back to my corner, I knew that something was different about me.

London can't be much further," Mark shouted, as the train hurtled through a tunnel, enveloping us in a long, screaming black hole. My skin tightened like a drum and my spine constricted against the narrow backrest. I felt as if I was suffocating. This trip was taking far too long. The train shot out of the mouth of the tunnel, and I noticed a tiny cluster of city lights in the dark distance. Since we'd left Newcastle, my body temperature seemed to have been rising, and the word "fuck" had been running between my mind like the stomping feet of an unruly child.

"What do you expect?" Mark swung his legs up onto the empty bench. "It's the Big City Saver. At least we've got plenty of leg room."

"But who wants to sit on a train that smells dank and of wet paint for ten hours, stopping at every station in England to drop off the post?" I said, wondering if the tiny cluster of lights was London or another small town that we would have to stop through. It was broad daylight when I'd left Newcastle on a full breakfast of sausage, beans and toast.

"And I'm frying up your favorite, Son!" Mam had shouted across the kitchen, stirring a pan of fried tomatoes. She had been shouting the same thing every morning for almost a week, ever since the Sullivan fight.

Dad had been volleying words back across the kitchen. "He nearly had ya, Son. He nearly had ya," and "You should have seen our Kev. He threw everything at him but the kitchen sink."

Today was different, and Dad's volley was a heavy one as he sat opposite me and scribbled on a piece of paper. "Now, this is your address and phone number. Keep it in your pocket, at all times, in case of an emergency."

"How come he gets to go to London?" Sandra walked into the kitchen. "I never get to go anywhere. It's not fair."

"Shush, Sandra, he's only going for a fortnight. He'll be back in no time," Mam said, as I winced at the thought of being back home so quickly.

"But a lot can happen in two weeks." Dad squeezed the piece of paper into my palm, and I could feel the weight of his hand on mine as if he were anchoring me to the table. I couldn't tell if it was his hand that made me feel the way I did or if it was something else.

Since the Sullivan fight, I'd sensed the notion that a puzzle was nearing completion. From the way I felt each morning when I woke for breakfast to the lump on my head that had shrunk to a comforting welt, to the stocky man with a red face and bowler hat who had squeezed into the dressing room after the fight and asked me to become a professional prize fighter. Fowler had chased him, shouting, "He's too young!" but it didn't matter. The very mention of it, that I might be good enough to be a professional, filled me with the same weighty sensation I had when Dad gripped my hand.

I could see the distant lights as the train made an arch in the darkness. A rush of heat rose in my stomach, the excitement of seeing the big city for the first time. Until then, it had felt like a distant dream. Something made me pull out the paper Dad had given me, and as the train leaned further into the arch, I traced the curved letters of Dad's handwriting. *What if I don't go back? What if I don't ever go back to Newcastle?*

"We will be arriving in King's Cross Station in approximately five minutes," the announcement chimed through the overhead speaker.

"Did you hear that?" Mark said. I stood up and reached above my head for the worn, brown leather suitcase Mam made me bring. Mark reached under his seat and grabbed his skateboard.

Sweaty and cramped, we squeezed our way down the narrow aisle as the train slowed. When I slid down the window of the carriage door and stuck my head outside, the last ten travel hours melted away. The wind brushed over my face.

"Fuck! I'm in London!"

The train inched its way into the floodlit station. Across the empty platform, another train rolled in at the same time, and it made me feel as if I was looking into a mirror.

"Push," Mark shouted, and I kicked open the heavy door. We jumped into the throng spilling out of both trains. The smell of diesel, the domed glass roof above us, and the bustle of the crowd, hurrying across the platform, entranced me.

"What does he look like?" I shouted.

"He's African."

"Well, that really narrows it down."

I laughed, excited that we weren't yet out of the station, and already I could count at least a dozen black faces ahead of us. We squeezed through the turnstiles and dropped our tickets into the palm of a white-haired Indian man.

"He's probably looking for us," I said, scanning the indifferent faces. And at that moment I expected to hear Isaac shout out our names or see a hand push through the crowd and grab our bags.

"Let's wait here." Mark sat on a bench, where we could see the scope of the platform and the clock that hung above our heads like a giant cube of sugar with Roman numerals. "It's just a matter of time. He should be here any minute," Mark assured. "It's still only nine-thirty." But it didn't take long before we were sitting in an empty station looking up at the cube of sugar.

"Fuck, it's nearly eleven o'clock," I said.

"I can't believe it."

"Are you sure he knew that we were coming?"

"Of course, he did," Mark continued. "But I'm wondering if he had an accident or something."

"Or maybe he just didn't bother to show up," I griped.

I felt a wave of nausea run through me, and Mark looked at me with a frown. He dug his hand into his pocket and pulled out a crumpled piece of paper, like a magician producing a trump card.

"This is Isaac's address. I don't have his phone number, but I have his address."

"Well, I don't feel like sleeping on this bench tonight." I wondered how it would feel to have to take the train back to Newcastle. The thought of it collapsed my pride. I felt numb as I visualized myself on an empty carriage, headed back and struck dumb by shock. "What choice do we have?"

"We don't have a choice." Mark stood up. "Maybe we can get some help, find out where to get a bus or something. Or a taxi. Or maybe it's close enough to walk."

"Maybe. I'll do anything." I picked up my suitcase, and our footsteps echoed as we walked through the empty station.

Before we made it to the exit sign, someone shouted, "It must be past your bedtime boys!" A balloon-shaped man with a flat cap and golf-ball eyes came half jogging towards us, panting and leaning to one side, as if one side of his body was holding up the other.

"Is he talking to us?" Mark asked.

"I don't know, but let's pick up the pace." That didn't help because the flat-capped man cut a diagonal across the floor and stopped us short.

"It must be past your bedtime boys. Do you need a taxi?"

"Oh, a taxi!" Mark smiled, relieved.

"How can I earn your business, gents?"

"Earn our business?" Mark said.

"Is there an echo in here? I could have sworn I just said that. Yes, earn your business. Take you somewhere? Give you a ride to your destination at this late hour of the night, chaps?"

"Well, we are trying to get to this place." Mark handed him the piece of paper.

"Elephant and Castle?" the man sniggered.

"What's wrong?" I said.

"It'll cost ya four quid. It's just down the road." He dropped the paper back into Mark's hand.

"I should have enough for that," Mark said.

"Right then, follow me." The man set off, one hand in the pocket of his sheepskin coat, and the other swinging by his side, as he walked his way to a rusty yellow car that was parked along the side of the road.

"Don't you drive one of those black cabs?" I pointed to a row of beetle- like taxis, as we slid onto the back seat of his car.

"Black cabs are not worth the money." He slammed the door shut and the car tilted on its side as he plopped himself down into the driver's seat. I could smell stale smoke as I looked out of the window, wishing that I could see more of London. The only view out my window was a black maze of slanted roofs and vertical buildings.

"I like to take the back alleys," he said. "Now, the black cabs, they'll take the long way, and you'll end up paying more."

Mark was silent, and the wave of nausea grew in my stomach. It reminded me of the feeling I had when I sat in the back seat of Fowler's car. I wanted to run, but I had no idea where I was. And so, I put my hand in my pocket to make sure that the paper that Dad gave me was still there.

"Those black cabs... you just can't trust them." The car rocked and came to a halt. And then he twisted his bulky frame and thrust his dirty palm forward. "That'll be four quid, please."

"Is this it?" Mark dropped two pounds into his palm, and I dropped two more.

"It's that one there, the big one." He pointed to a concrete tower. "It'll cost ya, but I'll wait for you if you want."

"That's a good idea," Mark said, as we pulled our bags out of the car.

And then the man opened his big palm and said, "A quid should cover it."

"A quid?" I said.

"That's cheap, the black cabs will cost ya more," he said as Mark dropped another pound into his palm and said.

"Good idea, just in case."

"I'll be parked right here." He leaned out of the car window as we climbed the dozen concrete steps to the tower. We stepped into the lift. It smelled like vomit. I was starving and I hoped Isaac would have something to eat.

"Here we are, eighth floor." Mark nudged me and we began to walk down the narrow corridor. It looked like a prison. I wondered how it would look in the daylight.

"I'm sure it will be fine." Mark pointed to a blue door. "This is it. 86 C." He rang the bell, sending a long buzz into the house. I crossed my fingers. I'm sure that Isaac just got the days mixed up, that's all. And I'm sure when the door opens, he'll greet us with open arms.

But the door didn't open. Mark looked at me. "Do you think he could be sleeping?"

"Ring it again!" I said, and he jabbed at the bell with his thumb. Then I jabbed at it with my thumb. And before we knew it, we were both jabbing and hacking away in a frenzy, sending wasp-like buzzes through the house, not caring if we woke him up, or the neighbors, or the whole tower block, for that matter. We continued until our thumbs were raw. And then we froze.

"Did you hear that?" Mark said. "It was a scream."

"Yeah, I swear I heard something."

"I bet that's Isaac," Mark said. "Thank God. It's Isaac!" And we laughed and patted each other on the back. I put my arm around Mark's shoulder in a sort of victory hug.

"That was close," I breathed out, wiping the sweat from my forehead comedically. "Now we can start enjoying our holiday."

The door opened, and out jutted a tall wiry man with insect-like arms, a square black forehead, and burning ruby eyes. "Who the fuck–?"

"Isaac!" Mark interrupted.

"Mark?" Isaac leaned back, taking a second look, his red eyes glaring. "What are you doing here?"

"You were supposed to pick us up at the station, Isaac."

"Oh, really? Who is this?" He pointed at me.

"'That's my cousin. Aren't we supposed to stay with you?"

"Isaaaaac!" a woman's voice shouted from inside the house. "Who is that? Who is at the door?"

"Look, Mark, this is not a good time."

"What do you mean 'not a good time'?" I said.

"We just came all the way from Newcastle," Mark explained.

"Isaac, don't make me drink alone," the voice screamed.

"You were supposed to meet us at King's Cross, Isaac. Me and my cousin, Kev!" Mark shouted, his voice rising.

"He's drunk Mark. I think he's drunk!" I snapped.

"Who the fuck...? Who you call~" Isaac reached for me, but Mark slapped his hand away. Mark's eyes blinked in shock that he'd just slapped Isaac.

"He's drunk!" I shouted.

Isaac pulled his wiry shoulders back, filling the doorframe, like a black mantis. Mark's eyes kept blinking as Isaac stepped forward.

"Run! Fucking run!" I shouted, and we were off, flying down the narrow corridor without looking back.

"To the car!" Mark wheezed, as we rattled down the stairs, dragging our luggage behind us.

"To the car!" I echoed, not caring if I twisted an ankle or a knee going down the stairs. If Isaac didn't catch us, we'd be safe in the car. I'd be happy to put every penny in that big dirty palm. We hit the ground floor and ran out of the building and down a dozen concrete steps. But when we got there, the street was empty.

"Where is he?"

"I don't believe it!" Mark dropped his skateboard on the ground. "He's gone."

"Fucking BASTARD!" I shouted into the empty street.

"What now?" Mark sat on the curb holding his head in his hands.

"I don't know."

Isaac hadn't followed us. But it might've been better if he had. I could have overcome his insect body and smashed him to smithereens, tearing him apart and grinding him into the ground until he was nothing more than pulp under my feet. I would be satisfied that he'd paid for everything—everything! "Let's see if that works," Mark pointed across the street to a phone box that sat like a lighthouse, glowing in the dark.

"Let's give it a go then," I said, thinking of Fowler, because that's what he'd tell me if I was knocked down and on my knees: keep going, Kid. Don't stop. We walked across the street and crammed ourselves into the small box that was plastered with business cards.

"It's ringing," Mark held the receiver to his ear. "It's me, Mark." I could hear the faint voice of Doreen from where I was standing. Mark explained what had happened, and she sounded calm and then her voice began to accelerate, and

Mark's head seemed to jolt back and forth from the impact of her words. He slammed down the receiver like a hammer.

"I think she wants to kill him."

"But what about us? What about now?"

"I don't know. She said to call back in ten minutes."

I felt trapped as we stood facing each other, pressed up against our luggage, in the tiny phone box. Over Mark's shoulder, my eyes landed on a card that read: Fuck me hard. Impulsively I said, "Did the other boys really sleep with Mandy?"

"Huh?" Mark's eyes dilated.

"You heard me. Did they sleep with her?"

"That's a crazy question," Mark peered into my eyes. "Why do you wanna know?"

I peered back without answering. And then I said, "Why not? Seems like a good time to know." And we both burst into laughter, howling like never before—laughing and laughing until the tears rolled down our cheeks. And then it stopped, and once again, we fell into silence. It seemed like an hour had gone by, and just as I was about to suggest we call Doreen, the door ripped open and Mark screamed. Before us was a black man with matted locks that shot out of an alien head, like the roots of an upturned tree. His eyes were sparkling, and his mouth of jagged gold teeth glistened.

"Easy Rastafari. Black man them cometh, Rasclot!" His voice filled the phone box. "Me name is Raymond, and Doreen sent me."

A golden crown is lowered onto my head. I've arrived in Marrakech. I'm alone, sitting in the ancient city. 'I'm the champ. I'm the champion of the world,' Ali's voice echoes in the background. Kweku slaps me across the face with a chicken claw. "I am not your father!" he screams out loud, while Steve Babbs warms up his legs in the background. Mam grabs my face and kisses me on the cheek. She says, "I don't love you. I idolize you," and then she turns and walks down the street. My eyes follow her, as she gets further away. I'll remember this moment for the rest of my life.

I struggled to open my eyes. A stream of blinding white light poured through a big glass window—there were no curtains. *Where am I?* My heart pounded and my back felt stiff as I sat up, fully clothed, in the recliner in which I'd spent the night. I could hear faint chatter and the smell of fish. Across a toy-littered floor, Mark lay on a leather sofa, groaning as he opened his eyes, "Where are we?"

I stood up, stretching the length of my body into the window while looking out across the rooftops to a silver sky.

"We're in London."

"Oh, yeah. It's all coming back now," Mark said. The door crashed open, and Raymond blew into the room, with his dreadlocks waving around.

"That woman no let me alone," he said, stopped in his tracks and smiled at us with a mouthful of gold. "Good morning, Rasta. Good morning, Rastafari. Me hope you slept well. Me hope you slept like kings!"

It was well past one o'clock in the morning when he'd pulled us out of the telephone box. As he drove us across London for an hour, he told us, "I'm a friend of Doreen and Rocky, long time pass. Now, you two gonna stay with me. Me can't believe that a grown man would leave two youth upon the street like that! Me see that rasclot, me cut him up!"

He seemed so mad that I wondered if he was crazy. But I was too tired to enquire about the meaning of "rasclot" or ponder what would have happened if he really did get his hands on Isaac. The thought of his dreadlocks flying everywhere while chasing after Isaac somehow put me at ease, so I didn't say anything. I also didn't care that our trip had taken a detour, because when Raymond turned the key and pushed open the door to his small, one- bedroom flat, I couldn't wait to collapse onto the recliner and shut my eyes.

The leather sofa squeaked as Mark sat up and Raymond's teeth glistened in the sunlight. "The way I see it, sometime the almighty Jah come and make tings go certain ways, when ya least expects them."

The door opened and in walked a short woman with a big Afro. She was wrapped in an orange cloth, carrying a crying baby in her arms. "Raymond, I need help in the kitchen."

"This is me wife and pickney," Raymond introduced them.

"Did you hear me, Raymond?"

"Yes, me hear you, darling, loud and clear. Me just talking to the youth."

"Well, you can talk to this youth." She plunked the baby down into his arms and turned to face me. "Hello, my name is Marilyn. Welcome to our home."

"I'm Kevin, and that's Mark," I pointed.

"I'm cooking breakfast," Marilyn smiled and turned to walk out of the room. A map of Africa was tattooed on the back of her naked shoulder.

Mark raised his hand. "Do you know where the Mad Dog Bowl is?"

"Mad what? What mad dog you talking about, bwoy?"

"It's a skate park, and I need to find it."

"Gw'on with yourself and ask the Mrs. Me not know about them tings. Me know where to find ganja and Rastafari."

"What's your baby's name?" I asked as Mark stood up and walked out of the room.

"Me pickney's name is Marcus, as in Marcus Garvey, the first true star of Jamaica. Garvey was da'man. He be a leader of Black Nationalism. He inspired a global mass movement of economic empowerment for Africa!"

"Really?" I said, amazed at how his language was so different than anything I'd heard, and yet somehow, I caught a similarity to Geordie. I remembered what Dad had said when we stood in the lift.

"Let me tell you something. Even da' Africans put a black star upon the flag of Ghana, in honor of Marcus. Yes, Rasta, look back to Africa."

"My father's from Ghana," I boasted, but Raymond didn't hear me over his persistent rhetoric and the cry of the baby. So, I just stood, being swallowed by the light that shone through the window, thinking of the black star. I wondered if looking back actually meant looking forward. Had I learned anything, searching to find my father? I had looked back to Africa, but had it made me wiser? If history is taught to remind us of our past, so we can clearly see which path to walk, then shouldn't I now have earned my right of passage?

"Breakfast is ready!" Marilyn popped her head around the door.

I walked into the kitchen and inhaled a sweet air of spices. Mark stood at the far end of the kitchen with the telephone pressed to his ear. He hung up and put his hands on his head, letting out a long, anxious breath. "I don't believe it. I just don't believe it."

"What's the matter? You look like you're gonna cry." I sat down at the table, beneath a rack of hanging pots, in the small square kitchen.

"I telephoned the Mad Dog Bowl, and a man answered the phone. He said they closed for business yesterday."

"Maybe there's some mistake," I said.

"No, it's just my luck. I could hear them in the background tearing down the half pipe. The man said 'You can always go to Meanwhile Gardens.'"

"In the meanwhile, you go to Meanwhile," Raymond laughed, shaking his dreadlocks from side to side.

"It's not funny."

"Too bad, Mark," I said.

"Eat." Marilyn slid four plates of steaming food onto the table and pulled the baby from Raymond, leaving his arms unoccupied. "I hope you like fried salt fish." She sat at the table, and her melon-sized breast fell out as she pulled down the orange cloth and lifted the baby's gaping mouth toward her black nipple.

"It's the first day of the carnival," Raymond said. "I'll take you both and you'll forget all 'bout the mad dog, and them tings."

"That's great, I can't wait to go," I shoveled the fork into my mouth and bit down into the crispy nuggets of fish.

"I don't want to go," Mark moaned. "I'd rather try to find the other skate park."

"Have it your way, Rasta. In the meanwhile, you go to Meanwhile." Raymond laughed again and pointed at me. "I and I will go to the carnival. Me no say 'you and I.' Rasta say 'I and I' because Rastafari believe that all men is one."

We dived into breakfast. And while all that could be heard was the scraping of forks on plates and the suckling of Marilyn's nipple, the words I and I lingered. Dad's voice revisited me, saying awkwardly as we stood in opposite directions, "Aye, sometimes Jamaicans sound like us Geordies."

"Aye," Raymond stood up when our plates were scraped clean. "Sun is shining, weather is sweet. Them the words of Marley. Now, boy, we go carnival!" While he stood in the kitchen exclaiming the lyrics, I had already washed and changed before he finished the song.

We clambered down the four flights of wooden stairs to the bottom of the building and stepped out onto the street. "My God! This is London," I praised.

"This is Kilburn High Street," Raymond pointed down a road that stretched through an endless row of shop fronts and high-rise towers. "We can walk there. It won't take long."

"Okay." A blur of red buses flew by, nearly sweeping me off my feet.

"A trillion people come last year, and a trillion more come this year. They all come down to the roots."

"The roots!" I repeated joyously, as I followed him down the cobbled street. For a moment, it felt like I was following Fowler to the ring. The sense of awe and the mystery of walking into the unknown mesmerized me. Raymond, like a zealous tour guide, pointed to everything that he didn't want me to miss. Fowler had done the same to make sure I was fully aware by the time I climbed through the ropes.

"We must be getting closer," I said, noticing more and more people gathering together. The crowd seemed entranced, collectively led toward the faint hum of music.

"So many people," I said. I turned to Raymond, but he was gone. I had lost him in the growing masses. "Raymond! Raymond!" I shouted. There was no sign of him, so I kept walking. I didn't mind that I couldn't find him.

It felt natural to just keep going, like the River Tyne. Dad would take me there and put me on his shoulders when the tall ships were sailing in. The quayside would be filled with people who wanted to clamber onto the decks of the ships before they set sail again.

"The river never stops," Dad would say. "If I had to do it all again, I woulda joined the merchant navy. I woulda sailed the seas, been a free man," as we stood at the edge of the pier, watching them drift down the bending river until they disappeared from sight.

I followed the curve of steel and cement, making my way through the winding streets. Above me, street banners strapped to the sides of buildings flapped in the wind. Megaphones at precarious angles stuck out of windows and dished out Reggae, as if it were an appetizer for what was to come.

"London Carnival. Largest celebration of all mankind! Come and get it!" A brown-skinned man wearing a sleeveless jacket shouted from across the street, as he waved a newspaper in the air. *Was he trying to wave at me?* I wondered, as I looked at him through the blur of pedestrians that sped past. "Come and get it! It's the biggest party in the world."

It must be enormous, I thought, looking at the gathering faces. There were faces everywhere, jutting in and out of focus as we crossed paths. There were black faces of all shapes and shades—Rastas and Afros and big curls with big accents that swept through the streets, bouncing along in broken rhythms that matched the bustle of our feet and the sounds spilling out of the speakers above us.

"Come and get it!" The sleeveless man's voice began to fade, and I glanced back to check if he was really waving at me. By now he was too far in the distance, and I was bending out of sight, the way those tall ships would bend out of sight as Dad and I waved them off.

"Where are you, Dad?" I wanted to shout, as I felt my throat swell with sadness. It was too late to turn back. Each step I took with the cheering crowd made me miss Dad more. I could feel Mam's grip on my arm when I walked out with my suitcase.

And I could hear Sandra's voice shouting, "Hurry up and come home!" as she ran down the stairs before I closed the front door.

What if I don't go back? I thought of how I bounced down the street on a cushion of air, leaving Sonia still and silent, sitting with her pink feather duster, after she admitted that my Dad was from Ghana. *Had she told me everything?* I wondered if it really mattered. I was here—in London—and I was surrounded by the masses. I and I, all men are one. I determined to look forward—not back— forward. Not even Kweku and the hope of finding my father could give me this. Maybe, here, I would need no one.

The pace of our crowd quickened as I passed hot-dog vendors, Caribbean fried-chicken vendors, sellers waving T-shirts in the air and shouting, "London Carnival, two for one!" I went past the police barriers, following the growing sound of drums and whistles that pulsed faster. The streets became narrower and the bodies thicker. Then as I turned one more corner, the streets erupted, and I became one in a trillion people. They pushed, pulled and grabbed.

"Fight your way!" someone shouted. My shirtsleeve tore as I was thrust into the throng of people. There was loud cheering, and a flock of red balloons rose into the silver sky. More cheers lifted up, following the balloons, and everyone lifted their hands in the air. I did the same, jostling along in what had become a river of yellows, oranges, and reds—like a dazzling, multicolored lava oozing through the concrete crust of London.

I could live here, I thought. My heart thumped, and I raised my hands higher, clapping them with zest. I was intoxicated, filled with the willingness to go deeper and deeper into the writhing river. The music grew louder and faster, and the uncountable parades of costumed dancers stretched endlessly. A hundred Aztecs dressed in orange plumes with paint on their bare skin swept past, followed by peacocks with feathers higher than any building. An army of men on stilts, dressed in the red silks of Sinbad, towered thirty feet high.

Could this be better than Africa? Would I ever find my father? That thought quickly spiraled off into the crowds while I stomped my feet harder. The trucks floated by, weighed down with frenzied dancers and steel bands that threw music onto the streets like confetti spilling over our heads.

"YES!" I shouted.

On and on I went, with the strange feeling that my body was becoming lighter—almost weightless—as the sweat poured out of me. I laughed at the thought that there was nothing holding me down. I pushed myself further, flinging my arms in the air again and again until I was filled and exhausted and forced to weave my way to the curbside where the current was not as strong. I waded onto the pavement, following the waft of spices and a voice that shouted, "Whole heap of food. We got a whole heap of it!"

There was still no sign of Raymond as I walked down the street of food stalls and souvenir booths. I had forgotten to look for him—I'd forgotten everything. It was as if it had all been pushed aside in the swaying and the bumping of the crowds.

"Jamaican Patty. Try one," a brown-light skinned woman with short curly hair, holding a tray of food, stepped in front of me.

"No thank you," I said, distracted, as I looked over her shoulder. A ship's mast sprung out of the midst of street-side stalls and was soaring into the sky. At the top, glistening in the sunlight was a golden boxing bell.

I walked past the pastry seller toward a stocky bald man holding a giant hammer above his head. "Everyone's a winner! Ring the bell! Win a goldfish! Prizes galore!" The man looked like Fowler, and the closer I got, the more his head turned toward me. He was staring right at me the way Fowler would stare at me when proving a point. "One quid to ring the bell, Kid! Win a prize! Tallest bell in the country. It's a boxing bell, so you better swing hard. Ha ha!" I dug into my pocket, pulled out a hand full of coins, and sifted a quid's worth into his palm.

"Swing it hard, Kid, and you've got a chance. Everyone's a winner!" I gripped the rough handle with both of my hands. The weightless feeling I had was gone. The hammer was heavy as I dragged it toward the foot of the mast where a battered strip of white tape marked the place to strike.

"X marks the spot. It's all in the way you swing it." He put his hand on my shoulder. As he stepped back into the small crowd that had gathered, I felt like I was standing in the ring. I looked up at the golden bell and remembered struggling to stand at the end of the fight, the lights burning down on me, knowing that the referee would raise my arm when the judges read out the scorecard. I remembered the way Sullivan had looked at me when I walked to his corner to shake his hand. Something inside of me was coming together.

"Hit it hard, Kid. X marks the spot. Ring that bell!"

I staggered, hoisting the hammer high above my head. Sweat dripped down my face, and the sun shone in my eyes. I leaned forward, swinging the burdensome mallet toward the target. My neck bulged, the veins in my arms rippled, and my teeth clenched as the hammer crashed onto the target and the wooden ball soared upward.

WORLD CHAMPIONSHIP

The tunnel was dark and filled with silhouettes of fighters. A dim light that opened to the main arena, and a hubbub of anticipation wafted through the darkness towards me. Thirteen thousand people was the number when I left the locker room. It was 15,000 when I climbed the stairs of the building, and by the time I entered the tunnel, the word was that 20,000 were crammed into the Hungarian Olympic Stadium. The thought excited me.

It took so long to get there, and I wondered if I could ruin it all. And yet, I was at ease, standing in the shadows, savoring the last moments before being led out. Beneath the layer of fear that rippled over my skin, there was a depth of serenity that surprised me. The voice in my head said, I've got nothing to lose. That went against my usual tide of having everything to lose. The thought compelled me to look down at my hands in the same way that I'd done as a teenager, telling myself, over and over. These are African Hands. It was those same hands that were wrapped with tape, eager to don the gloves for the world championship. I was transfixed as everything else around me faded away. I had the feeling that something great could happen, and if I was lucky I could gain something that could never be taken away from me. "It's time." Neville dropped his heavy hand on my shoulder, breaking my thought. My mind raced as he guided me through the tunnel. The feeling of safety was left behind in the shadows.

"This is it! Let's do it!" Neville's breath on the back of my neck, propelled me forward. "Just the German left."

I nodded my head, thinking of the German, who seemed more like an object to overcome than a person. I hadn't noticed him yesterday, when I left the arena filled with confidence after beating the Hungarian. Instead I had noticed the hung heads of the fighters who looked lost in the bleachers, gathering their belongings and packing their bags; their dreams were torn into rags and the chance of a lifetime gone. I'd taken a moment to thank God as I was swept out of the building, grateful that I was not in their shoes.

"Here we go." Neville squeezed my shoulder. I was punched in the face with a rush of sound, as we stepped out into the massive dome.

"Brewerton," an Eastern European voice echoed through the speakers, spitting my name out of its mouth distastefully. It felt like walking through a storm. The ground shook, and lights flashed all around me.

"We're here," Neville shouted into my ear. "Stay focused."

That's right, don't blow it. Don't mess this one up, the voice in my head told me. *Act like a champion.* I smiled, tricking myself, trying not to be overcome by another voice. *Who do you think you're kidding?*

"There it is!" Neville shouted.

The ring sat, illuminated, waiting for me in the distance. Longest walk I've ever taken. Neville threw a towel over his shoulder and led me across the floor.

For a moment, I asked myself if fate had brought me here. The night we departed from London to Budapest, the British team and myself had gathered in the airport terminal only to be told that the flight was cancelled indefinitely~ it was the only flight. If we couldn't make it to Budapest that night for the official weigh-in, we would have to forfeit the championships. I was shattered; I roamed the airport alone, trying to find solace. Over time, I looked up at the departure board, the flight was still cancelled, but I had noticed a separate flight departing to Marrakech. One of my teammates ran up and announced that someone had offered to fly us to Budapest on a private jet, so we left right away.

I climbed the stairs and into the ring, raising my arms, as if I'd already won. I'm going to take the world title, grab it, run with it, or steal it if I have to. I've come too far and worked too hard. Nothing else matters.

Loud cheers encircled me. My eyes briskly panned the stadium. I tried not to get distracted, and I told myself to keep focused. But fighting for the world title wasn't an everyday occurrence, so I scanned again, taking in the crowd of thousands who surrounded me. What a spectacle: waving flags, marching bands, beautiful women, protruding camera lenses, flashing lights. It seems like the whole country was there. I blew out into the relentless din to refocus.

"Big ring," Neville commented.

It was the biggest ring I'd ever seen. It had been raised six feet from the ground, and it was rope-less. The ring was rope-less! Someone could fall over the edge. I liked the possibility; it could prove useful to me. Confidence filled me as I gripped my feet into the matted ring, testing it. I imagined myself crashing into the German.

"You know what to do, Champ." Neville slid my glove onto my fist.

"Yeah," I nodded back. The glove felt tight. I knew the game plan. I'd been dreaming about it for the last two years, thinking about it while I brushed my teeth, ate dinner, and said my prayers. The night before, on the floor of the hotel, naked, on my knees, I prayed.

"Please God, give me the power. Give me the power to win."

I knew the game plan. The voice in my head was unstoppable: *Dismantle him, make no mistakes, break him down and, if given the chance, throw him right over the top of the ring and into the judges if you have to!* The crowd roared. Across the arena Haerrer, my German opponent, forced his way through the massive dome. A small pack of hunched bodies followed him. His chiseled face glistened like alabaster, and he wore a white satin robe with a black eagle stamped across his chest that fell from his rigid frame. I smiled harder, covering up the fear of losing, and the crowd began to roar loud as if he were a superstar. I felt like the underdog. *I like an underdog,* I thought. I noticed that all the aches and bruises from the day before were swelling up.

"Haerrer!" The announcer's voice filled the Olympic stadium, as my opponent climbed the steps. He rolled his neck, and his trainer pulled the satin robe away from him, like a magician revealing his prized trick. His wide shoulders and a tapered torso that was lean and muscular. His legs were long. He did some kind of rehearsed shuffle. It was mechanical and made me wonder if he was going to be a spoiler. I hated battling awkward fighters, especially the ones with long legs. It was hard work. It would make for a long night.

"Use your speed, Champ," Neville grunted in my ear.

The referee stood center ring in his white shirt, black bow tie, and white gloves. The closer I got, the taller Haerrer grew until we were standing face to face. I stared up into his narrow blue eyes.

"Clean fight now, please gentlemen." The referee's broken accent slid between us. Haerrer's stillness was unnerving, his smirk mocking, and his neck and shoulders were rippling, as if some serpent waited beneath his skin to be unleashed at the ring of the bell.

"Go now." The referee spread his white-gloved hands as if to mime the clearing of a table for a delicious meal, sending us back to our corners. The final seconds ticked away, while the crowd escalated with anticipation.

"You ready? You ready champ? Go get him now. Go get him." Neville's hand gripped my shoulder. He slid my gum shield into my open mouth. I turned to look across the ring, where the German was standing, already out of his corner, eager to attack.

The bell rang, and Neville's hand on the back of my shoulder thrust me out into the open ring as Haerrer came running.

This is it! The words streamed through my head. But there was no time to reflect on the moment, as the German threw a long looping sidekick that dug into my shoulder. *Do you really think so?* I shrugged it away and smiled at him. He smiled back, grinning as he threw another kick at me.

"Don't let him catch you. Close him down!" Neville shouted, as the German's kick flew past my head, leaving a smell of liniment in my nostrils. The crowd roared, and I danced around him, using the vast ring to move away from his thrusting legs. He moved in with that mechanical shuffle, trying to lock me in the corner, as his arms flew out like pistons. He lunged in with a straight sidekick, catching me on the hip, making me stagger.

Fuck. Wake up!

I stepped back. He moved in faster, spurred by the frantic cheering. He kicked out again; it was short, but another was on its way. His kick came at me as I was backed into a corner, almost out of bounds. I lunged forward, jamming his leg mid-stride and sending a solid straight right hand at him. He blew out of his mouth as the punch landed flush in the center of his chest. The crowd screamed as he stumbled back, and the referee waved the point with his white glove. It all moved fast, and I was lucid—more lucid than I'd ever been. The voice went off in my head. *This is for the world! This is for the world!* I ran at him as he moved back, flicking out the kicks to keep me at bay. His eyes were fixed and glaring. Jarring German words spilled out of his corner. Neville's voice strained to reach me from across the ring, "Go! Go! Go!"

The German came running at me. His jab flew past my head, and his front kick landed on my glove. I pushed it away, as if I were slamming a door shut. He swung around, trying to thrust his long arm at my head. But I moved to the side of him, leaving his arm to dangle in midair. A wincing sound resounded from the watchers as the thousands of them took in the thrust of his glove. The echo that rebounded back into the ring fueled me, as my fist crashed into his ribs. My opponent jumped back. His cornermen wailed, and he shuffled mechanically to straighten his posture. He bit down on his gum shield and narrowed his eyes into slits. I lunged, eager to launch another right hand, but his lancing-jab was already on its way and slammed into my face. My head snapped back into blackness, as I absorbed his glove, inhaling it. Shock waves raced through my body.

In a blink, the crowd was silent, the ring was a black void, and the smell of leather was all that connected me to the world. *Come on! Come on!* the voice in my head shouted, as my instinct forced me around the outskirts of the ring, close to the edge. I stayed on my feet.

Fucking wake up! Wake up! The voice in my head was sharp, while the sound of the crowd was warped and thick, like molasses in my ears. I felt the ring becoming firmer under my feet, and the blurry body of the German quickly came back into focus, a vivid white torso of writhing muscle, shuffling relentlessly toward me.

"Come on! Move!" Neville shouted.

I was on my toes, again, sweeping across the ring. The blow cleared my head and crystallized my focus.

When I left for London, it was clear. I shed those forlorn feelings of ever finding my father, shrugging them off my shoulders, like a jacket filled with anger and resentment that was weighing me down. *Fuck you!* I'd said, as it fell from my back and hit the floor with a loud thud. I felt lighter and free.

I was filled with hope by the voice inside me, *You can be anything you want. I want to be a champion,* I told myself. *That will be who I am. I don't have to be anything else but a champion.*

I left behind that old picture of myself, hopelessly searching for my father in Newcastle and replaced it with a different image. I was like Ali, the showman, the American, the pioneer. I took all of those things, for they were already embedded in me, and used them to define who I wanted to be. If finding my father and becoming a champion ran side by side, then I would go forth in victory, unstoppable.

My jab slammed into the side of his face. He moved back, throwing his arms up in a wall of protection. Fear forced my focus. I did not come this far to leave without a title.

The crowd cheered, as he shook off my punch. Sweat and spit spewed through the air. His face and neck were a map of bursting blue veins. More German words piled out of his corner. It sounded like the clatter of bricks being tossed into the ring, creating in him a hardness tougher for me to break down. My opponent danced, rolled his shoulders, and threw a front kick straight at my chest. I stepped to the side, letting the kick slip past my shoulder. The crease of his ribs filled my right fist as I drove it upward. He winced, buckling sideways, and weaving his body with mine. The smell of oil and menthol engulfed me. My arms were around his waist, and his arms were around my neck as we pushed against each other.

"Break. Break." The referee's voice came between us. The German squeezed his grip. His arms were strong and slippery. I buried my head into his throat. We were a contortion of elbows and arms, pushing and tugging and morphing into one body. Then suddenly, I was pulled away.

"Break! I say 'break.'" The referee threw his pointed finger back and forth at us, as we stepped apart, our eyes anchored in each other's, ready to fight the moment the referee stepped out of our way.

The noise was endless; a resounding cry of static, like the sensation of seashells against my ears. It was an infinite vacuum of whirling space and air— endless to the mind, endless to the imagination. And I was back in Newcastle, riding home from the beach on the train with Dad. He'd told me about the time he was captured by the Germans, and how Rommel, the Desert Fox, almost looked him directly in the eye, as he inspected the prisoners.

I wished Dad were out there in the crowd, watching me, witnessing my win. *Would it matter if I lost? Would he care?* "You're only as good as your last fight, Kev."

I saw him leaning back in the armchair, in his worn-out cardigan of faded green and knotted wool. *Or was it Fowler who'd said it? Or Babbsy? Or someone else I'd overheard? Or had I been telling myself, over and over, that I was only as good as my last fight?*

The referee tripped backwards, sprayed with my sweat, as I lunged, attacking the German. *Whoever wanted it the most would win. It's the law: he who has intention will win. Do you want it? If you fucking want it, take it then!* The voice demanded as my right hand bounced off the German's head. He fell back into a reclining jog, eyes wide and shocked. I stepped forward to follow through. But he glided back out of reach, leaving me only a blurry red glove, which flicked back and forth like an annoying fly, that I wanted to swat out of my face.

We swept across the ring, and the hands of my inner-clock ticked. This clock, ingrained in my DNA, counted down the three-minute round. It could be an eternity or a blink of an eye. *Am I in hell or am I in heaven?* The answer was always relative: who's thrown more blows? Who's hurting? Who's in control? And who's heart is filled with the knowledge that they'd left the very best of themselves in that ring? And even then, would that best be enough?

I'm ahead. I'm ahead, the voice said. I held onto that thought, as if it were a rudder of a ship in a raging sea. I was in the center of it all, me, Kevin Brewerton. *I can win. I can win the world championship.*

The German's glove spit at me. I bobbed and weaved, taking nothing more than the spray of sweat from the leather. He slid back towards his corner, recoiling his arms, then spit his fists back out at me with a methodical deliberation. It forced his neck and shoulders into a rigid mass. Another branch of veins streaked up through his face, as his eyes darted from side to side. He threw a right. I saw it coming and slapped it away. Then his left scraped past my ear, burning my skin. The sound of the room hollowed, as the impact of my fist reverberated against the bone of his chest. The bell rang and the referee scrambled between us, pushing us apart.

"Come on! Come on back, Kev!" Neville waved me in. His face was calm and his eyes were like tacks. "Looking good, good, good!" He said, pulling the gum shield out of my mouth and spraying water into my face. "You're too sharp for him. This is yours, it's yours." He sprayed more water in my face. It was cold and fresh, my reward for winning the round.

The stadium whirled around me, but in here, in our corner, we were focused and calculated. Not one word was wasted in those sixty seconds that would pass in a blink of an eye. A fight could be won or lost between rounds, as surely as a fight was supposed to be won before you stepped into the ring. "When that bell rings, there's just three more minutes. That's all—three more minutes and you'll leave here the next light-heavyweight champion of the world," Neville spoke with a clarity that I'd never before heard, and pressed a layer of grease across my cheekbones with the nub of his thumb. The thought intoxicated me and reduced the enormity of the whole thing to a minor procedure that would determine the rest of my life within the next 180 seconds.

"He's behind, so he's dangerous. He's gonna come out hard. He's gonna come out strong. He doesn't have a choice. He's gonna be out for blood. Don't let him muscle ya. Keep it tight. Keep it sharp," Neville admonished.

"Seconds out!" the referee shouted.

"This is yours!" Neville slotted the gum shield back into my mouth, while the voice in my head said, *Don't fuck it up! Enjoy this!* The bell rang, jolting my attention across the ring to the German advancing from his corner.

"Gw'on!" Neville shouted. And I shot out of the gate, biting down on my gum shield, leaving his voice trailing behind me. His words were lost in the babble of the crowd. The German was already in front of me, all fists and shoulders grinding up the air. His jab flashed towards my face. I knocked it away, feeling his searing intention as his arm swung past me. I moved sideways; he followed me, spinning around like a whip. His body was fluid, powerful, and the mechanical motion was gone. I threw a jab, which missed, and a torrent of red came back at me, pounding at my hands and shoulders like hot stones. I parried and moved from side to side, escaping his urgent demand for control.

Don't let him in! Don't let him fucking turn it! The voice in my head begged me as I dipped beneath his arm, burying my fist into his meaty torso. The crowd wailed. The German grunted and shuffled backwards, trying to look composed but his eyes filled with panic. His corner's screams into the ring were too late. I'd already launched a left hook that reached his head before their words could enter it. His neck torqued upon impact.

"Thank you!" I shouted. "Thank you!" The words spit out of my mouth, as the referee's white-gloved hand reached up into the dome. My opponent jogged back, shaking his head in frustration and pounding his gloves together. He returned with kicks that sliced through the air, trying to keep me out of arm's reach. But he failed again; I'd found my way inside, and my fist reached his chin.

"Thank you, thank you!" I rejoiced as he jolted backward.

The crowd's ovation churned back into the ring, but it was a different sound than before. It was an incomprehensible echo coming from deep within a cave, an amorphous rumble striving for definition. The German pounded his gloves together harder and advanced, but I got inside yet again.

"Thank you," I shouted as my fists reconnected with his ribs and face. The ringing from the crowd became audible, demanding my attention by surprise. The German shuffled to the outskirts of the ring. But I was my strongest and fastest. With every blow I landed, the crowd echoed back, clearer each time.

They shouted, "Thank you!" I was shocked and inspired. From ringside, my own words wheeled around the dome, through the 20,000, and crashed back into the ring, permeating my being. They drove me forward.

My opponent was confused. I attacked his rib cage, then his chest, then his jaw. I'd twisted his mouth into a grimace that revealed he could not defeat me. Every punch I threw flowed with ease, and all the struggle was gone. It was as if the divine hand of the gods had swept clear a table, leaving it blank. I had no walls to climb or obstacles to surmount. It was a miracle that expanded inside of me and poured out into the dome. We we're spinning in a euphoric explosion, bringing me to the core of this ring where the final seconds ticked away.

There was an ease I'd never felt before. *Will I ever feel this again?* I wanted to slow down time and savour every moment of it. I was in control of everything: the palpable air that swirled around me, the sound of laughter in the echo of the crowd, and the German who had acquiesced, no longer fighting to win.

He returned to the mechanical motion of a subordinate cog in a much larger machine. There was an effortlessness in his hunched shoulders and his hoisted gloves that obscured his face. He had surrendered. The pugnacious glare was gone and had been replaced with something more content, which went against the distant, frantic voices of his corner men.

Come on. Come on. The voice in my head returned, forcing the tension back into my body. *Stay alert! Stay sharp,* it spoke as I inched my way towards the German. But before I threw my punch, I was stopped by the sound of the bell.

That's it! That's it! the voice screamed. For a moment I had no idea what to do. Then I lifted my arms into the air. The dome ignited, and Neville ran into the ring. But before he could reach me, the German swept me off my feet, in an unprecedented manner. My body tensed in confusion, until I realized that he was celebrating my victory. He lifted me over his shoulder and spun me around in the center of the ring. *I'm the world champion,* the voice cried. *I'm the world champion.*

*H*ow did I get to be here? I ask myself. I'm sitting in a chair, facing the mouth of a fireplace that looks like it could swallow us both. *Is it because we're both fighters? Or is it something much deeper? Am I here merely by chance?* It feels like we are a mirror to each other, and somehow we're supposed to recognize something about ourselves from looking at the other.

Milton had spelled it out to me, loud and clear, while critiquing me in his acting class. "You're trapped," he said. "I see you trapped in a bubble, fighting to get out!"

How could he have seen that? I'd thought, imagining myself alone on stage, stuck in an invisible sphere. When I learned that Sonia was my mother I put up a wall, but it wasn't of brick and mortar, as one would expect. It was something far more elusive, like a shower curtain, which is worse because its translucent appearance makes you think it isn't there.

Was that the bubble Milton could see? The sphere that protected me and trapped me all at once. The sphere I'd been unable to step beyond to stop the violence, while Mam, over and over, fell to the floor. It was the translucent curtain that surrounded me, hovering and morphing, unseen, from one shape to another. *He could see it!*

If he can see it, I can break through it, I'd told myself, after Katselas had walked off stage at the end of the night. *Bust right through that fucking thing!* The voice in my head urged, but another, deeper voice was whispering, *Force will get you nowhere. Just let go.*

I could imagine myself on stage, the bubble dissolving around me as I stepped through it. I heard Mam's laughter while she pointed at the TV. "He does narf love himself, doesn't he? He loves himself. Boy, he really loves himself!"

Did I do it? Did I get through the bubble? I don't feel any different. Could it really be that easy, just love yourself? I mean, isn't that what Mam was really saying?

"I want to get out of here," M, whispers, exhausted.

I feel like standing up to shout in his face. *Do you know this is bigger than any title fight? You're fighting for your life! You're flat out on the canvas and being counted out. You're looking up at a referee counting to ten as fast as you can blink. He's already at nine! This is it, damn it. Get up!*

I choose not to say anything, saving those words for myself. All that moves is my armchair. It swivels as I shift my weight.

"There are a lot of people here who care about you. You know that?"

"I know," he admits, moving his weight around in his chair. He looks like he's gained a second wind.

"Who's your favorite fighters?" I ask.

"I like the little guys. Duran, Leonard, Hagler."

"I loved Ali. No heavyweight moved like him," I say.

"Yeah. He's a good man, too." He looks at me and casually flicks his hand in a gesture that tells me he knew Ali well.

"I remember watching him and Joe Frazier fight, the Thrilla in Manila. It was brutal. They said it was like walking into an oven, 105 degrees of heat. They punished each other. Ali said it was the closest he'd ever been to death."

"Frazier had to be admitted into a hospital right after the fight,"

"It was that fight that I realized how much they loved each other."

"It's true. Fighters can love each other."

"Ali came to my boxing gym when I was a kid." The memory flows through me, as if it had just happened a moment ago.

"That must have left an impression on you," he comments.

"It did. The only problem was I wasn't there when he came."

"No way." He looks confused.

"Yes, I know," I continue. "I still have no idea how that happened. I took it hard at the time, but when I was living in London years later, I learned that Ali was coming to town to promote his latest book. I knew there would be a lot of people there, so I called ahead of time and introduced myself over the phone to the promoter to see if he could arrange a meeting with Ali. He told me he'd take care of it if I showed up.

"I was married at the time, so I went with my wife Kema, and her niece, along with my son, Kolby, and a friend, Paul.. My daughter had yet to be born. Off we went. I took a copy of a book I'd written, called The Warrior Within. It's about how to win in a martial arts competition. I wanted to give it to Ali. When we arrived at the bookstore, there were hundreds of people there. The store had reached its capacity, so they weren't letting anyone else inside. I found the manager that I'd spoken to.

"'Come back in an hour, once things have quieted down. There's a side door, ask for me,' he said. So we returned an hour later. Black-suited security guards surrounded the entire building. I approached one of the men guarding the door.

"'I came to meet with Ali. The promoter told me to meet him here.'

The security guy looked at me, without even blinking and said, 'No one gets in.'

'But you don't understand,' I said. 'I'm a guest. It has been arranged.'

'No one gets in. Sorry.'

"We exchanged words, to no avail. A small part of me didn't care and I kind of liked that – all the pressure of meeting my hero released. Just then, as I stood outside the door, the figure of another black-suited bodyguard stepped up from behind. He looked at me.

"'Excuse me. Are you the Jedi? You're Kevin Brewerton, right?' Before I had a chance to answer, he turned to his colleague, and said, 'Do you know who this guy is? You have to let him in.' The doorman stepped aside, and we were ushered down a winding corridor."

"That's funny," M says. We both laugh. He points his finger up in the air. "If there was ever a time to be recognized."

"So, we followed the corridor," I continue my story. "I was holding the book in my hand as we arrived at a door, where another guard stood. He opened the door to a small backroom. It was minimal, a few chairs, white walls and beige carpet. I scanned the room. There were only five or six people standing around, casually chatting. And then I saw him. Ali was sitting down at a small table, resting. I couldn't believe it. I was in the room, ten feet away from Muhammad Ali. I was led over and introduced.

'Muhammad, someone is here to meet you,' the security guard said, before walking away, leaving me with him. Ali smiled at me. I sat next to him.

'What's your name?' He put his hand on my shoulder. His voice was calm.

'My name is Kevin. It's good to meet you. I love you,' I said, almost immediately, launching the words at him. I'd been holding them in for so long, and they slipped right out. I sensed intrigue flash across his face, as if he was wondering, Who's this man that's telling me he loves me, right off the bat, like that?' Although clearly taken aback, he put his arm around me and hugged me. I held onto him.

"'How old are you?'

'I'm thirty-two.'

'You're still a baby,' he looked right at me.

'I'm gonna come back and shake up the world!' he said. We laughed hard, and then I held up the book.

"'Muhammad, I've won several world championships in kickboxing. I wrote this book. I couldn't have written it without you. I want you to have this.' He took the book from me. I expected he would glance it over, but he held it in his hands and took his time looking through the pages, as if it was something of great value to him. I felt slightly uncomfortable, watching the greatest of all time look through the pages of my book, while I stood before him with my family. I introduced him to everyone, and we spent the rest of the time together talking and taking photos, as if we were long lost relatives. It was like time had yielded itself to me."

"Wow," M, says, looking at me from his armchair. He laughs gently and then we fall back into stillness.

"So, did you ever find your father?" he asks.

"I had stopped looking for him. I thought I didn't care anymore. I pushed away the desire to find him, and then one day, I had a change of heart."

"What happened?"

"When my daughter was born, something in me changed. I had a reason to share my family history because it was also her history and my son's. It was also because of Kema. We shared all of those similarities: being mixed race, the absence of our fathers, and the fact that her grandparents raised her. She was so proud of being half Ugandan and half Russian. It made me reconnect to all of those feelings that I once had. The yearning to find my father returned. For years I had never allowed anyone to know me intimately. When I became famous in the fighting world, I could keep people on the outside, only showing them what I wanted them to see. For the first time in many years, I let someone in. I wasn't ashamed to tell her about my life. I stopped hiding. I remember when I was eighteen, sitting in class at college while we discussed John Donne's poem, No Man is An Island. That title resonated in me at that early age. I knew that one day, I'd have to reconcile myself and integrate all of the parts of me that I'd once separated and compartmentalized. I'm still reconciling. It's like unfolding a piece of paper, over and over."

"It's never ending," he adds.

"I went to Africa, that's what I did. We were married by then, so I went with Kema and my daughter. She was three years old. We flew from Los Angeles to Ghana, through London. We were living here in Los Angeles, but somehow, I was able to track down a man who I thought was my father. He had a different last name, Odonkor, but everything else seemed to check out, and so I thought, maybe, Sonia had gotten the name wrong. All of those years ago, Odonkor, or Addo, might have sounded similar to a young girl from Newcastle. Kema had a friend, Sheila, who lived in Ghana. For over a year, I liaised with her. She was in communication with this man, Dr. Odonkor. She was convinced that she had found my father.

"We stepped out of the airport and watched the sun rising while we were chauffeured to Sheila's home in Cape Coast. There I was in Africa. It looked just like it did in the books I'd read. It felt like I'd reached home. Sheila greeted us and everyone made a fuss when we arrived. I remember walking into the room that we were staying in. I turned on the radio, and Eric Clapton was playing, 'My Father's eyes... Look into my father's eyes.' It seemed like the whole universe was telling me that it was time to meet my father. The following day Sheila drove us from Cape Coast to the capital city, Accra, where my father was located.

"When we finally arrived at the doctor's office, we walked into the lobby. 'Hello,' I said. 'I'm here to see Dr. Odonkor. We just flew in from London.'

"The receptionist looked shocked and calmly replied, 'I'm awfully sorry, sir, but the doctor is in London. He departed two days ago; he's gone on holiday.'"

"No way. You have to be kidding!" M says, looking at me, while he rocks forward in his chair.

"Yes. It hurt, man. It hurt a lot. I didn't know what to do," I say, while thinking of Fitzgerald's quote.

"What did you do? How did you not know that he was in London?" he asks me.

"I wish I knew. I'd been talking with Sheila the whole time and she was in communication with the doctor. I never found out why. I think some information between us just got lost in translation. I know it sounds crazy. We landed back in London, and the following day, we took a train to Mile End Tube Station. I always thought it was ironic that the station was called Mile End. It made me think I was at the end of my journey, and the reward would be there waiting for me.

"I had spoken to the doctor over the phone and I told him everything. He responded with, 'Let's meet in person and talk about this.' When I arrived at his house, he was very polite. He was a slim man, dark smooth skin, with a kind face. He was well-spoken and had a compassionate demeanor. We sat for a while talking about how I first learned that my father was African, right up until how I came to be in his office in Ghana. By the end of the conversation, we determined that he was not my father. He offered to help me find him."

"That wasn't the guy?"

"No, it wasn't him. But I don't regret it. We had originally flown into London on our way to Africa. The flight had been cancelled for twenty-four hours, so I decided to take the train to Newcastle for the day and surprise Mam. When I got there, I found her lying on the sofa. She was sick. She had intense stomach pains. I hadn't seen her for almost two years. She looked severely gaunt. I was furious that no one had told me. She looked like she was about to die. I carried her to the hospital, fighting for hours to get her an appointment with a doctor. She smiled when they rigged the I.V. to her, and she started to perk up.

"I got the chance to see her again and take care of her, so it was a beautiful moment. I told her about the trip to Africa to find my father. The last thing she said, as I left her bedside was, 'Good luck Son. I hope you find him.' Then she smiled right at me. That was the last time that I saw her. She passed away a month later. If I had not been going to Africa, I would never have been able to spend that last day with her.

"When she died, I flew back to England to be at her funeral. The service infuriated me. The coffin was on display in the church, and it was dusty. The priest gave a generic speech. It was clear he didn't know her; she wasn't a church girl anyway. I sat there the whole time, continually dismissing the urge to stand up and shout out, 'First thing you need to know about Mam is that she wouldn't want a dusty coffin.' I didn't do it. I told myself it'd be disrespectful. That was ten years ago."

"That's deep," he voices.

"That was a tough year, losing her right after I had returned from Africa."

"That is a big hit."

"You know something?" I reply. "This might sound crazy, but just a few months ago, before we met, I was invited to go to India to visit an orphanage and present them with funding and a new school bus. We spent a few days with the kids and then on the last morning, I was given the responsibility of standing outside of the building to await the arrival of the new school bus ~ it was a surprise. As I stood there, something caught my attention. Across the courtyard, about fifty yards away, a yellow bus was parked at the side of the building. It was empty, but something inside was moving. It looked like a black dot fluttering back and forth across the rear window of the bus. As I looked closer, I realized that it was a butterfly. It was trapped inside. It couldn't perceive the clear glass and it was trying to fly through the window.

"The butterfly was in a frenzy, fluttering and repeatedly slamming into the window. I stood there watching, controlling my desire to free it. I couldn't decide what to do. I'd been told to stay at my post. A short time went by, then the doors of the building opened behind me. I was ushered inside to have breakfast with the priests and the organizers of the event. I sat there the whole time, eating breakfast and being cordial, but constantly thinking of the butterfly.

"Eventually, to the surprise of everyone, I stood up, left the table and went outside looking for the bus. Someone had moved it further back into the compound. *Was I too late?* I ran over and peered through the rear window of the bus. At first, I didn't see anything, but I looked closer, and there it was, the butterfly, sitting in the corner of the window. I ran to the back of the bus. The butterfly was still sitting there. It looked paralyzed. I wanted to pick it up, but how do you pick up a butterfly? The wings are too delicate. So I placed my hand next to it. Without delay, it climbed onto my finger. I carefully walked over to the window and stuck my hand outside into the open air. I expected the butterfly to fly right off into freedom, but it didn't. It just sat there on my finger. Without words, this phenomenal creature was communicating with me. We stared at each other. I could feel it. It was like we were talking to each other telepathically. It was saying, 'Thank you, I know who you are.' And then it flew off."

"Man, that is crazy," M, says.

"Somehow, I like to think that butterfly was Mam," I confess.

"Man, what can I say? I wouldn't disagree. After all, Cus said, he'd come back and haunt me." We erupt with laughter, rocking back and forth, almost falling out of our chairs. Tears fill my eyes. We can't stop laughing.

"Enough, enough," I wave my hand gesturing to push him away. However, this only makes things worse and the laughter escalates into a crescendo, before falling into a silent resolution of heaving chests and shoulders, as we slowly regain composure.

"What happened with your father?" he continues.

"The doctor offered to help me look for my father."

"And did he?"

"Yes, he was amazing. Over the course of a few months he helped me track down an old college alumnus from Nigeria, who apparently knew my father. I managed to track him down via e-mail. He did verify that he knew a man with the name Anim-Addo, who studied medicine with him at Newcastle University. For the first time in my life, I had found the man with the name Addo. *Could it be him?* He had a medical clinic in Doncaster, England, just an hour from Newcastle.

"The first thing I did was pick up the phone and call him from Los Angeles. A strong dignified voice greeted me. He was very curious about my story. He asked me things about myself, and I could hear him painting the picture of what kind of man I am. By the end of the conversation, he said, 'I think you have found the right family, but it wasn't me, it was my brother. There were rumors that a child had been born.' He paused and then he said, 'I'm sorry to say, he died a few years ago.'"

"What? He died? Is that what he said?"

"That's what he said, but it didn't seem to add up. So I did some checking and found out that his brother wasn't studying medicine. He was in Newcastle during a different time period, which would make it impossible for me to have been conceived from him. A few months later, my intuition told me to call doctor Addo, again. The conversation started off well. I was polite and respectful. I told him that I had checked out his brother, and the timelines didn't match up. Then I asked him if he wouldn't mind taking a blood test, so I could eliminate him from my search. He immediately blew up on the phone, shouting, 'I am not your father. I've told you. I am not your father!' And then he hung up on me!"

"What did you do after that?"

"I left it alone, for about three years. I didn't do anything. Just got on with life. And then, one day, I was driving from Newcastle to London, visiting from Los Angeles. My daughter was with me. She was eight years old. As we drove south on the freeway, I saw a road sign for Doncaster. Something inside of me urged me to pull off and follow the road. I knew his address from the research I'd done, and so I decided to pay him a visit.

"I told myself, let's see what he looks like. I wanted to see if anything unexpected or revelatory would happen when we stood face to face. I wound through the streets of Doncaster. It was around 9pm on a Sunday evening. I found the house and parked at the top of the driveway just out of sight. I had my daughter stay in the car. She didn't know why I was there. I walked down the sloping path that led to a two-story home, which sat neatly between a well-manicured landscape of shrubs and trees.

"I had no idea how I would be greeted. *Be polite, calm, and respectful*, I reminded myself. Let your arms hang by your side, so as not to appear threatening in any way. I approached the front door and rang the bell. At first I heard nothing coming from inside, and then the door opened.

"A dark-skinned teenage girl with a ponytail, opened the door. 'Hello,' I said, 'Can I speak to doctor Anim-Addo, please?'

"She looked curious, but smiled and said, 'One moment,' then she returned, leaving the door slightly ajar. I stood there, thinking I could be about to meet my father for the first time. A moment later, the door opened wide, and there he was, standing in front of me. His dark face was slightly lit by the lamp on the porch. He had a short Afro combed backwards over his head. He wore casual trousers, house slippers, and a beige knitted cardigan. *Had I disturbed his Sunday evening?* His eyes pleasantly looked me over, curious of who I was and why I was standing at his door.

'Hello, may I help you?'

'Hi there!' I said, in the friendliest way possible. 'My name is Kevin Brewerton. We spoke-'

"'Oh yes,' he paused, recalling my name; I could see his curious smile quickly morphing into an uncomfortable glare. His voice became rigid. It was as if we had just hung up the phone three years earlier and no time had passed at all.

"'I just thought I would come and meet you in person. I thought it might make a difference if you were to see who I am,' I smiled.

"At that moment, his wife came walking up from the side of the house and stood about five feet away from me. 'Who are you?' She said.

'My name is Kevin ~'

'So did your mother send you?' He cut me off before I could continue.

'What? My mother? No. She didn't. I just wanted~'

"'Then why are you here?' He continued questioning me, while his wife stood like a guard dog at my flank, looking me up and down in defense of their territory. I kept my arms by my side. It was getting heated and I was trying not to react. Then out of nowhere a voice pierced the air, forcing us all to stop in our tracks and look up the driveway.

"'Dad! Are you okay, dad?' My daughter was standing alone watching. I didn't want her to see her father being humiliated while he was looking for his father. I put my hand out, gesturing for her to stop. I felt like I was standing between two worlds, holding together strings of a broken lineage.

"'Yes, I'm fine', I answered, attempting to make my voice sound casual.

'I'm okay, go back to the car, I'll be right there.'

'But Dad ~'

'It's okay,' I continued. 'I'll be right there, I promise.'

"She waited for a moment, then turned and walked back to the car. I turned to face the doctor. It felt like a truce had been formed. The doctor and his wife seemed more reserved. I considered my daughter's presence a stroke of luck.

'So that's your daughter?' the doctor said.

'Yes, she is,' I answered.

"He paused, looked at his wife, then at me, and raised his hand, pointing right at me. His mouth opened wide, as he sucked in enough air to fill his lungs to maximum capacity. Then he screamed, 'I told you I am not your father! I am not your father! I am not your father!'

"His voice was relentless. Anger flooded through me. I'd told myself that I would not react, but I clenched my fist and took a step forward. He stepped back; terror flashed through his eyes. I'd seen that look many times. I was right in front of him, face to face.

"'You wanna know something?' The words flowed out of my mouth. 'Even if you were my father, I wouldn't want you to be. You don't deserve me!' I stood for a second, looking into his eyes. He and his wife were frozen. I knew that the decision I made in the next few seconds would define me for the rest of my life, so I turned and walked away. The fear in his eyes turned to a blank look of relief. I didn't look back."

"That's heavy, man," M, says. "What happened then?"

"I left them standing there. I jumped in the car and drove towards the freeway.

'So, Dad, was that your dad?' my daughter's voice stretched from the back seat. I was surprised. *How did she know?* I had tried to keep it a secret. 'Are you crying, Dad?'

'It's okay,' I said, wiping away the tears, while looking back at her through the rear-view mirror. 'And no. He's not my dad.'

'Good,' she said, 'because I didn't like him!' We both laughed."

"Do you think that he was really the guy?" he asks as he leans forward towards me.

"You know that Shakespeare quote," I began. "'The lady doth protest too much.' I think it could very well be the case. Everything sort of pointed to him, even his reaction. Why would you react so harshly if you didn't have anything to hide? I mean, what kind of man wouldn't give another man two minutes of his time to help him find his father?"

"How about a blood test?" M, suggests.

"I thought about that. I could get a private investigator to follow him to a coffee shop or someplace, and pick up his cup after he drank from it. Then I'd have the DNA."

"Would you do it?"

"It was on my mind, but you know, that night as my daughter and I drove down the freeway, something happened to me. It was unexpected and something I'd never felt before. Just as easily as I'd changed lanes to merge into the flow of traffic, the yearning to find my father disappeared. It wasn't out of anger or frustration in the way it had been in the past, but more so, a sense of inner peace. I'd gained clarity by answering the question: what if that man is my father? Or what if, one day, I was to find my father only to discover that he's a jerk? That wouldn't be good. It's better to keep him in my imagination. As she and I continued to drive into the night the thought of Dad throwing away his medals came to mind. I laughed to myself, having finally found the answer. Dad wasn't a fool any more than Ali was when he threw his medals away. He'd done the right thing. It was time for me to let go too. I decided to no longer hold onto something that was not serving me.

"'Dad?' Kaivalya said. Her voice was eager and full of energy.

'Yes?'

'Can we get some ice cream?'

'But it's almost ten o'clock at night.' 'So?'

"'Okay, why not? Let's get some ice cream,' I said as we neared the end of the freeway and entered the outskirts of the city. Various roads lead off into different directions. Up ahead all of the traffic lights were green."

I would like to thank my Ancestors and my Higher Power, who has made all things possible. With gratitude, I thank all of those who helped me to fully realize this book and to bring it into existence: Milton Katselas, Mike Tyson, Andrea Paige, Kema Muyingo, Lisa Doctor, Allen Barton, The Beverly Hills Playhouse, Neville Wray, Steve Babbs, Bey Logan, Giuseppe Bivono, Bob Fermor, Lorna Partington, Sheila Flionis, Carol Mangione, Laurie David, Bob Sykes, Craig Pallister, Robert Tin, Myra Oiga, Linda Jones, Barbara Powell, Freya Adams, Adam McKay, Shira Piven, and Mark Byron. And there are others, including all of the writers who I sat with each week sharing stories at the Doctor's house. Thank you.

Printed in Great Britain
by Amazon

62184892R00132